# The Pattern &The Prophecy

**The Ancient of Days**

by William Blake 1794, from Europe: A Prophecy.

**When he prepared the heavens, I was there:**
**when he set a compass upon the face of the depth.**
Proverbs 8:27 (KJV)

# The Pattern & The Prophecy

## God's Great Code

James Harrison

 Isaiah Publications

# THE PATTERN AND THE PROPHECY
## God's Great Code

### By James Harrison

Published by: Isaiah Publications

P.O. Box 1221
Peterborough Ontario,
Canada K9J 7H4

**Canadian Cataloguing in Publication Data**

Harrison, James, 1936–
    The Pattern and The Prophecy: God's Great Code

1st ed.
Includes bibliographical references and index.
ISBN 0-9698512-0-0

    1. Symbolism in the Bible.  2. Numbers in the Bible.
I. Title.

    BS680.N8H37 1995     220.6'4     C95-900341-X

Cover design: Nora Mickee
Printed: Toronto, Canada

**To my mother,**

the bravest person I know

# ACKNOWLEDGMENTS

My daughter claims I have been writing this book all my life. Along life's path many friends and colleagues have helped me. My thanks to Jerry Larock and Larry Keeley for editing the early manuscript, and to Evelyn Andrews goes a special thanks for her advice on reorganization and general editorial comment. To Roger Smith, my appreciation for editing the manuscript with an emphasis on its content. To Alice Higham, my gratitude for a critique of the typesetting. I express my indebtedness to Jamie Skinner and Alexandria Carstens whose knowledgeable computer assistance made the actual physical process of writing and typesetting possible. And to my daughter Jennifer, a special recognition for fine-tuning the entire text. Lastly, my thanks again to Jerry Larock for his expert help with the indexes. To all my friends who have offered encouragement with this long task, my gratitude.

Much appreciation to Nora Mickee for the cover design and FIGURES 8.5 and 12.23: "The Fishes and The Net" and "An exploded view of the Cube of Truth's three parts." My thanks also to the young artist Michael Stewart for drawing FIGURES 9.8 (a) and 10.1: "The Apple's Core" and "The Ark on the Flood." Grateful acknowledgment is made for permission to reproduce FIGURE 13.1: "Taken from The NIV Study Bible. Copyright © 1985 by The Zondervan Corporation. Used by permission of Zondervan Publishing House." I am further indebted to Mr. Jean-Marc Hamou for FIGURE 12.5: "Where the Ancient Temple of Jerusalem Stood," *Biblical Archaeological Review*, VOL. IX NO. 2, Washington DC. Finally, my appreciation to Hugh Claycombe, artist of The NIV Study Bible, for the rights to use his fine drawings of God's Temples: FIGURES 12.1, 12.2, 12.4.

# TABLE OF CONTENTS

# CHAPTER — 1

## THE TRINITY

*Who has measured the waters in the hollow of his hand,*
*or with the breadth of his hand marked off the heavens?*
*Who has held the dust of the earth in a basket, or weighed*
*the mountains on the scales and the hills in a balance?*
Isaiah 40:12

All the universe is divided into three parts: length, width, and breadth; past, present, and future; proton, neutron, electron; Father, Son, and Holy Spirit. Our very existence tells us that at least once, God stepped out of eternity into time and created His Word and His Works. Both bear the imprint of The Trinity.

For centuries scientists have been on a quest seeking the mathematical meaning and structure of nature. At the smallest scale imaginable, they have detected a triangular grouping of quarks. In the other direction — the grand form of the universe — recent discoveries have shown a similar triad arrangement of the galaxies themselves.

Yet God has put as much mathematics into His Holy Word, the Bible, as scientists have found in His Holy Works, the earth and the heavens. It can be found from the first verse of Genesis to the last of Revelation. It can also be found in the relationship between these two sentences. Science and religion are coming to the same conclusion: both God's creations are threefold and reflect The Trinity. "Everything comes in threes" declares an ancient proverb, an old saying even in the days of King Solomon.

Δ
Δ  Δ

# OLD TESTAMENT TRINITIES

To learn more about the Bible, I had been reading a modern author's commentary on Genesis. His preface contained the following disturbing statement: "In the Old Testament, God is treated as a single entity." At that point I stopped reading this book and opened *The Book*, to let it speak for itself. Genesis 1:1 proclaims:

> *In the beginning God created the heavens and the earth.*

In the original Hebrew, the word used for God is *Elohim*, the plural form of Eloah. It is notable that this plural subject, *Gods*, is written with the singular verb, *created*. This act effectively prohibits any thought of polytheism (belief in many gods). More important, it implies The Trinity of the Godhead in the very first sentence. In the second verse of the King James Version (KJV), *The Word* declares:

> *And the Spirit of God moved upon the face of the waters.*

Here, the Bible introduces The Holy Spirit. (The word *waters*, in this context, means chaos, the opposite of cosmos or order.)

I propose to take a brief tour through the Bible in this chapter to show the ever-present "threeness" of our Lord. Later chapters will expand this inventory with deeper and richer examples. For now, consider the following.

Authorities differ over the identity of the 3 persons Abraham met in Genesis 18:2. Many scholars believe them to have been the Father, the Son, and The Holy Spirit, yet others feel they were the Lord and two angels. Remarkably, however, Abraham addresses them as both 1 and 3 like The Trinity. We read, "he said" and then "they said" and "the Lord said."

In Isaiah 6:3 (KJV), the great prophet wrote a famous verse that became the inspiration for a celebrated hymn:

> *And one cried unto another, and said,*
> *Holy, holy, holy, is the Lord of hosts:*

Three times the angels cried "holy," once for each Being in the coequal, coeternal, and indivisible mystery we call The Holy Trinity. These angels correspond to the "living creatures" of Revelation 4:8 who chant the identical phrase.

Isaiah 9:6 records one of the most transcendentally prophetic passages in all Scripture. Not only is Jesus predicted, but this passage affirms His equality with the First Person, the Father:

> *For to us a child is born, to us a son is given,*
> *and the government will be on his shoulders.*
> *And he will be called Wonderful Counselor,*
> *Mighty God, Everlasting Father, Prince of Peace.*

Each time, these verses praise the Second Person in The Trinity by titles with exactly two elements (i.e., Wonderful Counselor, Mighty God, and so on). As a writer interested in the Bible's numerical structure, I find that significant.

## NEW TESTAMENT TRINITIES

> *May the grace of the Lord Jesus Christ, and the love of*
> *God, and the fellowship of the Holy Spirit be with you all.*
> 2 Corinthians 13:14

Now that we have seen a few trinities in the Old Testament, let us look into the New Testament. Verses 10 and 11 (KJV) at the beginning of Mark's Gospel are famous passages illustrating the threeness of God. Jesus listens:

> *And straightway coming up out of the water,*
> *he saw the heavens opened, and the Spirit*
> *like a dove descending upon him:*

> *And there came a voice from heaven, saying, Thou*
> *art my beloved Son, in whom I am well pleased.*

Of course, similar and equally beautiful passages exist in the other Gospels. In Chapter 11 we'll explore the deep symbolism of the dove and discover its many levels of meaning.

Certain words are striking for the number of times they arise concerning the same topic. "Fullness" is such a word. Relating to the Godhead, it is found exactly 3 times in the entire Bible — this implies His totality at that quantity. These are the passages (KJV):

> *The fullness of God* — Ephesians 3:19.
> *The fullness of Christ* — Ephesians 4:13.
> *The fullness of the Godhead* — Colossians 2:9.

Even the word "Godhead" itself is found only 3 times.

Jesus told us how to pray in Matthew 6:9; He even stated 3 petitions, one to each part of The Trinity:

> *Give us today our daily bread* — the Father.
> *Forgive us our debts* — the Son.
> *And lead us not into temptation* —The Holy Spirit.

The following verse from Matthew 28:19 explicitly states the threeness of the Godhead. Jesus speaks:

> *Therefore go and make disciples of all nations,*
> *baptizing them in the name of the Father*
> *and of the Son and of the Holy Spirit:*

## JESUS AND THE NUMBER THREE

Concerning the Father, the Son, and The Holy Spirit, 3 occurs a startling number of times. Consider the following examples, just about Jesus:

- During His 3-year ministry, Christ raised 3 people from the dead.
- Satan tempted Jesus 3 times.
- The Transfiguration of Jesus took place before Peter and the brothers James and John — 3 people in all.

- Peter denied Christ thrice.
- On Calvary 3 were crucified.
- Amazingly, it was at the 3rd hour that Jesus was crucified.
- And for 3 hours darkness shrouded the earth.
- On the 3rd day, like Jonah from the whale's belly, Jesus rose from the earth. Symbolizing this future Resurrection, the earth itself rose out of the waters (chaos) on the 3rd Day of Creation.

This list could be widely expanded, but let's be satisfied with 7 examples for the time being.

Some skeptical readers may still doubt the essential threeness of the Godhead. Perhaps they consider the above summary resulted only from long research. In that case, I would ask them to complete a similar list of equally important events based on any other number. Their choice, of course, is legion.

Every Christian knows that you only approach the Father through the Son under the inspiration and guidance of The Holy Spirit. To deny this fundamental threeness of the Deity is a basic misunderstanding of Him and our relationship to Him. Threeness or triangularity is an ever-present element in God's Word, Works, and Being. The Father sent the Son to shed His blood on Calvary so that we might have life eternal, and He left His Holy Spirit to dwell among us.

# CHAPTER — 2

# GOD AMONG THE SCIENTISTS

*Science without religion is lame,*
*religion without science is blind.*
Albert Einstein (1879-1955)

*I believe that when I die I shall rot,*
*and nothing of my ego will survive.*
Bertrand Russell (1872-1970)

*Knowing that Christ being raised from the dead*
*dieth no more; death hath no dominion over him.*
Paul, Romans 6:9 (KJV)

## GOD AND SCIENCE: PRESENT

Concerning men and women of science, there is a question every Christian has quietly asked: Why are so many scientists unbelievers? Statistics show that most scientists in North America do not accept the Christian faith. The situation is even darker in Europe and completely black in the former Soviet Union. Although in the latter case, this may be rapidly changing. A few quotations will forcibly show the attitude of most modern scientists.

Humanist philosopher/scientist Bertrand Russell said in his book *Why I Am Not a Christian*:

> *I cannot myself feel that either in the matter of wisdom*
> *or in the matter of virtue Christ stands quite as high as*
> *some other people known to history. I think I should put*
> *Buddha and Socrates above Him in those respects.*[1]

Russell's influence has spread over most continents and persisted for at least seventy years.

Isaac Asimov (1920-1992) was an extremely popular science writer and for many years the leading editor of *The Humanist* magazine. This publication directs the flood of anti-Christian propaganda on abortion, removing school prayer, evolution, situational ethics, and so on. In a 1982 interview Asimov revealed:

> *I am an atheist, out and out. It took me a long time to say it. I've been an atheist for years and years.*

This century's most vehement attack on Christianity occurred on the front page of the *New York Times*, 15 October 1980. A group of sixty-one prominent scientists placed an advertisement entitled *A Secular Humanist Declaration*. This statement expressed skepticism toward "supernatural claims," "traditional views of God," and the "divinity of Jesus." Some of the signers were Francis Crick (biologist), Albert Ellis and B.F. Skinner (psychologists), Henry Morgentaler (abortionist), and Paul Kurtz (writer of the Declaration and main Humanist representative). Such is our world in these latter days!

# GOD AND SCIENCE: PAST

What were the attitudes and beliefs of past scientists toward God and His Word? The famous Italian scientist Galileo (1564-1642) was of quite a different mind than his modern counterparts. Despite his problems with the Roman Catholic Church he was a most devout Christian. Galileo sincerely believed that by studying the natural world he was entering into The Works of God. For that reason, he declared the study of nature to be as pious an act as reading the Bible. The following quotation comes from his book *The Assayer*:

> *Nature is written in that great book which ever lies before our eyes — I mean the universe — but we cannot understand it if we do not first learn the language and grasp the symbols in which it is written. The book is written in mathematical language, and the symbols are triangles, circles and other*

*geometrical figures, without whose help it is impossible to comprehend a single word of it; without which one wanders in vain through a dark labyrinth.*

Galileo showed that the language of God in His Works is mathematics. I propose to show that the language of God in His Word is also mathematics.

The celebrated astronomer Johannes Kepler (1571-1630) believed space has 3 dimensions (length, width, and depth) because The Trinity has 3 parts. In his youth Kepler studied to be a minister and he remained extremely pious throughout his difficult life.

John Napier (1550-1617), a contemporary of Kepler, discovered logarithms and used them on the numbers in the Apocalypse. They change the more difficult operations of multiplication and division into the easier ones of addition and subtraction. Calculators in our time have done for dreary computation what logarithms did in theirs. Kepler welcomed them in his study of the Lord's heavenly handiwork, the stars and the planets.

But the true hero of the mechanical universe and the major source of our modern technology was born prematurely on Christmas Day, 1642. His discoveries are legendary in number and breathtaking in scope: the most important are his three laws of motion and *the* calculus. However, the modern writer Aldous Huxley once called him "a failure as a human being." If this hero had done for God's Word what he accomplished for God's Works, our present society would be an entirely different and better place. That man was Isaac Newton.

Sir Isaac was profoundly religious. He once defined God as "eternal, infinite, and absolutely perfect." As well as Napier, mentioned above, Newton wrote widely on biblical matters. This includes his largely forgotten *Observations upon the Prophecies of Daniel and the Apocalypse of St. John.* Like all the scientists of his day, Newton knew that by studying nature's mathematical form he was dealing directly with God's Holy Works. Since divine attributes were to be read in the book of nature, scientific study was, by itself, an act of devotion. At Proposition VI in his most famous book *Principia Mathematica* Newton wrote:

> *There exists an infinite and omnipresent spirit in*
> *which matter is moved according to mathematical laws.*

As Newton noted, this passage is almost identical to Paul's speech in Acts 17:28.

Sir Isaac had a series of fifteen rules for the correct scriptural interpretation. His ninth rule has been my guide for this book:

> *It is the perfection of God's works that*
> *they are done with the greatest simplicity.*

Newton thought the 6 Days of Creation were just that, and not some poetic part of an ancient myth. The great man's knowledge of the First Temple overshadowed that of all his contemporaries, and he believed Solomon constructed it on divine proportions. He read the New Testament in Greek and the Old Testament in Hebrew as easily as the Latin in which he wrote his scientific papers. Although no one of his time had such a deep knowledge of the Bible, his superficial use of that knowledge is strangely curious.

# A FALLING AWAY

Yet every man falls short of the Lord, whether he is the grand Sir Isaac Newton or the most humble peasant. What was the outstanding error in the life of this emperor of science? Well, I think I know. And it was this error that prevented Newton from mathematically unlocking The Word of God in the same brilliant manner he had unlocked The Works of God. Simply put,

*Newton intensely denied the reality of The Holy Trinity.*

Because of the apparent subordination of Christ's Will to that of the Father in the Garden of Gethsemane, Newton obstinately refused to believe They were coequal. The great man thought the doctrine of The Trinity had corrupted Christianity. So, in truth, he rejected the divinity of Jesus, not realizing that to be *anti-Trinity* is to be *anti-Christ*. This spiritual error blinded Newton to the full implications of the Scripture's numerical patterns.

To become a full professor at Cambridge University in those days, each candidate had to be an ordained minister. If Newton's Unitarian views had been openly expressed, the college would have revoked his professorship. On ordination day he had to reveal his position or be a hypocrite. As luck would have it — just before that day arrived — he received a special exemption from holy orders, and so he kept his secret.

Such was Newton's passion for the Holy Scriptures that he wrote over one million words on them; unfortunately, most of it is still unpublished. Many of these writings, which he guarded in a black trunk in his private rooms, were anti-Trinitarian pamphlets. In 1888 the council of the University Library at Cambridge gave away the mathematical portion of these papers. Fifty years later, Sotheby's auctioned off the biblical writings, mostly on Daniel and Revelation. These are now dispersed around the world, never to be published.

With his mastery of ancient texts and his phenomenal memory, Newton knew huge sections of Scripture by heart and in their original languages. However, because he did not accept the reality of The Holy Trinity, he missed that indispensable *code word* for a deep understanding of the Bible. Without the pattern of The Trinity, as we shall see, it is impossible to discover the beautiful mathematical designs in God's Word.

By failing to uncover these forms and patterns, and by dismissing two persons from The Trinity, Newton is partly responsible for the atheistic state of modern science. It is significant that since Newton's time scientists have totally neglected any detailed study of the Bible.

The second major agent in the decline of faith was/is Charles Darwin. With the publication of his *On the Origin of Species* (1859) and *The Descent of Man* (1871), Darwin set the stage and prepared the materials for today's disbelievers. Most scientists claim we need billions of years in the earth's history for evolution to take place. Therefore, Genesis is simply false, and the Creation Week, a childish myth. Furthermore, they insist, God did not create Adam and Eve, but instead, both descended from apelike ancestors.

Biologists call the driving force of evolution "natural selection" or "survival of the fittest." This dogma directly opposes the Golden

Rule of our Lord. How is it possible to love your neighbor as yourself and still be in savage competition with him? You cannot have both Christ and Darwin!

To be perfectly fair, it must be said that not all 20th century scientists have been, or are, godless. Some of the greatest were fervently devout. Newton's modern equal, Albert Einstein, was very fond of stating what God *could do*. So fond, that a colleague once reprimanded him for telling God what *to do*.

Scientific man started as religious and God-fearing. Yet, due to the diligence of anti-Trinitarians, the single-mindedness of Darwinians, and the predominance of Humanists, he has lost his true self. Now he "wanders in vain through a dark labyrinth."

Life has its bizarre and curious twists; yet few can be more strange than the following. Out of the many institutions at Cambridge University, Sir Isaac Newton taught and lived in *Trinity College*. In fact, every day when he left his private rooms, he walked straight out the Great Gate of the college and paraded up *Trinity Street*.

# GOD AND SCIENTISTS: FUTURE

It is a commonplace to say we live in a scientific age. The mass of men respect and, yes, even worship the leaders of modern science. Everyone seeks their opinions and judgments. Whether we as followers of Christ like it or not, the public thinks that "religion without science is blind."

This angry divorce between science and religion has deeply harmed both camps. Still, Christianity need not fear the truths of science. How can God's Word and Works be at war? Hasn't modern archaeology fully supported the Old Testament?

In these special times we must endeavor to return scientists to their former reverential attitude toward the Lord's Word and Works. One possible way to do this is to take the methods of science and apply them directly to the Holy Bible. Mathematics is the basic tool for all scientific research. So, this is the central question: Is it possible to discover a simple, beautiful structure — a great code — in the numbers and Words of God? If so, then men of science will return and bring millions with them.

The Book of Daniel (12:4) has a striking passage implying that in the *end times* knowledge will grow:

> *But you, Daniel, close up and seal the words*
> *of the scroll until the time of the end.*
> *Many will go here and there to increase knowledge*

It seems meaningful that only *now* are we discovering the magnificent mathematical designs in God's Holy Word. I believe the book you are presently reading will show some *small part* of His glorious pattern. Armed with this design — revealed from Genesis to Revelation — everyone will give a hearing to Jesus' message. Then at last, we can completely carry out Christ's final commandment and Great Commission:

> *Therefore go and make disciples of all nations.*

# CHAPTER — 3

# TRIANGLE NUMBERS

*From the intrinsic evidence of his creation, the Great Architect of the Universe now begins to appear as a pure mathematician.*
Sir James Jeans (1877-1946)

U p to this point, I have only alluded to the mathematical form in God's Word. Now we shall begin to discover it. The triangle with its 3-in-1 structure (three sides but one figure) perfectly represents The Trinity. The 6 Days of Creation and the 28-day average of the moon's revolution are also, surprisingly, triangle quantities. And from the miraculous fishing scene in John 21:11 comes the most interesting triangle number in the entire Word of God, 153. God's Holy Spirit has 1081 as its triangle quantity. Yet perhaps the most bewildering of all such numbers is that of the Antichrist, 666.

What are these numbers?
Why are they called triangular?
Why should Christians know and understand them?

Numbers that can be arranged as shown in the figure below are triangle numbers. The reader can see from the diagrams that these are just the sums of the ordinary numbers. With a handful of pennies you will quickly find all these patterns.

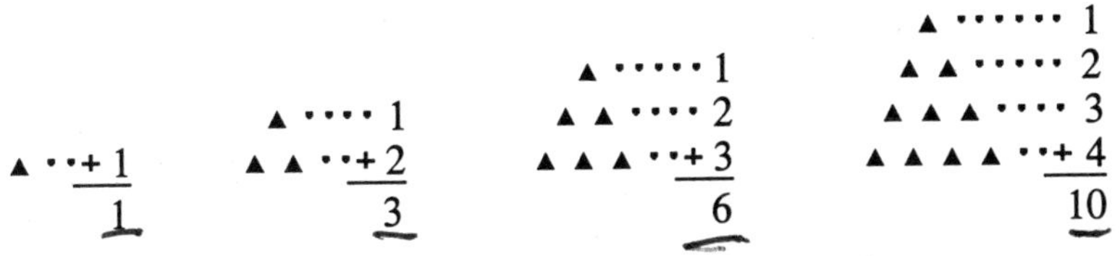

1, 3, 6, 10 are the first four triangle numbers.

FIGURE 3.1

For future reference, here are the first 46 triangle numbers. As we explore the Holy Scriptures, you will have many occasions to use this table.

## THE FIRST 46 TRIANGLE NUMBERS

| | | | | |
|---|---|---|---|---|
| 1. **1** | 2. **3** | 3. **6** | 4. 10 | 5. 15 |
| 6. 21 | 7. 28 | 8. 36 | 9. **45** | 10. 55 |
| 11. 66 | 12. 78 | 13. 91 | 14. 105 | 15. 120 |
| 16. 136 | 17. **153** | 18. 171 | 19. 190 | 20. 210 |
| 21. 231 | 22. 253 | 23. 276 | 24. 300 | 25. 325 |
| 26. 351 | 27. 378 | 28. 406 | 29. 435 | 30. 465 |
| 31. 496 | 32. 528 | 33. 561 | 34. 595 | 35. 630 |
| 36. **666** | 37. 703 | 38. 741 | 39. 780 | 40. 820 |
| 41. 861 | 42. 903 | 43. 946 | 44. 990 | 45. 1035 |
| 46. **1081** | - - - - - - | - - - - - - | - - - - - - | - - - - - - |

FIGURE 3.2

Triangle numbers are not common. Up to 1000, *only 4 percent* are such. When the numbers get even larger, these special ones become extremely rare. For example, in the first 2 million numbers, fewer than 2000 are triangular — on the average that is only 1 in 1000.

Instead of individual triangles, we can picture these quantities as the infinitely large pattern of FIGURE 3.3. Different triangle numbers are formed by cutting off top portions of the figure. To produce the triangles 10, 66, and 153, draw lines as illustrated. The number **1** is the crowning triangle quantity. Accordingly, the point at the summit of this arrangement shows God's position, while the first 3 points represent The Trinity.

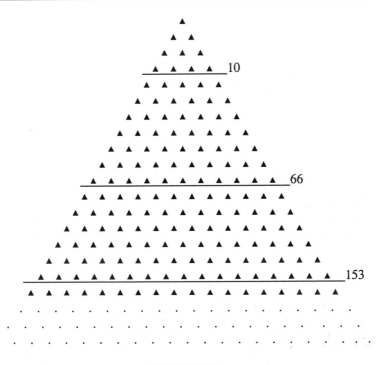

FIGURE 3.3

To find the Bible's favorite quantities, however, it is not necessary to draw diagrams or add up long lists of numbers. If you wish to produce the 6th triangle number, say, just do the following:

STEPS  1. Multiply 6 by itself (i.e., 6 x 6).
          2. Add 6 to your answer from STEP 1 (i.e., 36 + 6).
          3. Divide your answer from STEP 2 by 2 (i.e., 42 ÷ 2).
          4. Congratulations, you have found 21, the 6th triangle.

Try another example, say the 10th triangle number:
STEPS  1. Multiply 10 by itself (i.e., 10 x 10).
          2. Add 10 to your answer from STEP 1 (i.e., 100 + 10).
          3. Divide your answer from STEP 2 by 2 (i.e., 110 ÷ 2).
          4. Again congratulate yourself for finding 55, the 10th triangle number.

# DOES GOD PLAY DICE?

*I shall never believe God plays dice with the world.*
Albert Einstein

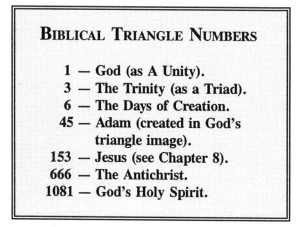

## BIBLICAL TRIANGLE NUMBERS

  1 — God (as A Unity).
  3 — The Trinity (as a Triad).
  6 — The Days of Creation.
 45 — Adam (created in God's triangle image).
153 — Jesus (see Chapter 8).
666 — The Antichrist.
1081 — God's Holy Spirit.

FIGURE 3.4

The reader must be wondering why 45 is Adam's number and 1081 is The Holy Spirit's. I found these exact values by using the almost lost science of **gematria**. *God's Word* provides the authority for gematria's use; the Apostle John explicitly mentions it. From Genesis to Revelation, it links all outstanding biblical verses. The very words of the Bible contain it. Simply stated, every character in the ancient Hebrew and Greek alphabets did double duty as both a letter and a number. So, *every word was also a number*. This practice is familiar from Roman numerals. The Romans, however, used only the letters I, V, X, L, C, and D as numbers. We will examine this fascinating, ancient topic in Chapter 6.

Consider the 7 triangle numbers in FIGURE 3.4. How do we know the authors of the Holy Scriptures put this pattern into the Bible under The Holy Spirit's inspiration? Couldn't it just be a mathematical accident? What are the odds favoring all the most prominent numbers in the Lord's Word being triangular?

Good questions are as important as good answers, and the previous ones can be rephrased as follows. If you randomly choose 7 numbers less than or equal to 1081, what is the probability they are all triangular? Because these calculations can be complicated, the details are in the Chapter Notes. The results, however, are given here:

> **By chance alone, the probability all 7 numbers are triangular is only 1 in 6,271,067,535 or roughly 1 in 6 billion.**

FIGURE 3.5

Do we really know how large a billion is? How many hours, days, or even years must pass to have a billion seconds? The answer isn't obvious or intuitive. Amazingly, it takes over 32 years to produce just 1 billion seconds. Therefore, it would require more than 200 years (32 x 6.271) to have 6.271 billion seconds. So, the probability these 7 numbers are triangular — by luck alone — is the same as picking **one particular second from 200 years of seconds.**

Such results are inconceivable! Nevertheless, they are based on only a few of the extremely numerous triangle numbers in God's Word. For example, the number of books in the Bible is 66; the length of Noah's Ark, 300 cubits; the number of God's Commandments, 10; the number of disciples in the Upper Room, 120; the total number saved in Paul's shipwreck, 276; and so on. All are triangle numbers!

We should have expected to find a mathematical design in God's Word. After all, as Sir James Jeans said, "the Great Architect of the universe now begins to appear as a pure mathematician." Surely what is true of the Lord's *Works* must also be true of His *Word*! What surprises is the beauty and simplicity of this triangle structure. As Newton wrote "It is the perfection of God's works that they are done with the greatest simplicity."

Our God is all-knowing. For that reason, it is almost blasphemous to say He would give us His Holy Book without any underlying design. After all, if numbers were not important, why is The Holy Trinity a major tenet of our relationship with God? Naturally, we will not understand all the mathematics involved. We can only hope to comprehend a tiny needle point on the mighty garment of His Creation. We do what we can; God does what He pleases.

# HOW ACCURATE ARE
# THE SCRIPTURES?

*In the beginning was the Word, and the Word was with God, and the Word was God. He was with God in the beginning.*
John 1:1

Gematria is only as accurate as the text on which it is based. Can we trust the words and numbers found in our present versions the Testaments? Has the original inspired Word been added to, deleted from, or altered somehow?

At life's plummeting pace today, it is impossible for us to truly understand an ancient culture. Yet we can achieve some knowledge of the fantastic dedication of the early copyists by studying the Masoretic texts. The Masoretes were the traditional Jewish scholars concerned with the correct copying, interpretation, and pronunciation of the Holy Scriptures. Original Hebrew texts often contain their detailed marginal notes.

Several years ago I had dinner with a biblical scholar who has a thorough knowledge of Hebrew and Greek. From him I learned about the extreme care and devotedness of these Masoretes. After supper we were discussing the accuracy of the copied (not translated) Hebrew Holy Scriptures. To illustrate Masoretic exactness, my friend opened an edition of the Old Testament in Hebrew. He turned to a certain page and pointed out two words. According to the marginal note, these were the *middle two words* (Levitcus 10:16) of the entire Pentateuch! I was impressed, but my friend wasn't finished. Again he flipped to a nearby page and indicated a single letter as the *middle symbol* (ו = vau) of these same books. Such dedication by copyists and commentators seems incredible in our hurried world.

The priests allowed the scribes a single error; of course, it had to be corrected. If a second mistake was committed, then they burned the entire manuscript, and the unfortunate copyist had to start over at Genesis 1:1. With this kind of devotion, who can truly say additions, omissions, or errors have crept into the Lord's Holy Word? I believe the Bible, in its original manuscripts, is the inerrant Word of God! As 2 Timothy 3:16 (KJV) says:

*All scripture is given by inspiration of God.*

# BLAISE PASCAL

Pascal (1623-1662) was a famous French scientist, mathematician, and religious writer. In his short life, he produced a wealth of inventions and discoveries, including the hydraulic pump and the first mechanical computer. Yet he did not discover the triangular pattern of FIGURE 3.6 named after him. Poets and writers knew it six centuries earlier. Yet he was the first to prove many of its intriguing properties.

**PASCAL'S TRIANGLE**

```
0
1   0
1   1   0
1   2   1   0
1   3   3   1   0
1   4   6   4   1   0
1   5   10  10  5   1   0
1   6   15  20  15  6   1   0
1   7   21  35  35  21  7   1   0
1   8   28  56  70  56  28  8   1   0
1   9   36  84  126 126 84  36  9   1   0
1   10  45  120 210 252 210 120 45  10  1   0
1   11  55  165 330 462 462 330 165 55  11  0 .
1   12  66  .   .   .   .   .   .   .   0 . .
1   13  78  .   .   .   .   .   .   .   0 . .
```

FIGURE 3.6

If you inspect the third column (highlighted) of the above figure, you will notice it contains nothing but triangle numbers (1, 3, 6, ...). By expanding this design downward, any triangle can be found.

New rows are easily produced by adding the two quantities directly above and to the left. For example, consider the highlighted trio **21**, **7**, and **28** (i.e., 21 + 7 = 28). Strikingly, you can generate the entire design in this fashion except the 1 at the apex. Those interested may find the next row; the answer is in the Chapter Notes.

Nothingness, represented by the zeros, surrounds the triangle. So it is possible to view "0" as the *first* triangle quantity.

The full, glorious significance of this figure will be obvious only after Chapter 7, "The Triangle of Creation." In the fourth column are all the 3-sided pyramid numbers — really just 3-dimensional triangle quantities. They can be constructed by stacking tennis balls on a three-sided base. And the fifth column represents all the 4-dimensional triangle numbers, which only God can see. The remaining columns include all the triangle numbers in every higher dimension. So, remarkably, each entry is a triangle. Therefore, Pascal's pattern represents all triangles in all dimensions. Its very shape mirrors The Trinity itself, which also contains all things.

# CHAPTER — 4

# THE RULE OF THREE

*"Come now, let us reason together, " says the Lord.*
Isaiah 1:18

*For now we see through a glass, darkly.*
1 Corinthians 13:12 (KJV)

*So we fix our eyes not on what is seen, but on what is unseen.*
*For what is seen is temporary, but what is unseen is eternal.*
2 Corinthians 4:18

## THE THREE LEVELS

All Christians want to understand The Word and The Works of God. The Lord gave us the gift of reason that we should use it to strengthen our faith and spread the Good News. Our spiritual life and confidence will grow as our knowledge of The Word increases. I am using *knowledge* in the special sense of the Bible's numbers and their half-hidden form and meaning. Armed with this irrefutable logic, Jesus' message can then break down the last walls of resistance. And finally Christ will gain a hearing in the halls of science and the homes of unbelievers everywhere.

In this scientific age people are much more skeptical than in earlier times, even to the point of cynicism. Everyone has a show-me attitude. To get beyond this initial resistance, **you must prove the Bible contains hard scientific facts**. Only then will today's man give the testimony of Jesus' divine message its rightful consideration.

To change a man's mind you must *first* appeal to his reason, said the ancient Greek philosopher Aristotle. Only after this do you use moral and ethical evidence to persuade and convert. Some four hundred years after the Greek sage, the Apostle Paul used this method when he gave his matchless sermon on Athens' Hill of Mars (Acts 17:16-34). Paul's teaching began by complimenting the Athenians for having the good sense to build an altar "to an unknown god." By praising their reasonable actions, he gained an audience for Christ's message. I could do no better than to follow his example.

Only in these latter days is the mathematical design in God's Word being uncovered. Scientists, however, have studied the Lord's Works for centuries and written about them in countless scientific books, papers, and journals. To parallel this I will prove The Word is also a paradise of numbers and design. But we are late arrivals with much to do and little time to do it in. So let's get started.

The Holy Scriptures have many levels of meaning. From a mathematical viewpoint, I discern at least three. These are as follows:

---

## THE THREE LEVELS OF INTERPRETATION

**Level 1.** References to quantities, times, measurements, and the number of occurrences of important words, phrases, and events.

**Level 2.** The gematria of the words.

**Level 3.** The triangle form of God's Word as revealed by the Triad Rules.

---

FIGURE 4.1

In Isaiah 45:15 the prophet says:

*Truly you are a God who hides himself,*
*O God and Savior of Israel.*

To learn what treasures God has buried beneath the surface of His Word, we shall inspect each level in turn. Please keep your Bible and a calculator handy to verify the references and the computations.

# LEVEL I: NUMBERS IN THE BIBLE

Consider two interesting and related examples that dramatically show the Bible's use of numbers.

## EXAMPLE ONE: THE PERFECTION OF GOD

By creating the world in precisely 6 days, God intentionally introduced *symbolic* numbers. The Lord repeated the creation formula 6 times, once for each day. Now it is obvious our omnipotent Godhead could have produced the universe in an instant, a day, a million years, or any time period He wished. So, why did He choose 6 days? The question is still valid no matter how long you interpret the "biblical day."

In Chapter 3 we discussed the triangle quantities that our Lord used to show the form of His Holy Word. If you look at FIGURE 3.1, you'll see that 6 is the third such quantity. Beyond being triangular is the intriguing fact that 6 belongs to a very small but unique group of numbers called "perfect." This is the true reason for the 6 Days of Creation, and not one of God's infinite other choices.

I can almost hear the reader asking, "What is a perfect number?" It is a quantity equal to the sum of *all* the different numbers that divide into it exactly (not including itself). Consider 6, the first perfect number.

*[handwritten: 1, 2 + 3 can all be divided by 6]*

1, 2, and 3 all divide 6,

and 1 + 2 + 3 = 6.

Therefore, 6 is a perfect number.

1, 2, 3 divide 6,

6     and

1 + 2 + 3 = 6.

## THE 6 DAYS OF CREATION

The next perfect quantity, 28, is the average number of days the moon takes to circle God's perfectly created earth. Coincidence? Not likely! The Lord does not design randomly like some modern artists by hurling paint at a canvas.

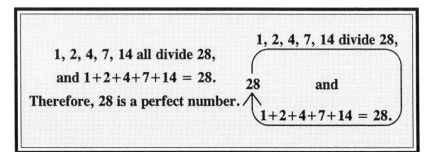

## THE 28-DAY AVERAGE OF THE MOON'S REVOLUTION

Perfect numbers are only a single thread in the immense Garment of God's Creation. No matter what we learn there is always more to discover. Let's illustrate. While doing this research, I noticed that not only are 6 and 28 perfect quantities, but, surprisingly, both are also triangles. I wondered if the following few perfects were triangles as well. A quick check showed that indeed this was the case. Naturally, the next question was "Is every perfect number also a triangle number?" Unexpectedly, the answer is again, yes! The group of all perfects rests like a smaller bowl within the larger bowl of triangle numbers. This unusual piece of information will be useful later.

Even with our modern supercomputers, we know only 32 perfects. The largest of these has a phenomenal 455,663 digits! By replacing every letter and space on this page by a digit, this number would require almost 125 pages to print. The sum of all the fundamental particles in the entire universe is much, much smaller. For a mathematical proof that every perfect number is also a triangle number and a list of all those presently known, see the Chapter Notes.

For reasons that will be apparent long before you finish this book, I predict just **37** perfect numbers exist. Presently, only God knows the remaining ones.

## EXAMPLE TWO: THE SONS OF ISAAC

Let's briefly recall the wonderful story of Jacob and Esau, the battling twin sons of Isaac and Rebekah. Representative of their later struggles, Genesis 25;26 tells us the second-born Jacob came out of the womb grasping his brother's heel. Three verses later, we learn how the grown Jacob traded a bowl of soup for his starving brother's entire birthright. Later, by deceitful means and his mother's help, the second son obtained his father's final blessing. This additional offence enraged Esau to the point of murder; so Jacob wisely fled north to the land of his uncle Laban.

On this journey Jacob had his famous vision of the staircase to Heaven (Genesis 28:10-15). During this, God spoke to him and repeated the great 7-fold promise He had given to Abraham:

> *There above it stood the Lord, and he said:*
> *"I am the Lord, the God of your father Abraham*
> *and the God of Isaac. I will give you and your*
> *descendants the land on which you are lying.*
>
> *Your descendants will be like the dust of the earth,*
> *and you will spread out to the west and to the east,*
> *to the north and to the south. All peoples on earth*
> *will be blessed through you and your offspring.*
>
> *I am with you and will watch over you wherever you go,*
> *and I will bring you back to this land.*
> *I will not leave you until I have done what*
> *I have promised you. "*

This revelation and blessing must have given Jacob a wonderful sense of confidence and destiny.

In Laban's land Jacob labored 7 years for Rachel. Yet on their wedding night, he discovered that the crafty uncle had substituted his eldest daughter, Leah, for her younger and more beautiful sister, Rachel. Laban it seems, as well as Jacob, was something of a trickster. After working another 7 years and finally marrying Rachel, the nephew and the uncle quarreled. With a mixture of anger and fear, Jacob collected his wives, children, and livestock and immediately began another trek. This time it was back to the dangerous land of Canaan and Esau.

Now this story takes a curious twist. On his fearful journey to encounter Esau (Genesis 32:1), we learn of a conference between Jacob and some "angels of God." Strangely, we are not told what took place at this meeting. However, no passage in the Bible is without purpose and meaning; consequently, we should closely examine the verses following the first. Do we find anything unusual? Yes, in verse 14!

In what unexpectedly turns out to be a successful effort to regain Esau's friendship, Jacob sends him a gift of **220 goats**. Of all conceivable numbers, this is the most symbolically important he could have given. This quantity is the smaller half of what mathematicians call a "friendly pair" of numbers, the larger part is **284**. The properties of friendly and perfect numbers are almost identical. If the sum of the divisors of one quantity equals another, and vice versa, then the two are called a friendly pair. See the Chapter Notes for others. This pair, 220 and 284, is the smallest possible. Consider them.

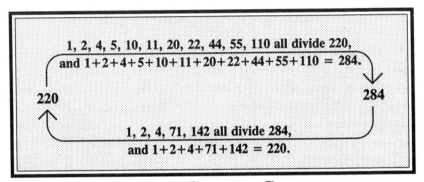

$$1, 2, 4, 5, 10, 11, 20, 22, 44, 55, 110 \text{ all divide } 220,$$
$$\text{and } 1+2+4+5+10+11+20+22+44+55+110 = 284.$$

220

284

$$1, 2, 4, 71, 142 \text{ all divide } 284,$$
$$\text{and } 1+2+4+71+142 = 220.$$

## THE FIRST GIFT: 220 GOATS

Now let's realize this is approximately 2000 B.C., and Jacob is a semi-nomadic herdsman. Such traveling flock-keepers lived a life of severe hardship, carrying with them everything they owned. There was only enough time to learn what was necessary for survival: mending the tents, guarding the flocks, and getting them safely to the next green pasture. For these reasons, it is totally impossible Jacob could have known the properties of friendly numbers without help. So the "angels of God" from verse one must have told him.

In the early centuries of the Christian Era, it was a common practice for two people to each wear one of these numbers, signifying their friendship. Outside the Bible these quantities were first mentioned by the Greek mathematician Pythagoras around 550 B.C. — 1500 years after Jacob.

The Scriptures pointedly emphasize this quantity by a second gift of **220 sheep** (Genesis 32:14). Still, Esau probably never counted any of these animals. Even if he had, the exact number would have meant nothing to him. God alone knows the past and the future; therefore,

*1, 2, 3 can all be divided By 6:*
*and 1 + 2 + 3 = 6, then 6 is a* *Perfect #*
The Rule of Three / 29

the numbers are for our benefit not Esau's. This implies the Lord must have softened the heart of Jacob's brother. And The Holy Spirit depicted that softening by using what would be called friendly numbers. Remember, God promised Jacob the land of Canaan, not death by Esau's hand.

As another example of triads, note the following. Each quantity dresses itself as the exact sum of precisely three significant triangle numbers. To verify these results refer to the table on page 16.

$$220 = 1 + 66 + 153$$
$$284 = 3 + 28 + 253$$

$\}$ All triangle numbers

Jacob's peace offerings hold still more surprises! In the verse following 14, a third gift is prepared consisting of **140 animals**. This quantity is the smaller half of what mathematicians call a "semi-friendly" pair of numbers, the larger part is **195**. These quantities differ very slightly from the former by not including 1 in the sum of their divisors. As before, 140 and 195 are the smallest possible such pair. Compare them to the previous couple.

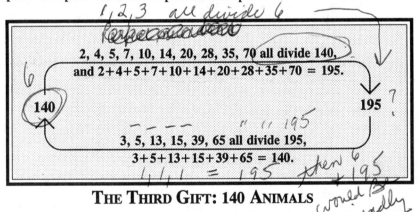

*1, 2, 3 all divide 6*
*Perfect number*

2, 4, 5, 7, 10, 14, 20, 28, 35, 70 all divide 140,
and 2+4+5+7+10+14+20+28+35+70 = 195.

6

140                                    195 ?

3, 5, 13, 15, 39, 65 all divide 195,
3+5+13+15+39+65 = 140.

*1, 1, 1 = 195 then 6 + 195 would be friendly*

### THE THIRD GIFT: 140 ANIMALS

Since Jacob's flocks were not inexhaustible, each time he gave the smaller half of the smallest pair. Nevertheless, the numbers did not influence Esau; God did. Clearly, the "angels of God" instructed Jacob to present 3 gifts of exactly these sizes. How else could he have known them? The Lord promised Jacob the land of Canaan, and a multitude of descendants. For that reason He could not allow Esau to murder him. Man may break promises; God does not. These numbers are uniquely symbolic; they offer mathematical evidence of the presence of God's Holy Spirit in the Scriptures.

Even these last two numbers can be expressed as the sum of exactly three triangles each, and with similar patterns.

$$140 = 10 + 10 + 120$$
$$195 = 21 + 21 + 153$$
$$\left.\right\} \text{All triangle numbers}$$

# LEVEL II: GEMATRIA

Now that we have explored the borders and margins of Level 1, we shall descend to deeper territory. At the second level the landscape is so unusual and unknown that recent centuries have only hinted at its existence and treasures.

You could ask a thousand people what the word *gematria* means before getting a single correct reply. Even if someone had the right answer, it is extremely doubtful they could explain gematria's connection to the Bible. So here is a good dictionary definition: Gematria is the ancient science of using the numerical values of Greek, Hebrew, and Latin letters to change words into numbers.

Strange? Not really. Even the title for this section illustrates it. The "II" are two capital letters "i" with a number value of **2**: this is an example of Roman gematria. From public school you may recall that only a few Latin letters have a numerical value. On the other hand, in the Greek and Hebrew alphabets *every symbol* did double duty as both a letter and a number. Any Webster's dictionary under "Special Signs and Symbols" will provide a full list of the Roman and Greek letters with their numerical values. The Hebrew number/letter code is more difficult to find. However, E. W. Bullinger gives a complete listing in his *Number in Scripture* (Kregel Publications, Grand Rapids, Michigan, 1967, page 48). Also, by inspecting any Hebrew edition of the Pentateuch, you will notice that every chapter and verse is numbered with the letters from their alphabet.

The authors of both Testaments knew their gematria; they used it widely in their writings. We can be certain of this because the Bible tells us so. Here is a famous example from Revelation 13:18:

*This calls for wisdom. If anyone has insight,*
*let him calculate the number of the beast,*
*for it is a man's number. His number is 666.*

John is instructing us to add the numerical values of each letter in a certain man's name and the total will be **666**. The Apostle had to write in code for reasons of personal safety. Yet his followers would have known exactly whom he meant, and we shall also. God's Word contains thousands of instances of gematria, many of which we will examine and decode.

In modern biblical studies, a truly incredible shroud of silence envelops the topic of gematria. I have often asked myself, "Why?" "Do we not want to fully understand God's word?" To omit gematria from any study of the Bible is equivalent to trying to appreciate a glorious sunset with your eyes shut. If you want to understand the full depth and power of the Holy Scriptures, then gematria is crucial. For that reason, and because it is such a neglected subject, I have devoted all of Chapter 6 to it.

# LEVEL III: THE TRIAD RULES

*For there is nothing hidden that will not be disclosed, and nothing concealed that will not be made known or brought out into the open*
Jesus, Luke 8:17

We will use three rules or functions to reveal what we could otherwise only dimly perceive. Each rule has the same simple form. First, choose a number from the Bible (the pre-image), and then do some operations on it (for example, $+$, $-$, x, or $\div$) to get a second number (the image). That's it! These functions project murky figures into clear bold pictures.

Our first rule is follows in very formal attire. You may recognize it, however, from page 17. There it casually dressed itself in work clothes while constructing the 6th and 10th triangle numbers.

---

## RULE ONE: THE TRIANGLE NUMBER FUNCTION

$$n \text{--------} > 1 + 2 + 3 + \ldots + n$$

pre-image                    image

---

FIGURE 4.2

Ancient mathematicians had a simple formula to avoid needless addition of long lists of consecutive numbers. Their technique was just a generalization of what we did in the two examples on page 17. If you wish to see this formula and a short proof, turn to the Chapter Notes.

For our first example here, let 3 be the pre-image:

$$3 \text{--------} > 1 + 2 + 3$$
$$= 6$$

So, 6 is the 3rd triangle number. Consider a second example: *ADD all Triangle #'s*

$$36 \text{--------} > 1 + 2 + 3 + \ldots + 36$$
$$= 666$$

This shows that the mark of the Antichrist, 666, is the 36th triangle number. As a third instance, choose 17 as the starting quantity:

$$17 \text{--------} > 1 + 2 + 3 + \ldots + 17$$
$$= 153$$

*153 is the 17th Triangle #*

Therefore, the number of fishes from John 21:11 is a triangle number. I will frequently refer to **153** and as the **Fish** or **Celestial Number**. The properties of this quantity are spectacular.

I propose to prove that the entire Word of God forms a symbolic triangle structure, *an image of The Trinity*. The Lord said, "Let us make man in our image" and for poetic emphasis added "after our likeness." Since God fashioned man on The Trinity, it is reasonable that His Holy Spirit should have fashioned the Bible on The Trinity also. As this book goes on, you will learn of the abundant triads in all the Bible's key names and critical events. This will enrich your mind, elevate your spirit, and confirm your faith.

Scholars call our second rule *casting out nines*. They have found it in first century A.D. manuscripts involving gematria. It is the simplest of the Triad Rules; you merely add up the digits of your starting number (pre-image) to arrive at your final number (image). For simplicity assume the "n" of Rule One has three digits abc.

---

**RULE TWO: THE DIGITAL ROOT FUNCTION**

$$n = abc \text{ --------> } a + b + c$$
pre-image                    image

---

FIGURE 4.3

For example:

$$153 \text{ --------> } 1 + 5 + 3$$
$$= 9$$

So the digital root of the Fish Number is 9. Usually this function is repeatedly applied until only a single digit remains. Consider the large triangle number 57,291:

$$57,291 \text{ --------> } 5 + 7 + 2 + 9 + 1$$
$$= 24$$
$$\text{and again, } 24 \text{ --------> } 2 + 4$$
$$= 6 \text{ (final root)}$$

The previous two results can be concisely written as follows:

$$57,291 \text{ --------> } 24 \text{ --------> } 6$$

Triangle            Root            Final Root

If the digits begin at 1 and increase regularly, then the image is always a triangle number. For instance:

$$1,234 \text{ --------> } 1 + 2 + 3 + 4$$
$$= 10 \text{ (see page 16)}$$

In dealing with his fellow man, Sir Isaac Newton was the essence of arrogance. Yet when studying The Works or The Word of God, he had the humility of a saint. He once said:

*I do not know what I may appear to the world; but to myself
I seem to have been only like a boy playing on the seashore,
and diverting myself in now and then finding a smoother
pebble or a prettier shell than ordinary, whilst the great ocean
of truth lay all undiscovered before me.*

This is the proper attitude for any seeker after the truth. For the oceans of
ignorance are everywhere, while the ponds of truth are scattered and few.

Rarely — perhaps once or twice in a lifetime — the seeker may
stumble upon a large lake or an inland sea. Discovering, the Third
Triad Rule was such a time for me. This function is a mighty search-
light illuminating deeply into the oceans of truth. Like the second law,
you add up the digits, but first raise each to the Trinity Number 3.
FIGURE 4.4 introduces this rule in full formal uniform, while the
examples following show how it works.

---

### RULE THREE: THE TRINITY FUNCTION

**This idea will play the central role in unveiling Holy
Scripture. Again consider any three digit number, abc.**

$$abc \longrightarrow a^3 + b^3 + c^3$$

pre-image            image

---

FIGURE 4.4

In the above figure, the small 3 at each letter's upper right is a
compact way to show repeated multiplication. For example, $a^3$ means
a x a x a. Let's illustrate:

$$
\begin{aligned}
276 \longrightarrow \quad & 2^3 \;+\; 7^3 \;+\; 6^3 \\
= \;& 2x2x2 \;+\; 7x7x7 \;+\; 6x6x6 \\
= \;& 8 \;\;+\;\; 343 \;+\; 216 \\
= \;& 567
\end{aligned}
$$

If you are unfamiliar with mathematics, this must appear a most
unusual rule. Its outstanding feature is the general *threeness*. Also, no
matter how you scramble the pre-image digits, the image will always
be the same. Consider 726, a mixed up version of 276:

$$726 \text{-------} >\quad 7^3 \;+\; 2^3 \;+\; 6^3$$
$$= 7\text{x}7\text{x}7 \;+\; 2\text{x}2\text{x}2 \;+\; 6\text{x}6\text{x}6$$
$$= \;\;343\;\; + \;\;\; 8 \;\;\; + \;\; 216$$
$$= 567 \text{ (as before)}$$

This function will allow us to see clearly through a dark glass into a world of marvelous symbolism and beauty. You will appreciate the unbelievable clarifying value of this rule and the profound insights it allows into God's Holy Word after Chapter 8, "The Fish."

# THREE IN ONE

The driving force in modern science (especially physics) is the reduction of all rules to a single, grand, unifying law. Whenever this is possible, the many rules are then special cases of one general law. The ancient mathematician Euclid, in his book *The Elements*, tried to deduce all his propositions from just a basic ten. These he called self-evident truths. He failed, but scientists ever since have honored his method by imitation. Yet, men of science could more wisely have followed the identical process, set forth much earlier, in God's Holy Word.

For instance, in North America we have thousands upon thousands of criminal and civil laws. These are so numerous and complex that most people need highly trained lawyers just to interpret them and to tell us our do's and don'ts. If we just followed God's original Ten Commandments, however, we could fantastically simplify the legal system. Our laws are — or should be — just special cases of God's basic ten.

In a few sentences, Jesus reduced even these ten to only two. Unlike Euclid, they remain as true today as they were then. You will find them in Matthew 22:37-39 (KJV) and in the hearts of Christians everywhere:

*Jesus said unto him, Thou shalt love the Lord thy God with all thy heart, and with all thy soul, and with all thy mind.*

*This is the first and great commandment.*

*And the second is like unto it,*
*Thou shalt love thy neighbour as thyself.*

By obeying Jesus' Two Commandments, we could render thousands of laws unnecessary. There are no lawyers in Heaven.

Similarly, we can reduce the three mathematical rules, explained on the previous pages, to just one. Strikingly, the Triangle and Digital Root Functions derive as special cases from the Trinity Function. *So, the third rule expresses the most general and powerful law — in effect it fathers the other two.* The Chapter Notes have a proof of this.

Far East of Eden, God created a second paradise: His Holy Word. By using our knowledge of numbers, the ancient science of gematria, and the Triad Rules, we will ascend and descend the Three Levels of Interpretation in this new garden. We shall not leave a second time. Reason will guide our steps, but The Holy Spirit will move us. Come, read for yourself, and marvel at the creations of our Lord.

# CHAPTER — 5

# THE SEVEN PILLARS

*And God blessed the seventh day and sanctified it.*
Genesis 2:3

*Wisdom hath built her a house; she has hewn out its seven pillars.*
Proverbs 9:1

*Lord, how oft shall my brother sin against me,
and I forgive him? till seven times?*
Peter, Matthew 18:21-22 (KJV)

## THE ROOT OF SEVEN

E veryone perceives something unusual about the number seven, even if they cannot explain what it is. The Hebrew word for *seven* is *shevah* from the root *savah* meaning to be full, satisfied, or have enough of. This root dominates the true use of the word *seven*. On the seventh day God rested because His Works were complete, full, and perfect. No addition to, deletion from, or alteration of could have changed them without harm. The derived word *shavath,* meaning to desist, cease, or rest became our *Sabbath*, the day of rest.

Probably the reader sees a similarity between *shevah* and *seven* and wonders whether this is accidental. The answer is a definite no! To show how languages are related, linguists regularly use the extraordinary stability of number names. The following chart illustrates this curious stability for *seven* throughout the centuries.

| | Hebrew | Sanskrit | Greek | Latin | German | English |
|---|---|---|---|---|---|---|
| 7 | *shevah* | *sapta* | *hepta* | *septem* | *sieben* | *seven* |

Man abhors any mutation of his numbers. The basic constancy of the word *seven* is startling evidence of this.

# THE OLD TESTAMENT AND SEVEN

*In the beginning God created the heaven and the earth.*
Genesis 1:1

In the original Hebrew, Genesis 1:1 contains exactly **7 words** composed of **28 letters**. As we know, 28 is the second perfect number and equals $7+7+7+7$. Also, it is the sum of the first 7 digits (i.e., $1+2+3+4+5+6+7=28$); therefore, by definition it's a triangle. The number symbolism here is evident: God's Creation was *complete* and *perfect*. The Bible's first verse holds many wonders. This pattern of 7s continues into the second verse with 14 ($7+7$) words, and so on.

The Old Testament is a mighty forest of majestic patriarchs like Enoch, the 7th from Adam, and Abraham, blessed by the Lord 7 times. Consider Enoch's great-grandson Noah who loaded the clean animals by 7s and then spent 7 days in the Ark before the rains came. Even after the Flood this deluge of 7s continued:

- Moses was called by the Lord on the 7th day (Exodus 24:16).
- When God instructed Moses on the building of the Tabernacle, there were to be 7 gold lampstands, each with 7 branches for 7 candles (Exodus 25).
- Jacob labored 7 years for Leah and 7 more for Rachel (Genesis 29:18, 30).
- Leviticus 25:8 speaks of the Year of Jubilee that comes after the following: "Count off 7 sabbaths of years — 7 times 7 years — so that the 7 sabbaths of years amount to a period of 49 years."
- Joseph correctly interpreted Pharaoh's first dream of 7 fat and 7 lean cows, and his second of 7 full and 7 thin heads of wheat (Genesis 41).
- The fiery furnace was made 7 times hotter than usual in an attempt to destroy Daniel's three friends (3:19).
- Nebuchadnezzar went insane for 7 years: "he lived with the wild donkeys and ate grass like cattle (Daniel 5:21)."

- In our future, the most important 7 will be Daniel's
  famous prophesied 70th week of 7 years (9:20).

This just a short list from a wealth of Old Testament choices. Even the actual word *seven* and its variations occur only in multiples of 7:

> *Seven* occurs 287 times or 7 x 41.
> *Seventh* is found 98 times or 7 x 14.
> *Seven-fold* occurs 7 times.
> *Seventy* is used 56 times or 7 x 8.

To complete the Creation Week, the Lord labored for 6 days and rested on the 7th. Beyond completeness, this implies there is something meaningful about viewing 7 as 6 work days plus 1 rest day — both triangle numbers.

| 6 | + | 1 | = | 7 |
|---|---|---|---|---|
| Days of Creation | | Day of Rest | | Complete Week |

Before leaving the Old Testament, let's recount one last, memorable example, Joshua and the walls of Jericho:

> *March around the city once with all the armed men.*
> *Do this for 6 days. Have 7 priests carry trumpets of rams'*
> *horns in front of the ark. On the 7th day, march around*
> *the city 7 times, with the priests blowing the trumpets.*
> Joshua 6:3-4

And, yes, the walls did come tumbling down, according to the latest archaeological data. Bryant Wood of the University of Toronto claims new research evidence is consistent with Scripture. Wood said, "It looks to me as though the biblical stories are correct." [1] These latest findings were published in the 1990 March/April issue of the *Biblical Archaeology Review*. Those interested can also find a short summary in *Time* magazine (5 March 1990), under the title "Score One for the Bible."

> **As its root suggests and all the examples show,**
> **7 in the Bible symbolizes completeness.**

# SEVEN IN THE NEW TESTAMENT

Good beginnings and endings are important for books and for life; momentous words and events should accompany each. For that reason Genesis 1:1 and Revelation 22:21 will both receive a detailed analysis, the former in Chapter 12 and the latter in Chapter 15. But here we will consider the first verses of the Gospels.

Recall that Matthew begins the New Testament by tracing Jesus' lineage from Abraham to David. These initial sentences — like those of Genesis — have a substructure entirely composed of 7s. We know Matthew was aware of this because in 1:17 he says:

*Thus there are fourteen (7+7) generations in all from*
*Abraham to David, fourteen (7+7) from David to the exile*
*to Babylon, and fourteen (7+7) from the exile to the Christ.*

That is just the obvious part. Let's go deeper — beyond the English — right into the original Greek words and letters. When we do, and consider the first 28 triangle generations (up to the Babylonian exile, verse 11), what we find is truly remarkable. Judge for yourself!

- Only 49 (7 x 7) different words are used.
- Of these, 28 (7+7+7+7) begin with a vowel and the remaining 21 (7+7+7) with a consonant.
- Of the 49 different words, 35 (7 x 5) occur more than once and 14 (7 x 2) occur only once.
- These words are composed from 266 (7 x 38) letters, including 140 vowels (7 x 20), and 126 consonants (7 x 18).
- The verses contain 42 (7 x 6) nouns and 7 nonnouns.
- In the genealogies, 35 (7 x 5) proper names are used and 7 common names. Of these proper names, 28 (7 x 4) are male ancestors of Jesus, and 7 are not.

Succeeding verses are also imprinted with 7s. However, the point is clear: the Gospels constantly use 7 as a major theme.

The Lord's Prayer contains 7 petitions: 3 relate to God and 4 to man. In the 10 Commandments there is a similar division: the first 3 refer to God and the remaining 7 concern man. When Jesus rephrased the Decalogue into its more general form, mentioned in the previous chapter, He recognized this division. The triad relating to God became the Great Commandment:

> *Love the Lord your God with all thy heart*
> *and with all your soul and all your mind.*

The 7 affecting man were changed to the well-known Golden Rule:

> *Love your neighbor as yourself.*

Without doubt, the most sublime and immortal words (statements) ever spoken are the last 7 by Jesus from the Cross. At the beginning of time, God had determined that only 7 would be voiced on that transcendent day:

---

### THE LAST 7 WORDS FROM THE CROSS

1. Father, forgive them, for they know not what they do.
2. I tell you the truth, today you will be with me in paradise.
3. My God, my God, why have you forsaken me?
4. Woman behold thy son [John] . . . Behold thy mother!
5. I thirst.
6. Father, into your hands I commit my spirit.
7. It is finished.

---

FIGURE 5.1

Throughout the Bible this insistence on 7 is all encompassing. It begins in Genesis. It flourishes in the Law and the Prophets. It is resplendent in the Gospels and the Epistles. It bursts into glorious bloom, however, in the Apocalypse. Here the mystery of God is complete with 7 seals, 7 trumpets, 7 vials — 777.

# SEVEN AMONG THE GREEKS AND ROMANS

The ancient Greeks played a central role in Paul's writings. He witnessed to them. He suffered for their salvation. He named his Epistles after their cities. Tradition says he wrote 21 (a triangle) of these formal letters.

The following examples show how truly fond the Greeks were of using 7 as the quantity implying completeness:

- The 7 Wise Men.
- The 7 Wonders of the World.
- Ulysses spent 7 years as a prisoner of the witch Circe.
- The 7 Against Thebes.
- The 7 Sisters (daughters of Atlas).
- Even their horses' iron shoes were fastened with 7 nails.

From time to time, the keepers of lists changed particular Wise Men and certain Wonders of the World by deletion and addition. Yet, the outstanding point is that the number of each was always kept constant at 7. This implies the greater priority of the list's total over who or what might actually be in it.

The Romans had their own 7 Sages, not to be confused with the Greeks' 7 Wise Men. Legend says 7 followers of Romulus raped 7 Sabine women and afterward took them for brides. (This is the basis for the Broadway musical *Seven Brides for Seven Brothers*.) Since the Romans built their city on 7 hills, they could hardly avoid this number. You may recall the passage about the Harlot of Babylon (Rome):

> *This calls for a mind with wisdom.*
> *The 7 heads are 7 hills on which the woman sits.*
> Revelation 17:9

Philo Judaeus was a renowned Jewish philosopher from the time of our Lord. He believed the Greeks, at an earlier period, had derived their number knowledge from Moses or his descendants. We do know that by 500 B.C. the Greek thinker Pythagoras had an extensive mathematical philosophy. And the practical Romans picked up what little number sense they had from the Greeks.

# SEVEN AND OUR CULTURAL WORLD

*Measure seven times before you cut.*
Old Russian proverb       ·

Our western culture is adorned with a great variety of 7s. We see 7 colors in the rainbow. The beautiful constellation of stars called the 7 Sisters or Pleiades consists of only 6 naked-eye objects. Yet we insist, to keep the number right, that the 7th is hiding. On more earthly matters, biologists divide the animal kingdom into 7 parts. Musicians sing do, re, me, fa, so, la, ti and start the scale over with another do, an octave higher. Writers pen plays about the *7 Ages of Man*, and sailors speak of the *7 Seas*. Movie producers say, and legends affirm, it is always *Snow White and the 7 Dwarfs*. Seven is considered a lucky number. To be born the 7th son of a 7th son of a 7th son is said to be a triple blessing.

Since the triangle is the symbolic form of The Trinity, it's intriguing that only 7 basic types of triangles are possible. A list of these and a diagram are in the Chapter Notes.

From ancient times we have had 7 days in our week; any other length seems unnatural. The French, at the time of their revolution, rashly metricized the week into 10 days. The tormented citizens, however, only briefly tolerated this outrage.

Nevertheless, we could choose to have 6 colors in our rainbow as the Cree and Natchez Indians did, or even 3, as some other cultures do. Hindus divide their musical scale into many more parts than 7. Yet, if Christian civilization is your heritage, then you unconsciously insist on 7 sections for each. Other cultures use other numbers. The previous examples imply that the divisions are *totally arbitrary*, and therefore culturally learned. Nonetheless, for Christians 7 is a powerful image.

The Islamic people, the descendants of Abraham through his illegitimate son Ishmael, have also inherited this number tradition. Their religion tells them they must — at least once in a lifetime — go to Mecca and circle their sacred cubical rock (the Kaaba) exactly 7 times.

I cannot end this chapter without recounting a wonderful instance of this number in an English children's riddle. Each item is complete at 7.

> *As I was going to St. Ives*
> *I met a man with 7 wives.*
> *Every wife had 7 sacks,*
> *Every sack had 7 cats,*
> *Every cat had 7 kits.*
> *Kits, cats, sacks and wives,*
> *How many were going to St. Ives?*

Since the first man was going to St. Ives and the others (he met) were leaving, the correct answer is one. Versions of this riddle occurred centuries earlier in medieval Italy and ancient Egypt, and all were based on 7.

# A NATURAL SEVEN

Do we find the number 7 in The Works of God? I have read and studied mathematics and science for most of my adult life. Yet, I cannot recall a single instance of a true connection between 7 and the natural world. Even something as simple as the number of petals on a flower shows no 7s. We have plants with 3, 4, 5, 6, and 8 petals, but not 7. Search long and hard and you may find a 4-leaf clover, but never one with 7 leaves.

Curiously, Shakespeare knew all this centuries ago. In his celebrated play *King Lear*, there is a scene where the Fool and the King discuss the number of stars. (These are probably the 7 stars of the constellation Orion/Nimrod referred to in Revelation 1:16: "In his right hand he held 7 stars.")

The Fool speaks first:
> *The reason why the 7 stars are no*
> *more than 7 is a pretty reason.*

And the wise King replies:
> *Because they are not 8.*

The Fool says:
> *Yes indeed. Thou wouldst make a good Fool.*

Shakespeare's wise Fool said it exactly right. We should not force our cultural predispositions on the natural world, which is better described by other numbers. The Lord chose 7 for His Holy Word, not for His Holy Works. God dominates numbers, numbers do not dominate God.

# CHAPTER — 6

GEMATRIA

*And even the very hairs of your head are all numbered.*
Jesus, Matthew 10:30

*Thou* [God] *hast ordered all things in measure and number.*
The Wisdom of Solomon 11:20, Old Testament Apocrypha

*Prove all things; hold fast that which is good.*
Paul, 1 Thessalonians 5:21 (KJV)

For most people life is plain, even flat at times. The great mountain peaks of existence are either far behind us or on the distant horizon. Occasionally, with a rush of excitement, we remember the intoxicating heights of our first date, the birth of a child, or our rebirth in Jesus. For me, discovering gematria was an event of that magnitude, an Everest in importance.

In Chapter 4, I briefly referred to gematria as the Second Level of biblical interpretation. We defined it as the ancient science of adding the numerical value of a word's letters to arrive at a sum. That sum provides additional information in greater depth, but always harmonizing with the word's obvious meaning. To clarify this idea, I will give many examples.

The Old Testament was written in Hebrew, the New Testament in Greek. *Both languages did not have number symbols; instead, they used letters of their alphabets for counting.* The reader is already familiar with this practice: everyone has made a table of items and numbered/lettered them a, b, c, and so on.

This is not hidden or unusual knowledge. *Webster's New World Dictionary* under "Special Signs and Symbols" lists the entire Greek alphabet, giving the numerical value of each letter. Although not hidden, gematria is definitely not used. In our century religious writers have universally avoided this topic. At the close of this chapter, I will give some possible reasons for this evasion.

## ROMAN GEMATRIA

First, start with what we know. Most churches, likely yours, have dedication blocks marked with inscriptions and dates. Usually the date is in Roman numerals, for example, MDCCCCL means 1950. This is an instance of gematria, but unlike the Greek and Hebrew alphabets, only a few Roman letters have a value. Here is a list:

$$I = 1, \quad V = 5, \quad X = 10, \quad L = 50, \quad C = 100, \quad D = 500$$

Quite late in the Roman Empire, scholars introduced M for 1000, probably to complete the list at 7. However, DD or other variations were originally used. Consider the following three words and their Roman numeral values:

LIVID = 50 + 1 + 5 + 1 + 500 = 557.
CIVIC = 100 + 1 + 5 + 1 + 100 = 207.
LEGION = 50 + 1 = 51 (E, G, O, and N have no value).

Many Roman words were numbers, but not every Roman number was a word. Yet, because neither Testament has any Roman numerals/letters, let's quickly move along.

## GREEK GEMATRIA

Secondly, investigate what we may not know. Please read over the following table of Greek letters and their corresponding numerical values (FIGURE 6.1). You do not have to memorize anything. Just reflect on it for a moment and note the page or figure number for future reference. Anyone familiar with the Greek alphabet will notice three letters besides the normal twenty-four. The numbered notes after the chart explain these and other unusual points.

# THE GREEK ALPHABET

| UNITS | TENS | HUNDREDS |
|---|---|---|
| Alpha<br>A $\alpha$ = 1 | Iota<br>I $\iota$ = 10 | Rho<br>P $\rho$ = 100 |
| Beta<br>B $\beta$ = 2 | Kappa<br>K $\kappa$ = 20 | Sigma<br>$\Sigma$ $\sigma$ $\varsigma^4$ = 200 |
| Gamma<br>$\Gamma$ $\gamma$ = 3 | Lambda<br>$\Lambda$ $\lambda$ = 30 | Tau<br>T $\tau$ = 300 |
| Delta<br>$\Delta$ $\delta$ = 4 | Mu<br>M $\mu$ = 40 | Upsilon<br>Y $\upsilon$ = 400 |
| Epsilon<br>E $\epsilon$ = 5 | Nu<br>N $\nu$ = 50 | Phi<br>$\Phi$ $\phi$ = 500 |
| Stigma<br>$\varsigma^1$ = 6 | Xi<br>$\Xi$ $\xi^2$ = 60 | Chi<br>X $\chi$ = 600 |
| Zeta<br>Z $\zeta$ = 7 | Omicron<br>O $o$ = 70 | Psi<br>$\Psi$ $\psi$ = 700 |
| Eta<br>H $\eta$ = 8 | Pi<br>$\Pi$ $\pi$ = 80 | Omega<br>$\Omega$ $\omega$ = 800 |
| Theta<br>$\Theta$ $\theta$ = 9 | Koppa<br>$o^3$ = 90 | Sampsi<br>$\text{♊}^5$ = 900 |

FIGURE 6.1

[1] The letter $\varsigma$ (stigma) was not in the Greek alphabet. Why it should be used for the number 6 is uncertain and not a little mysterious. If the numbering pattern had been orderly, then 6 would have been denoted by $\zeta$ (zeta).

During times of intense religious feeling, "stigmata" are said to appear in the palms of the devout. Of course, these marks recall the nails driven through the hands of our Lord Jesus Christ.

$^2$ Because of its shape, this character is called the serpent letter and was seldom used.

$^3$ This is an obsolete letter whose lower case form is identical to omicron. In rare cases, the gematria meaning of a passage is clear only if 90 is used for "o."

$^4$ The two lower case forms have the same value: ς is only used at the end of a word and σ elsewhere. We will also see this practice with the Hebrew alphabet. Outwardly the terminal letter sigma looks like stigma.

$^5$ This is another obsolete letter, used only as a number. Omega is the final letter in the Greek *writing* alphabet.


Karl Menninger is the world's foremost authority in the field of ancient alphabets and number symbols. According to him (see *Number Words and Number Symbols* published by M.I.T. Press, 1970, p. 270) the Greeks always used an abbreviation for the letters στ. Normally στ would have a value of 200 + 300 or 500. However, Menninger says that when these two letters occurred together at the beginning of the word, the Greeks always replaced the 500 by a value of 6 — the value of stigma. For example, consider the *stadion*, σταδιον, a Greek unit of measurement equal to 600 feet. Examine its full gematria value:

$$
\begin{array}{llllll}
\text{st} & \text{a} & \text{d} & \text{i} & \text{o} & \text{n} \\
\sigma\tau & \alpha & \delta & \iota & o & \nu \\
6 \ + & 1 & 4 & 10 & 70 & 50 = 141
\end{array}
$$

The most important word in the life of any Christian is **JESUS**. The most important word in the Bible is **JESUS**. Remarkably, Joseph and Mary did not even choose it. In a scene commemorated by many famous artists, the archangel Gabriel announced to an astonished Mary:

> *You will be with child and give birth to a son,*
> *and you are to give him the name Jesus.*
> Luke 1:31

If gematria is to have any deep meaning at all, it must begin with this Most Holy Name. Using the original Greek from the Gospels, let us find the *number value* of His name:

> **This divine name cloaks life's greatest mysteries: life, death, and resurrection.**
>
> ## J E S U S
>
> I η σ ο υ ς
>
> 10  8  200  70  400  200  = **888**

FIGURE 6.2

I still remember the exact day and hour when I first learned of this beautiful threefold regularity in our Savior's number. It transfixed my soul with wonder and emotion! Here was a mystery worth chasing. This book is the result of that pursuit.

Before learning more gematria, we will investigate why the number **8** was chosen for association with **JESUS**.

# THE EIGHTH WONDER

The 1st Person in The Trinity is related to the 1st number cubed (1): $1^3 = 1 \times 1 \times 1 = 1$. The 2nd Person in The Trinity is related to the 2nd number cubed (8): $2^3 = 2 \times 2 \times 2 = 8$. The 3rd Person, as we shall see, has a similar relationship to the 3rd number cubed (27): $3^3 = 3 \times 3 \times 3 = 27$.

The emphasis implied by the 3 repetitions in 888 shows a close connection with the Trinity Number 3. Furthermore, by applying the Trinity Function (FIGURE 4.4) to 888, this closeness to triangle numbers becomes unmistakable:

$$
\begin{aligned}
888 \dashrightarrow \quad & 8^3 \;+\; 8^3 \;+\; 8^3 \\
= \; & 8 \times 8 \times 8 + 8 \times 8 \times 8 + 8 \times 8 \times 8 \\
= \; & 512 \;+\; 512 \;+\; 512 \\
= \; & 1536
\end{aligned}
$$

Except for its first three digits, 1536 seems an uninteresting image. Nonetheless, by reapplying the Trinity Function to 1536 and to each new image, something quite extraordinary occurs. Consider:

**888 ---->1536---->369---->972---->1080---->513---> 153**

**The image of 888 becomes the triangle number 153, the number of fishes in the net from John 21:11.**

FIGURE 6.3

Notice that this process involves 7 numbers, implying *completeness*, and 6 transformations, indicating *perfection*.

If 7 is the number of completeness of a list, then 8 begins a *new* list. To learn how and where the Bible displays this relationship of *renewal* and *rebirth*, read the following examples:

- All the Gospels say that Jesus rose from the dead "on the first day of the week." For Jews this was Sunday, the 8th day of their week.
- The Ark contained 8 souls: Noah, his wife, his three sons, and their wives. When these 8 stepped out of the Ark onto a new world, they had to start a new order and regenerate all life on earth.
- The Jewish ritual act of circumcision had to be done on the 8th day (Genesis 17:12). Concerning that, Luke 2:21 says: "On the 8th day, when it was time to circumcise him, he was named Jesus, the name the angel had given him before he was conceived."
- Aeneas, a paralytic, was healed in Jesus' name and rose out of his bed after 8 years (Acts 9:33-35).
- Jesus' brilliant Transfiguration took place 8 days after the first announcement of His future sufferings. Exactly three disciples witnessed this showing of the glory to be at the Second Coming.
- The entire Bible details 8 resurrections, distinct from our Lord's and His saints:
  - 3 in Old Testament (1 Kings 17, 2 Kings 4 and 13)
  - 3 in the Gospels (Matthew 9, Luke 7, John 11)
  - 2 in Acts (9 and 20)

- The Resurrection is the 8th "great sign" in John's Gospel.
- In Greek, the word *Lord* is 800 or 8 emphasized.

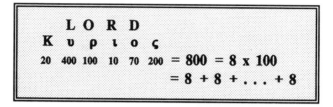

- Eventually we will learn all the incredible gematria surrounding the title CHRIST; for now observe only that, like JESUS, it is also a multiple of 8:

$$
\begin{array}{c}
\textbf{C H R I S T} \\
\textbf{X}\ \rho\ \iota\ \sigma\ \tau\ o\ \varsigma \\
600\ \ 100\ \ 10\ \ 200\ \ 300\ \ 70\ \ 200 \ = \ \textbf{1480} \ = \ \textbf{8 x 185} \\
= \textbf{8 + 8 + \ldots + 8}
\end{array}
$$

Summary: LORD, JESUS, and CHRIST are all multiples of 8, and the New Testament uses them in exactly 8 combinations:

| | |
|---|---|
| 1. Lord | 5. Lord Christ |
| 2. Jesus | 6. Jesus Christ |
| 3. Christ | 7. Christ Jesus |
| 4. Lord Jesus | 8. Lord Jesus Christ |

Since each of these names is composed of 8s, their sum is also a multiple of 8.

- During the church's early days, believers used the first and last letters, Xς, of *Christos* (*Christ* in Greek) as a contraction for the entire name. This short form is just 8 emphasized:

The many instances involving 8 and Jesus could be continued for several pages, but the preceding list is sufficient to make the point:

> **In the Bible, 8 is the number of resurrection and renewal.**

# THE NUMBER OF THE BEAST

Now that our detour has shown the prominence of 8 in our Savior's life, death, and resurrection, let's return entirely to gematria. As previously stated, The Holy Spirit distinctly gave divine sanction for gematria's use in Revelation 13:18:

> *This calls for wisdom. If anyone has insight,*
> *let him calculate the number of the beast,*
> *for it is man's number. His number is 666.*

In this often quoted passage, John tells us the sum of the letters in the Beast's name totals 666. Yet, why didn't he just clearly state who the Beast was? Scholars would have saved countless hours of speculation and calculation. However, bluntly naming the Beast would have meant an assured and painful death. Personal safety was the issue. John is the only disciple believed to have escaped martyrdom. We may be confused by this verse, but the author's contemporaries would have known the code and, therefore, this Antichrist's real name. In those days, literate Greeks and Jews commonly practiced gematria.

The NIV Study Bible gives an interesting note on Revelation 13:18: it identifies the probable Antichrist as the emperor Nero Caesar. This despot was the first to persecute the early Christians; his cruelty eclipsed that of all previous emperors. Under his orders Christians became lion bait in public arenas and human torches in private gardens. By using the emperor's common Greek name, both given and family, we have:

FIGURE 6.4

The above sum is apparently not the number we are seeking, but a moment's reflection reveals its true nature. As John says, "If anyone has insight . . .":

$$1332 = 666 \times 2 \text{ (or)}$$
$$= 666 + 666$$

So, his gematria is just the sum of two 666s.

By Satan's standards, Nero's inhuman actions wholly qualify him as *an* Antichrist. I purposefully used *an*, because history has seen many; 1 John 2:18 clearly states this:

*even now many antichrists have come.*

In the *last days* we can expect the final and most terrible Beast.

It may be significant, assuredly it is unusual, that the sum of all the Roman numerals amounts to precisely 666. This symbolizes the cruel, merciless behavior of the entire Roman Empire, past and future.

$$\begin{array}{cccccc} I & V & X & L & C & D \\ 1 + & 5 + & 10 + & 50 + & 100 + & 500 = 666 \end{array}$$

Many Christians believe the last Antichrist will rule the revised Roman Empire that we call the European Union. We are living in such turbulent times; anything seems possible.

For the present, we have finished our short tour of the New Testament world of Greek gematria. Accordingly, we will turn our attention to the equally fascinating Hebrew.

# HEBREW GEMATRIA

The Jewish alphabet contains twenty-two letters with five variations used only in the last position. This makes twenty-seven number/letters, available, exactly like the Greek.

## THE HEBREW ALPHABET

| UNITS | | TENS | | HUNDREDS | |
|---|---|---|---|---|---|
| Aleph | א = 1 | Yod | י = 10 | Koph | ק = 100 |
| Beth | ב = 2 | Kaph | כ = 20 | Resh | ר = 200 |
| Gimel | ג = 3 | Lamed | ל = 30 | Shin | ש = 300 |
| Daleth | ד = 4 | Mem | מ = 40 | Tau | ת = 400 |
| He | ה = 5 | Num | נ = 50 | Koph | ך[1] = 500 |
| Vau | ו = 6 | Samech | ס = 60 | Mem | ם[2] = 600 |
| Zayin | ז = 7 | Ayin | ע = 70 | Num | ן[3] = 700 |
| Cheth | ח = 8 | Pe | פ = 80 | Pe | ף[4] = 800 |
| Teth | ט = 9 | Tsaddi | צ = 90 | Tsaddi | ץ[5] = 900 |

FIGURE 6.5

[1,2,3,4,5] These finals occur only at the ends of words: they are variations of five previous letters. The actual Hebrew aleph-beth has only 22 *writing* characters.

From Genesis to Malachi, countless examples of Hebrew gematria abound. In this chapter we will investigate a few, but many more will be given later. In Genesis 1:26 the Lord declares:

*Let us make man in our image, in our likeness.*

"Adam," the first human (the Hebrew means man or mankind), possesses a very instructive gematria. Notice that Hebrew reads from right to left.

$$\textbf{A D A M}$$
$$\text{מ ו א}$$
$$\textbf{45} = 40 \quad 4 \quad 1$$

FIGURE 6.6

The Bible uses the plural form "our" with "in our image," and for emphasis and poetic effect repeats this as "in our likeness." Among other things, this means the image of The Trinity, the likeness of the triangle. In Chapter 3, I showed the extraordinary frequency of a triangular form in the Lord's Holy Word. Since God created Adam in the image of The Trinity, then *Adam* should also be triangular. *And he is!*

To confirm the triangle nature of 45, see FIGURE 3.3 or read on. By applying the Triangle Function to the pre-image 9, we find the following:

$$9 \text{ --------> } 1 + 2 + 3 + \ldots + 9$$
$$= 45$$
$$= \text{a triangle number}$$

So 45 is the 9th triad, implying you can arrange that number of identical objects into a triangle. It's no accident that the *last* creation of God was the 9th (see Chapter 15). A symbolism more beautiful than our Lord's is difficult to imagine.

After this brief look at Genesis, let's turn our attention to the Book of Daniel. Consider the rewards of great faith so wonderfully illustrated by the story of Daniel and his three friends Hananiah, Mishael, and Azariah. Perhaps you know them better by the names their Babylonian masters gave them: Belteshazzar, Shadrach, Meshach, and Abednego. (It is noteworthy that the gematria of these names has no symbolic meaning whatsoever.) As the biblical story unfolds, Daniel tells how his companions refused to bow down and worship Nebuchadnezzar's statue. Their disobedience so angered the king that he cast them into "the fiery furnace." While in this inferno, they remained unharmed, and a mysterious fourth figure joined them. Most believe this to have been Jesus (see Daniel 3:25).

Their miraculous escape from certain death serves as an everlasting model of faith's great rewards. Also, Daniel's incredible survival in the lion's den and his rapid rise to prominence as Babylon's first minister speak loudly of divine protection and counsel. The total gematria of their true Hebrew names is equally striking:

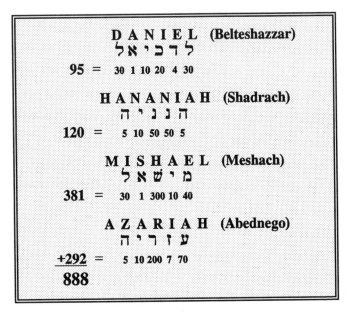

FIGURE 6.7

This startling and meaningful sum, 888, links the supernatural escape of the faithful exiles with Jesus — the other figure.

Sometimes too many examples can detract from a position rather than lend it support. Nevertheless, at the risk of overstating my case, I will present two more: one Hebrew, the other Greek. First, return to the original example of Nero, to find the value of his common Hebrew name:

FIGURE 6.8

So there it is, the name of the Beast. Whether in Greek (see FIGURE 6.4) or Hebrew, the answer is identical: Nero Caesar/666.

This gematria result implies the author of Revelation had a knowledge of Hebrew. He purposefully divided his Apocalypse into 22 parts, corresponding to the number of Hebrew letters. Later, these parts became the chapters.

The second example illustrates the connection between 888 and 666 — Christ and Antichrist. One exceeds and the other falls short of the most sacred symbol in all Christendom, the Cross.

FIGURE 6.9

This result should be unusual enough to shake even a militant atheist into questioning his belief that the Bible is *just like any other book.*

# THE JEWELS OF GEMATRIA

I will attempt to summarize these ideas and tie them together, by giving my limited vision of God's magnificent design.

Most Christians sadly underrate Satan's power and place in our future and our past. The Devil is so clever he can even fool men into denying his very existence. For humanity always finds it easier to smell the roses than touch the thorns. Originally, Satan was one of the Lord's three created archangels, endowed with a free will and awe-inspiring powers. Being part of the first creation, his triangle number, 666, reflects potent features. When he fell "like lightning from heaven," he lost his place and his number, but not his strength. In the final years of the coming Tribulation, Lucifer will mock God by somehow associating his original celestial number, 666, with his apprentice, the Antichrist.

Nothing in our Lord's Holy Word happens by accident. When that old Gospel song says "He has the whole world in His Hands," take it quite literally. So the occurrence of 666 in Revelation's 13th chapter and 18th verse is no chance event. Historically, 13 has always been considered a very unlucky number; part of this is superstition, but part has a rational, biblical basis. Also, presumably, verse 18 was chosen to represent 6+6+6 — see below.

Consider the following gems from God's gematria:

| ANTICHRIST | CROSS | JESUS |
|---|---|---|
| **666** = 18 x 37 | **777** = 21 x 37 | **888** = 24 x 37 |
| or (6+6+6) x 37 | or (7+7+7) x 37 | or (8+8+8) x 37 |

FIGURE 6.10

The above figure reemphasizes each number as the sum of identical digits, but it also introduces the quantity **37**. As you read this book, the importance of **37** will become apparent. This number is the supernatural key that unlocks the mathematical power of The Word. As a foretaste, notice that *Christ*, like *Jesus*, is built entirely of **37s**:

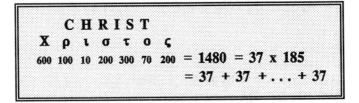

CHRIST
X ρ ι σ τ ο ς
600 100 10 200 300 70 200 = **1480** = 37 x 185
= 37 + 37 + ... + 37

FIGURE 6.11

The NIV Study Bible provides a further engrossing comment on Revelation 13:18: "Others take 666 as a symbol for the trinity of evil and imperfection — each digit falls short of the perfect number 7." As accurate as this note is, I believe the ideas should be expanded to include the Resurrection Number, 888. Surely everyone agrees 7 is the number of completeness. Therefore, 777 must represent absolute completeness of whatever you are measuring — here, good and evil are on the scales. Figuratively, 888 is one beyond each 7, while 666 falls short in every digit:

```
    666 <--- 777 ---> 888
 Antichrist   Cross    Jesus
```

Another symbolic truth is crucial in this situation. The Cross is the noble emblem of Christ's sacrifice for man's sins. It is a mighty bulwark against the unholy trinity of Satan, the Antichrist, and his False Prophet. The sign of the Cross stands forever immovable between good and evil, the first subduing the second. Between Satan and the sinner stands only the Cross.

This wonderful symbolism of man's protection from Satan's power is further highlighted when 777 is expressed as the sum of 3 meaningful triangle numbers:

```
 777  =    45     +     66    +    666
        Mankind <--- Bible ---> Antichrist
        or Adam
```

For now, this ends our journey into the wonderful world of gematria. In closing, we will look at some broader aspects of its use, purpose, and history.

## CRISIS AND CONCLUSION

Earlier, I promised to comment on the present lack of interest in gematria. It was not always so! Gematria has a long and honorable history, originating with the writing of Genesis. From then, through the first century to the late Renaissance, Christians have recognized gematria's great value: it provides a second level of meaning to God's Holy Word.

Why the present silence? I believe it is all part of religion's immense problem: turning its back on science. This avoidance of anything scientific or mathematical is based on the completely unfounded fear that logic and reason will prove our faith false. Newton, Kepler, and Galileo had no such timidity. Contrary to what almost all Protestant leaders and followers secretly believe, Christianity and science are not at war. They are just different divisions in the same army.

Despite his great biblical scholarship, Newton's forceful anti-Trinitarian writings worried many Christians and alienated them from his other achievements. And Charles Darwin's evolutionary "theory," founded on the social chaos of "survival of the fittest," began the official separation of science and Christianity. As well, modern secular movements like humanism and communism have labored mightily to make this separation into a final angry divorce. What are their motives? Quite simply, they fully recognize the tremendous power of science and mathematics in today's world. They know this divorce will have a profoundly crippling effect on our religious life and our success at evangelizing. Do not allow them to separate us from God's Holy Works!

In Christian circles, unfortunately, a general feeling of uneasiness surrounds anything even faintly mathematical. This book will attempt to help any believer, who might have these groundless fears, to overcome them. By so doing, he can share in the feast God has prepared in the magnificent structure of His Writings. Surely anyone would be disappointed at a grand meal that skipped the dessert course. Similarly, he should be gloomy about missing some courses in God's great banquet of The Word.

It is a curious twist of history that since Christianity has given up on gematria, science has adopted it. All modern computers use a coding system identical to gematria. For example, in the *A*merican *S*tandard *C*ode for *I*nformation *I*nterchange (*ASCII* for short) *a* is 97, *b* is 98, *c* is 99, and so on. Since computers recognize only numbers, some such code is essential.

Besides this, embassies and military installations regularly use gematria to send secret scrambled messages from country to country or between army bases. Even large companies use it. Of course the computer accomplishes all this. When the Apostle John sent an encoded message to his readers on their Antichrist's identity, he anticipated by 2000 years the workings of modern society.

One modern book has been written on just the topic of gematria: Lucas and Washburn, *Theomatics* (Stein and Day, New York, 1977). It is not my habit to be critical of other writers, especially Christians. Their book, however, leaves the reader with the totally false view that they invented gematria. Maybe that was not their intention, but it is their message.

Only in these *last days* is the mathematical framework of God's Word being understood. Perhaps that is part of His Blueprint as well. After all, history records the progressive revelation of His Plan. Compared with the early Christians, who possessed Jesus' full message, the patriarchs of the Old Testament had limited knowledge of God's designs. Paul says as much in Colossians 1:25:

> *I have become its servant by the commission*
> *God gave me to present to you the word of God*
> *in its fullness — the mystery that has been*
> *kept hidden for ages and generations.*

Since we have all 66 books as a foundation, our view of the Lord's Plan is larger even than Paul's. Yet, if we see further than others, it is only because we stand on the shoulders of giants like Paul. Over the centuries, the devout have made more and more insights. This is happening even as world events fulfill the prophecies that pave the wide path toward the *end times*. Centuries earlier Daniel 12:4 (KJV) said it best:

> *But for thou, O Daniel, shut up the words, and seal*
> *the book, even to the time of the end: many shall run*
> *to and fro, and knowledge shall be increased.*

Just as our knowledge of His Works, created in 6 days, advances and improves, so our understanding of His Word, recorded in 66 books, increases and deepens. Both numbers are triangular.

Christians are supposed to walk by faith, because without belief it is impossible to please God. Therefore, the reader should not use gematria, or the other mathematical patterns in this book, as a substitution for faith. Treat these designs as additions, not replacements. Followers of Jesus, however, should use these scientific insights into the different symbolic levels of Holy Scripture to evangelize. They provide a basis for a sympathetic first hearing and often the saving of another soul for Christ. Use, not abuse, is the key.

As experts in logic say, it is impossible to prove a universal negative. Still, no one has shown any book to possess a design remotely approaching that of the Bible. From Book 1 to Book 66, the mathematical patterns harmonize with each other. This agreement is so great that only the inspiration of The Holy Spirit can account for it. The reader may be certain that we know only a tiny portion of the entire structure. The Lord's Word is an organic whole. Its multiple pieces fit together in a *great code* to form an eternal, universal masterpiece.

In FIGURE 6.3 the Trinity Function displayed the link between **888** and **153**, the former as the pre-image of the latter. As completely unexpected as this relationship was, what follows surpasses it. Apply the Trinity Function one last time:

**The terminal image, 153, reveals the true nature of 888. Here's why!**

$$153 \dashrightarrow 1^3 + 5^3 + 3^3$$
$$= 1 \times 1 \times 1 + 5 \times 5 \times 5 + 3 \times 3 \times 3$$
$$= 1 + 125 + 27$$
$$= 153$$

**The pre-image and the image are identical. God incarnated as man!**

FIGURE 6.12

Each time 153 simply resurrects itself!!! There is no further image. Therefore, the Trinity Rule has uncovered the symbolic bond between 153 and the Resurrection.

# CHAPTER — 7

# TRIANGLE OF CREATION

*The heavens declare the glory of God;*
*and the firmament sheweth his handywork.*
Psalm 19 (KJV)

*For the invisible things of him from the creation of the*
*world are clearly seen, being understood by the things*
*that are made, even his eternal power and Godhead.*
Romans 1:20 (KJV)

God is all that is, or ever was, or ever will be. Throughout the ages men and women have sought God to explain their existence and to give it meaning. The Godhead is the deepest of all mysteries. We approach this subject with a sense of awe and an awareness that we are in the presence of the most sacred and divine.

God gives form and content to our daily lives. Without Him we are lost in an endless forest, without a purpose for this life, without any hope for the next. Not only has the Lord given form and content to our lives, He has done the same for the entire universe. After all, the Lord created the cosmos out of the chaos. How do we know this? Genesis 1:2 tells us:

*And the world was without form, and void.*

Everything had a beginning except The Trinity: three parts, coexistent, coequal, and coeternal. God just is. **"I am who I am."** Scientists are finding that the entire universe points back to a beginning in the Big Bang. That instant in time when God said **"Let there be,"** and there was.

To fully understand the Holy Scriptures, the reader must pay close attention to individual words as well as their meaning in context. When Genesis says God is "**dividing**" and "**separating**," it means He is creating the *form* of the cosmos. The Old Testament authors used the Hebrew word for *create* only with the Lord and never for human activity.

I claim the *form* of God's Word and Works is ultimately triangular. If my theory is correct, then the Creation itself must also be modeled on The Trinity. How could this be? This seems an extraordinary thing to say. Yet, the Lord has given us the means to prove this most astonishing fact. Not only does a unique triangular image exist for the Creation, but it also explains the following attributes of the Deity:

- How God created order out of chaos by separating and dividing.
- God's infinite qualities.
- God's perfection.
- God's omnipresence.

Consider a time before time. Before Adam and Eve, before matter existed, before the Big Bang, before anything man can know. Only the presence of The Holy Trinity pervaded the infinite void. At this point I ask myself the following two questions:

*Why did God create the universe? Why do I exist?*

Daily we experience the mystery of the second question. I mean that sense of "me-ness" feeling joy and pain while the world hurriedly goes its own thoughtless way. That sense of self that falls upon the thorns of life and bleeds. Why I exist is as puzzling as why the universe exists. No one knows the answers to these questions. God keeps these secrets to Himself. But at least once our Lord stepped out of eternity into time and created for 6 days. We have the privilege of viewing that grandeur and glory. Let's consider it.

As *an image* of the actual creation, the **Triangle of Creation** could have been formed in the following majestic fashion. Regard our portrait of The Trinity as a triangle *anywhere* in the immensity of the void. Call the vertices after the First, Second, and Third Persons of the Godhead.

In the beginning, God created an initial particle somewhere in space. This first particle can be viewed from any part of The Trinity, say The Holy Spirit. The distance between the particle and The Holy Spirit is then divided in half creating a second particle. By chance, this new speck can again be viewed from any part of The Trinity, say the Second Person. Now this new distance is divided in half to produce a third particle. If continued, this seemingly chaotic process will generate a spectacular triangular image of God's actual creation. I have sketched the process in the figure below.

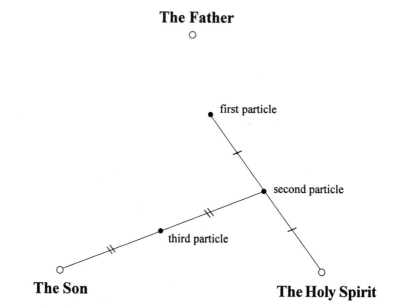

## The Father

first particle

second particle

third particle

**The Son**

**The Holy Spirit**

The following steps summarize this process.

1. Create an initial particle *anywhere* in space.
2. *Randomly* choose any part of The Trinity, say The Holy Spirit.
3. Divide in half the distance from the particle to The Holy Spirit. This division marks the position of the second created particle.
4. Again *randomly* choose any part of The Trinity, say the Son.
5. When this new distance from the second particle to the Son is divided in half, a third point is created.
6. To produce the beautiful Triangle of Creation, simply continue in the above manner for as many particles as desired.

These 6 steps define a process most quickly executed by a computer. In the Chapter Notes you will find a simple program to produce the images shown below for any number of particles. The following diagrams deliver some of the unexpected beauty of the design's formation.

No form visible from 10 created particles.

With 100 particles, some basic
patterns begin to appear.

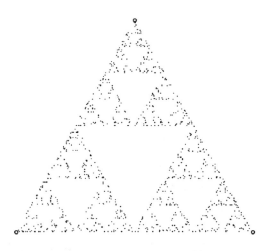

At 1000 particles the entire shape appears.

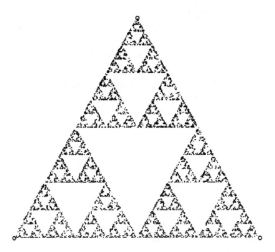

10,000 reveal considerable fine structure.

# THE TRIANGLE OF CREATION

At 100,000 particles the whole
magnificent pattern springs to life.

FIGURE 7.1

By just *dividing* we have produced this remarkable figure. Not only is this an image of the Creation, but it also has the same properties as the Godhead. Like The Trinity itself, any part that resembles the whole is the whole. In depth it is infinite; in size it is omnipresent. See the Chapter Notes for a detailed description of these and other properties.

# THE TRINITY AND THE TRI-UNI-VERSE

The Triangle of Creation possesses all those qualities listed at the beginning of this chapter that illustrate our Lord's Glory. For these reasons, it is *an image* of God's original Creation in the Big Bang. At that moment the Godhead transformed some of the Tri-Unity's infinite energy into our universe. But is there any concrete evidence of a Tri-Unity in the real universe and not just in our image, the Triangle of Creation?

Science deals with the natural world: the world of matter, energy, space, and time. Ever since Einstein's most famous equation, $E = mc^2$, we have known that energy (E) and mass (m) are interchangeable (c = the speed of light). This means the natural world is really a tri-unity comprising three basic aspects:

$$\text{matter-energy, space, and time.}$$

So, the answer to the question is a definite yes! The most magnificent divisions of the universe *do* reflect the Tri-Unity of The Trinity.

Scientists believe the world is a continuum of matter-space-time. None of the three can exist without the other two; accordingly, they were created simultaneously. Genesis 1:1 announces this fundamental truth:

> **IN THE BEGINNING [time] GOD CREATED**
> **THE HEAVENS [space] AND THE EARTH [matter].**

The foundation verse of the Bible is the foundation verse of science. It is all there in the original Hebrew in the very first statement. This initial sentence consists of 7 words, implying completeness, and the words themselves contain 28 letters, indicating triangularity and perfection.

The Godhead is a trinity, not just three separate gods or a triad. The parts of The Holy Trinity are like the three sides or points of a triangle: just different aspects of the same figure, the same mysterious Transcendental Being. However, if God existed only as an ultimate mystery then man could never know Him. For that reason He revealed part of Himself through His Son Jesus. Perhaps the Son is all we shall ever truly know of the Father. Yet, The Trinity dwells in The Works of Creation as well as The Word. Paul said as much in this chapter's opening quote:

> *For the invisible things of him from the creation of the world are clearly seen, being understood by the things that are made.*

Our world is not a MULTI-VERSE but a TRI-UNI-VERSE of matter-space-time, parallel to the very nature of the Creator. Remarkably, each of the natural world's elements is also a trinity:

**MATTER-ENERGY** has many transformations and forms. The most obvious is motion, which we experience as events. Matter-energy occurs everywhere in space. As momentum it is universally conserved — none has ever been created or destroyed since the Big Bang. Jointly, these and other forms make up the phenomena of our physical lives.

**SPACE** is 3-dimensional, wrote the great Renaissance astronomer Johannes Kepler, because it is a necessary counterpart of the Divine Trinity.

**TIME** is an arrow emerging from the distant past, hurdling through the present moment, to land in some uncertain future. And biblical prophecy is the true revelation of that future.

These arrangements are summarized below:

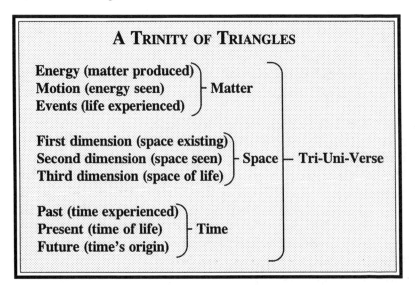

### A TRINITY OF TRIANGLES

Energy (matter produced)
Motion (energy seen)         ├ **Matter**
Events (life experienced)

First dimension (space existing)
Second dimension (space seen)   ├ **Space** ├ **Tri-Uni-Verse**
Third dimension (space of life)

Past (time experienced)
Present (time of life)       ├ **Time**
Future (time's origin)

# THE DAYS OF CREATION

God's Creation lasted 6 days, a perfect triangle number, and to complete the week He rested on the 7th day. These 6 days were broken into two groups of 3. The first set corresponds to the latter as shown by the arrows below. God divided and gathered on days 1-3, giving form to the formless. He made and filled on days 4-6, giving life to the lifeless. Genesis 1:2 proclaims these twin aspects of form and filling.

*And the world was without form and void* [empty].

### DAY ONE --------------> DAY FOUR
**(forming)**                           **(filling)**

*And God said, Let there be light: and there was light. And God saw the light, that it was good: and God divided the light from the darkness.*

*And God made two great lights; the greater light to rule the day and the lesser light to rule the night: he made the stars also.*

This mysterious first light may be related to the background radiation recognized by scientists as energy left over from the Big Bang explosion. The darkness had to be divided from the light because pure light is invisible. Only by shade and shadow can light be perceived.

### DAY TWO --------------> DAY FIVE
**(forming)**                           **(filling)**

*And God made the firmament, and divided the waters which were under the firmament from the waters which were above the firmament.*

*And God said, Let the waters bring forth abundantly the moving creature that hath life, and fowl that may fly above the earth in the open firmament of heaven.*

On day two He created the sky and the waters, which He then populated on day five with birds and fishes.

DAY THREE  ---------------->  DAY SIX
(forming)                        (filling)

*And God said, Let the waters*
*under the heavens be gathered*
*together unto one place, and let*
*dry land appear.*

*And God said, Let the earth*
*bring forth the living*
*creature . . . after his kind.*

*And God said, Let us make*
*man in our image, after our*
*likeness.*

On the third day He brought dry land into existence. On the sixth, He
fashioned the mammals and the insects — last of all, God created man.

The first day of each group is one of *forming* and *framing*, while
the corresponding day is one of *filling* and *furnishing*. The relationships between the days are both horizontal and vertical, clearly
showing the orderliness of God's Genesis. There is much disagreement
among biblical scholars concerning the length of these "days." They
may be 24 hour periods or immense geological eras — the Lord does
not view time like man. Nevertheless, the first 3 gave form to the
Creation, while the second 3 filled the void.

The Lord's further division of the 6 Days into two groups of 3
days expresses 7 as the sum of three triangle numbers:

| 3 | + | 3 | + | 1 | = | 7 |
|---|---|---|---|---|---|---|
| **Days of** | | **Days of** | | **Day of** | | **Complete Week** |
| **Forming** | | **Filling** | | **Rest** | | |

*God created order out of chaos;*
*Satan forges chaos out of order.*

# THE HONEYCOMB OF HEAVEN

We have seen great evidence of God's triangular patterns in the universe's fundamental fabric. And astounding news (15 February 1990) relating to this appeared on the front page of Canada's most respected daily newspaper, *The Globe and Mail*. Stephen Strauss of the *Globe* wrote the article, and most of what follows is from his report:

*A stunning observation of a seemingly inexplicable order among the galaxies is causing astronomers to rethink their theories of how the universe was formed.*

*Within the next few weeks, a paper by two teams of British and U.S. astronomers will present observations suggesting part of the cosmos looks more like a regular patterned* **honeycomb** *[emphasis added] than a random explosion of matter.*

*Looking across at least six billion light-years, the two groups independently have shown that vast galaxies apparently are clustered in a regularly spaced pattern.*

The article continues with a great deal technical data on the observations. Complete details can be found in the February 1990 edition of the British scientific journal *Nature*. Before publishing, the American and British teams collected information for 7 years to confirm their startling results. The chief discoverers of this gigantic pattern made the following comments:

*"We may be living among huge honeycomb [hexagonal] structures or cells," astronomer David Koo of the University of California at Santa Cruz said.*

*Joel Primack, a professor of physics at Santa Cruz, said: "It looks like a piece of corrugated cardboard . . . I cannot come up with any plausible explanation for the galaxy clusters."*

The American group surveyed the northern sky from Arizona, while the British team searched the southern from Australia. These two separate, independent groups arrived at identical conclusions: the large scale structure of our universe consists of hexagons. The report concludes with these statements:

> . . . *in any case the result could alter theories of what followed the cosmic expansion — the so-called Big Bang — in which the universe is assumed to have been born . . . It implies that a stable pattern emerged and fixed itself very early in the universe's expansion from its assumed primal state of extremely high temperature and density. This pattern, somehow appearing in the first fraction of a second before the newborn universe exploded from a size less than that of an atom to roughly that of a basketball, would now be discernible in what Prof. Koo refers to as a "fossilized texture or imprint," the regularity of galactic structures.*

The perplexed reader must be saying to himself: what do hexagons have to do with the Triangle of Creation? Let's see.

Scientists tell us that natural laws, when fully understood, have the utmost simplicity and economy. This need for fundamental simplicity is ingrained in the minds of scientists. For instance, if one set of facts has several competing theories to explain them, they always prefer the least complicated. Logicians call this preference "Occam's Razor," or cut the theory thin. It is as if a great craftsman had labored over the laws until they could be simplified no further. This is the nature of the Lord's Works.

Consider the Triangle of Creation. At the instant when God said **"Let there be,"** our universe started as a primal point. And the entire triangle structure formed milliseconds later — like the article says. After that no new matter-energy has ever been created or destroyed. But what became of the original triangular structure, "the fossilized texture or imprint," as the universe expanded with the energy of the Big Bang? The answer is wonderfully simple, natural, and inevitable:

> **The Triangle of Creation immediately formed the hexagons confirmed by modern astronomy.**

See for yourself in the diagram below. When the triangles fly apart, hexagons appear as a completely natural result of this expansion:

## THE HEXAGONS OF HEAVEN

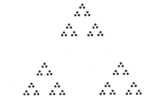

FIGURE 7.2

The image of the original Genesis was the Triangle of Creation. When the unimaginable energy of the Big Bang forced the particles apart, they became the hexagonal design recently discovered by astronomers. As the Psalmist said:

*The heavens declare the glory of God*
*and the firmament sheweth his handywork.*

# WORLDS WITHIN WORLDS

Up to this point, we have looked at our Lord's universe on the grandest scale imaginable and found it to be triangular in origin and hexagonal in growth. Let us now turn our attention in the opposite direction and examine God's smallest, most minute creations.

What could these be? Consider the 92 or more elements that form the material universe of the physicist. In this incredibly small world understanding becomes difficult, but most people are aware that every atom is constructed from a subatomic trinity:

proton, neutron, and electron.

So, even at this basic level, the triadic nature of the Lord's Creation confronts us.

As fundamental as these particles are, during the 1970s and 1980s, scientists found excellent reasons for believing they were not the ultimate pieces of God's Genesis. Researchers now know that every proton and neutron is itself composed from exactly 3 smaller particles called "quarks." Again we have uncovered a trinity within a trinity. And how many distinct quarks are there? Precisely 6, our first "perfect" triangle number. With a humorous twist, scientists have named these different quarks *up, down, strange, charmed, beauty, and truth.* Here is a breakdown of the composition of the two nuclear elements:

proton = *up* + *up* + *down* (3 quarks)
neutron = *up* + *down* + *down* (3 quarks)

The electron belongs to another set of 6 particles called leptons, and scientists further classify these by pairs into 3 groups. Beyond quarks and leptons are gluons, the binding force among all particles.

In conclusion, the material universe — at its most infinitesimal level — is formed from a fundamental trinity of indivisible building blocks called

quarks, leptons, and gluons[1].

This triumvirate of strangely named objects makes up the physical universe. Truly, everywhere man looks he can find the template of God's Trinity Creation.

# ONE TRIANGLE OR TWO?

Previously I said that God's natural laws, the laws of science, are always economical and simple. For example, light invariably travels from object to eye in the *least possible* time. Interestingly, that is not always the shortest path in distance, but it is always the quickest in time.

Earlier we discussed Pascal's Triangle and its intimate connection with triangularity and biblical numbers. The remaining chapters will show many other relationships between the Triangle and The Book. In this chapter, however, we have dealt exclusively with the Triangle of Creation. Accordingly, we have two designs: one dealing with God's Works, the other with God's Word:

> **GOD'S WORKS: TRIANGLE OF CREATION**
> **GOD'S WORD: TRIANGLE OF PASCAL**

When I considered our Lord's great economy in His natural laws, it was disturbing to have two ultimate triangles rather than just one. Scientists have only a single dominant theory or model to explain each aspect of nature. Granted, this model changes from time to time; nevertheless, only one theory rules in any decade. So, why does God do less than the scientists? Why does the Lord have two triangles? For many days I wrestled with this paradox before realizing the dualism was just an illusion reflecting my personal limitations.

Occasionally everything comes together and abruptly you understand part of the mystery of life. Then the world seems fresh, new, and alive. This was such a time. For allowing me this inspiration, I gave profound thanks to The Holy Spirit.

Consider FIGURE 7.3 on the next page. *This is Pascal's Triangle after a shaded dot has replaced every odd number and an unshaded dot every even number*. With this simple act, the deeper pattern buried in Pascal's Triangle (FIGURE 3.6) springs from the page. This replacement reveals our Lord's true design. By comparing FIGURES 3.6 and 7.3 with FIGURE 7.1, this gift from The Holy Spirit should be clear:

---

## PASCAL'S TRIANGLE IS
## THE TRIANGLE OF CREATION.

---

In variety we have discovered unity, implying the transcendent mind of a Celestial Architect behind The Word and The Works. To repeat, our world is not a *multi-verse* of unrelated parts with no purpose but a *Tri-Uni-Verse* of order, structure, and meaning. Look for yourself.

# PASCAL'S TRIANGLE

This is Pascal's Triangle with each odd number replaced
by a shaded dot and each even number by an unshaded dot.

FIGURE 7.3

Down the center (and elsewhere) of FIGURE 7.3 runs a series of unshaded triangles, containing the following *number* of dots: 1, 6, 28, and so on. Expand the figure and every "perfect" number will appear here — more of God's design. By their very nature, every unshaded shape represents a triangle number. See the Chapter Notes.

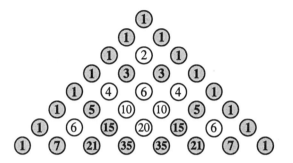

So that the meaning of FIGURE 7.3 is obvious, consider the diagram above. This is the top section of Pascal's Triangle (FIGURE 3.6) with all the numbers circled. Now, replace all the odds (i.e., 1, 3, 5, 7, 15, 21, 35) by shaded dots and all the evens (i.e., 2, 4, 6, 10, 20) by unshaded dots. Then Pascal's Triangle becomes the Triangle of Creation.

The sublime pattern of FIGURE 7.3 is curiously reminiscent of the *forming* and *filling* during the Creation Week. The odd numbers (shaded dots) provide the triangular *framework* for the entire structure while the even numbers (unshaded dots) deliver the *furnishing* in every triangle. It seems significant that just as the content is triangular in appearance, so the *Tri-Uni-Verse* is triangular in reality. This beautiful and meaningful image is a gateway into a paradise of understanding and insight.

The Triangle of Creation generalizes to a space-containing 3-dimensional structure with all the former properties. An explanation and a diagram can be found in the Chapter Notes.

Logic and mathematics will bring doubters to the great fountain of faith where they can find true peace and understanding. God's grace has given us the capacity for belief, but He created us with the ability to reason. From the magnificence of the heavens to the infinitesimal world of atoms, we are enveloped in His patterns — and still we do not believe.

CHAPTER — 8

# THE FISH

*Simon Peter climbed aboard and dragged*
*the net ashore. It was full of large fish, 153,*
*but even with so many the net was not torn.*
John 21:11

*Something deeply hidden had to be behind things.*
Albert Einstein

Long before television, VCRs, and CD players my home town had enormous old movie theaters for entertainment. Their ceilings were so high, it felt as if you were out-of-doors under a clear sky. In these beautiful buildings, I enjoyed many films now considered classics. Among my favorites were *The Robe, Quo Vadis, Ben Hur,* and *The Ten Commandments.* During one of these epics, the leading star outlined an unusual symbol on the sand. No words were spoken; yet the actors exchanged knowing looks. Also, the audience seemed to understand its meaning, but I certainly did not. The cryptic image on the beach resembled a fish: ⌒⌒ . Years passed before I learned that this was an early Christian symbol for Jesus Christ. Behind the imagery of the fish are reasons both wonderful and profound.

The Lamb, however, is the familiar symbol for our Savior. This derives from the Passover sacrifice of Exodus (12:1-11). John's Gospel speaks of Jesus as the Lamb that takes away the sins of the world. To this day, the ceremonial killing of the Passover Lamb parallels Christ's Crucifixion. It ideally symbolizes God's sacrifice of His Son for our sins.

The significance of the Lamb is clear, but what are the origins and meanings of the Fish? My research has uncovered many unusual sources for this watery, otherworldly image. Let me share with you all that I have learned.

In Matthew 7:7 (KJV) we have an unusual arrangement of words:

*Ask, and it shall be given you;*
*Seek, and ye shall find;*
*Knock, and it shall be opened unto you:*

For added emphasis the first letters of the lines spell out the word **ASK**. Although this may have been done unknowingly by the translators, it is very appropriate. Writers call this type of literary device an acrostic.

In the center of the Bible stands a triad of beautiful Psalms that are unique in their chapters and verses. The first of these, the 117th, has the distinction of being both the shortest and the exact middle chapter. The next, the 118th (KJV), contains the precise central verse of the entire Bible:

*It is better to trust in the Lord*
*than to put confidence in man.*

Important passages deserve important positions. This middle verse directly opposes the core of humanistic philosophy that takes its credo from the Greek Protagoras who said:

*Man is the measure of all things.*

In many ways, however, the most unusual Psalm is the 119th: it is the longest chapter in the longest book.

| Psalm 117 | Psalm 118 | Psalm 119 |
|---|---|---|
| The shortest and the middle chapter of the Bible. | Contains the Bible's middle verse. | Longest chapter in the Bible's longest book. |

This third Psalm is an extraordinary acrostic poem consisting of 22 stanzas of 8 verses each. In the original Hebrew the first 8 verses begin with the letter *aleph*, the second 8 with *beth*, the third with *gimel*, and so on. In this fashion the psalmist continues through the entire Hebrew aleph-beth. Therefore, this design stamps this Psalm with the number 22, the quantity of letters in the Hebrew alphabet.

This longest chapter sings of God's Word to man and man's praise of God. It is, in truth, a poem in praise of the Lord's Word. The number 8 — the length of each stanza — speaks of rebirth and regeneration throughout the ages. By the Word of God, man is born again of incorruptible seed (1 Peter 1:23).

So, by example, the Bible gives a seal of approval to acrostics. The world's most important example, however, cannot be found in Holy Scripture. Yet it flourished in the early Church, and it lives today in the hearts of Christians everywhere:

---

Ιησους Χριστος Θεου Υιος Σωτηρ

**This translates as "Jesus Christ, Son of God, the Savior." The initial letters of the five words spell out ΙΧΘΥΣ (ichthus), which is Greek for fish.**

---

FIGURE 8.1

What a striking symbol is ◁, for what a wonderful acrostic, from such a transcendent phrase. For early Christians it served a special purpose: secret symbols for your faith meant personal safety. Since Roman emperors demanded worship as gods, they ruthlessly slaughtered all competition. To be discovered as a Christian in ancient Rome was a death sentence. The symbol of the Fish implies a whole range of ideas, information, and emotions told in a concise, secretive manner.

Modern businesspeople know the value of a company or product symbol. Even small firms hire expensive graphic designers to develop suitable logos. When John wrote of the infamous Beast, he also used a symbolic code, and safety (as mentioned earlier) had to be a major consideration. His contemporary readers knew exactly whom he meant. By using gematria we have also discovered one such Beast; in later chapters we shall find others.

Although the preceding example inescapably associates Jesus with the image of the Fish, it is not the only possible illustration. Let's turn our eyes from the earth and water to the sky and stars.

Our Lord's Nativity was announced by the famous Star of Bethlehem. It has been a beacon to wise men of all ages and a light onto the world. But is there a corresponding astronomical event surrounding Jesus' Resurrection? What would be appropriate? Possibly a great occasion in outer space, somehow celebrating rebirth, renewal, and resurrection. God speaks about the stars in Genesis 1:14 (KJV):

> *Let them* [the stars] *be for signs,*
> *and for seasons, and for days, and years.*

Also in Jeremiah 10:2 (KJV) we read:

> *And be not dismayed at the signs of the heaven;*
> *for the heathen are dismayed at them.*

In other words, look to the heavens for good news, but do not be fooled by astrology, the false science of the New Agers. Our fate lies in our own hands — in the choices we make now — not in the distant twinkling of a star. Yet God, as Genesis tells us, uses the stars "for signs" to express a continuing message concerning man's redemption. What historical event could be more important than the Resurrection?

Early studies of the heavens revealed a rare astronomical (not astrological) event that takes place only once every 2,160 years. Like a gigantic child's top, the earth wobbles on its axis. One complete wobble (precession) every 25,920 years. This so-called precession means the sun's position moves backward through the constellations. So spring (the vernal equinox) comes 20 minutes earlier each year causing the sun to move through one constellation every 2,160 years (25,920 ÷ 12). Today, spring/rebirth takes place in the constellation of Pisces. It seems remarkable that at the time of the Resurrection the sun was leaving Aries the Ram and entering Pisces the Fish[1].

God refers to these great astronomical signs in Job 38:32:

> *Can you bring forth the constellations in their seasons?*

The Lord spoke these words directly to Job. They strongly imply He designs events to bring forth the constellations when He pleases. Even Pisces, the Fish, at the time of the Resurrection.

The phrase "Jesus Christ, Son of God, the Savior" speaks of both parts of our Lord's being. "Son of God" refers to His coeternal existence with God the Father as the Second Part of The Holy Trinity. "The Savior" tells of His incarnation as a man, His Crucifixion, and His final victory over death. By this sacrifice our sins are washed away; by this triumph over the grave our hope still lives. For that reason, the Resurrection of our Lord is the central fact of the Christian experience. Simply put, it is the most outstanding event in all human history. This is the heart of our faith. If we cast our nets on the right side and follow Him, we have the assurance of eternal life.

It is amazing just how much of Jesus' life was associated with fish and fishing. Even the very occasional Bible reader will recall such instances. For example, our Lord's ministry begins and ends at Galilee with a miraculous catch of fish. In Luke 5:4-7 we read:

*When he [Jesus] had finished speaking, he said to Simon,*
*"Put out into deep water, and let down the nets for a catch."*

*Simon answered "Master, we've worked hard all night*
*and haven't caught anything. But because you say so,*
*I will let down the nets."*

*When they had done so, they caught such a large number of*
*fish that their nets began to break. So they signalled their*
*partners in the other boat to come and help them, and they*
*came and filled both boats so full that they began to sink.*

In the last chapter of the last Gospel, again at the Sea of Galilee, Jesus encounters 7 disciples. This appearance of the risen Christ to His followers was the 3rd and last. It was also the 9th "great sign" of John's Gospel (the 8th being the Resurrection). In John 21:6 (KJV) and following, we find:

*And he said unto them, Cast the net on the right side*
*of the ship, and ye shall find. They cast therefore, and*
*now they were not able to draw it for the multitude of fishes.*

. . . . . . . . . . . . . . . . . . . . . . . . . . . . . . . . . . . . . .

> *Simon Peter went up, and drew the net to land full of great*
> *fishes,* **an hundred and fifty and three** [emphasis added]:
> *and for all there were so many, yet was not the net broken.*

Every detail of this supernatural catch has great importance and should be intensely studied. As a devout reader of the Bible and as a mathematician, I find the exact counting of the fish a very curious and unusual event. *Fishermen do not count their fish!* Man very rarely counts anything beyond 100. The only possible reason for doing so here was to introduce this number **153**.

If the Gospel writers had recorded the number of fish at 150, we would have given it no thought. The distinctiveness of this number springs from the extra 3. Beyond that, John tells us no fish escaped from the net, again implying this number's prominence.

> **Consequently, the outstanding question is**
> **why 153 fish and not some other number?**

The remainder of this chapter is an answer to this 2000 year old puzzle. From my research you will learn of the magnificent properties of 153. I will also compare it to, and contrast it with, the number 666 to shed new light on both. Finally, from an infinity of possible numbers, we will uncover properties totally unique to 153. Properties so special and meaningful that your spirit will soar at their beauty and significance.

Historically, Augustine of Hippo gave one of the first mathematical explanations. He began with 10, the number of the Commandments and a symbol of the old Mosaic dispensation. To this he added 7, the number of the Gifts of The Holy Spirit and the new dispensation. Therefore, by adding the old and the new he arrived at 17, and the sum of the first 17 numbers is 153:

$$1+2+3+4+5+6+7+8+9+10+11+12+13+14+15+16+17 = \mathbf{153}$$

The preceding comes from Augustine's *Tractates on the Gospel of Saint John*. Curiously, however, the famous bishop missed the crucial point of his own reasoning!

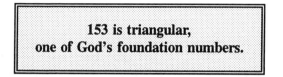

**153 is triangular,
one of God's foundation numbers.**

FIGURE 8.2

The intense triangularity of 153 reveals itself in every direction. Consider the following. Instead of writing 1 x 2 x 3, scientists write 3! (called factorial 3). With this type of notation it is possible to express our number as the sum of factorials:

$$
\begin{aligned}
1! &= 1 & &= & 1 \\
2! &= 1\text{x}2 & &= & 2 \\
3! &= 1\text{x}2\text{x}3 & &= & 6 \\
4! &= 1\text{x}2\text{x}3\text{x}4 & &= & 24 \\
5! &= 1\text{x}2\text{x}3\text{x}4\text{x}5 & &= +& \underline{120} \\
& & & & 153
\end{aligned}
$$

Therefore, 1! + 2! + 3! + 4! + 5! = 153

Some mathematicians refer to numbers expressed in the above manner as supertriangular. The Antichrist's quantity is not among them. Yet the first two supertriangular numbers are 1! = 1 and 1! + 2! = 3, our old friends unity and tri-unity.

# THE COUNTERFEIT OF CHRIST

*With the work of Satan displayed in all kinds
of counterfeit miracles, signs and wonders.*
2 Thessalonians 2:9

In the following sections, we will discover that 153 and 666 share many rare properties (see Chapter Notes for more):

- Both are triangle numbers.
- Both are reversible triangle numbers.
- Both are truncated triangle numbers.
- Both are expressible as the sum of three important triangle numbers.

This seeming similarity between **153** and **666** is deeply disturbing and must be explained.

The answer rests near the heart of black magic, whose evil essence forever desires to profanely mimic the good, the pure, and the holy. In satanic rituals the practitioners read the Lord's Prayer backward, place the pentagram upside down, invert the sacred cross, and so on. Even witches ride their broomsticks backward. Throughout these next sections we will follow the trail of this mocking rebellion.

We cannot, however, pretend to fully understand these titanic forces of good and evil that battle even with numbers. Ever cunning and powerful, Satan strives to show that 666 has properties equal to 153. "Diamatics," the mathematics of the Devil, marshals against "deomatics," the mathematics of the Deity. Yet, these forces duel on two separate fields of battle. On the lower one, Satan parades as the Dark Angel — this we shall survey first. The higher plane is forbidden territory to the strutting Rebel. It is the realm of the Fish Number — this we will investigate second.

The great English poet John Milton summed up Satan's attitude when he had him declare in *Paradise Lost*:

> *Better to reign in Hell than serve in heaven.*

This warrior ethic had its origin in pride, its practice in parody, but its outcome in Hell.

## REVERSE TRIANGLE NUMBERS

Not only is 153 triangular, but its reverse, 351, is also (see FIGURE 3.2). As we shall discover, 351 has a nature totally dissimilar to 153. Numbers with different digits that remain triangular when written backward are exceedingly rare. Of course, if the triangle number has identical digits, like 666, then it is automatically reversible. For a list of these numbers, turn to the Chapter Notes.

What biblical justification or precedent do I have for reversing digits and claiming this process has any spiritual or symbolic meaning? None except — in the style and form of their prose and poetry — the authors of the Bible did the same from Genesis to Revelation. Page 119 shows how the Psalmist used it in the famous 23rd. Or see Chapter 14 for a detailed explanation with other examples. Secondly, much important gematria has this symmetrical property.

## TRUNCATED TRIANGLE NUMBERS

Truncating 153 (cutting it into smaller pieces) further emphasizes its intense triangularity. "To truncate" means to slice off without rounding up or down. For example, 7.821 is rounded to 8, but truncated to 7. Let's show why 105 is a truncated triad. The symbol "/" means "a cut":

$$1/05 \text{ gives } 1$$
$$10/5 \text{ gives } 10 \qquad \text{All triangle numbers}$$
$$105/ \text{ gives } 105$$

From a set of infinite possibilities, only 6 numbers prove to be truncated triangle numbers (see Chapter Notes). Amazingly, 153 is one of these. Recall from a previous paragraph that 666 is, necessarily, a reversible triangle quantity. Strikingly, it is also found among the 6 truncates. Here is the *entire* list of these quantities and their triad parts:

| Truncated Numbers | Triangle Pieces |
|---|---|
| 15 -------------> | 1 and 15 |
| 36 -------------> | 3 and 36 |
| 66 -------------> | 6 and 66 |
| 105 ------------> | 1 and 10 and 105 |
| 153 ------------> | 1 and 15 and 153 |
| 666 ------------> | 6 and 66 and 666 |

# HEXAGON NUMBERS

*Quantities that can be arranged*
*in six-sided figures are hexagonal.*

The Chapter Notes have a proof that all (vertex centered) hexagonal numbers are also triangular. Imagine a set of bowls in your kitchen cupboard; let the largest one represent all the triangle numbers. Then the second sized bowl (because it is contained by the first) stands for all hexagonal numbers. And the third bowl (inside the first two) holds all the perfect numbers. Here is a short list of hexagonal numbers:

| 1. 1 | 2. 6 | 3. 15 | 4. 28 |
|---|---|---|---|
| 5. 5 | 6. 66 | 7. 91 | 8. 120 |
| 9. **153** | 10. 190 | 11. 231 | 12. 276 |
| 13. 325 | 14. 378 | 15. 435 | 16. 496 |
| 17. 561 | 18. 630 | 19. 703 | 20. 780 |

FIGURE 8.3

Inspection of this table affirms two facts:

- It is entirely composed of triangle numbers.
- Christ's number occurs, but the Antichrist's does not.

God created all the triangle numbers and their properties. He made 6 and 28 "perfect." Swollen with pride, however, by *appearing* thrice "perfect," 666 chose to rebel. Nevertheless, 6 and 66 should not be found guilty by association. You can see from the above table that these last two are both hexagonal.

As our degenerate society stumbles toward the end of the millennium, the most potent image of apostasy is the pentagram, Satan's five-pointed star. Pentagonal numbers are not contained within the triangles; they are a separate creation. We will explore the Devil's association with them in the next chapter.

## TRIANGLES WITHIN TRIANGLES

Investigating 153 and 666, as sums of triangle quantities further shows Satan's sacrilegious mimicry.

153 = 3 + 45 + 105
       Trinity     Adam     truncated number

666 = 15 + 300 + 351
    truncated 153   Tau Cross   153 reversed

So, we have expressed 153 and 666 as the sum of three triangle numbers each (i.e., a triangle equal to a trinity of triangles). Remarkably, the three that add to 666 clearly parody Jesus.

In Chapter 6 we learned that the gematria of *cross* was *777*. Yet, in the above equations I have used *cross* as *300*. Why the contradiction? The explanation involves the Greek or Tau Cross that was always a capital **T**. A quick dictionary reference to *Tau Cross* will confirm this design. This Greek letter has a value of 300 (FIGURE 6.1). Throughout ancient times, it served as a simple, alternative name for the Cross. The Romans crucified Jesus on the **T**au.

# THE PARABLE OF THE NET

*"Once again, the kingdom of heaven is like a net that was let down into the lake and caught all kinds of fish. When it was full, the fishermen pulled it up on shore. Then they sat down and collected the good fish in baskets, but threw the bad away. This is how it will be at the end of the age."*
Jesus, Matthew 13:47-49

Up to this point, we have shown a few of the unusual properties of 153 and some of the parody by 666. Now we enter an expanse forever barred to the Devil's triad and every other quantity, except the Fish Number. Nevertheless, the next 3 characteristics do not exhaust what might be written on 153 (interested readers should again turn to the Chapter Notes).

The wonderful attributes already discussed are just a preamble to our 3 main ideas. In Chapter 4 we read about the Triad Rules and how they reveal the buried mathematical treasures in God's Holy Word. The third was the Trinity Function. Consider the actions and outcomes of this rule on 666:

$$666 \longrightarrow 6^3 + 6^3 + 6^3 = 6\times6\times6 + 6\times6\times6 + 6\times6\times6 = 648$$

Nothing surprising. Yet, when we used this function on 153 (see FIGURE 6.12), the result was truly remarkable. Recall:

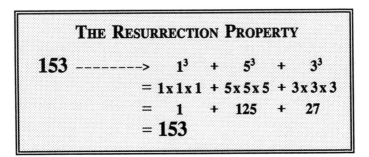

FIGURE 8.4

The Trinity Rule displays the constancy of Jesus' Number. It is neither transformed, altered, nor changed. Reapplying the rule each time simply shows how 153 resurrects itself. On the other hand, the Antichrist's number *is transformed*, but not by much: i.e., $666 \longrightarrow 648$. If a 2 had been taken from the 8 and given to the middle 4, then the parody would have been complete: i.e., $666 \longrightarrow 666$. Satan may imitate, but not equal, Christ.

> *"In the whole land," declares the Lord,*
> *"two-thirds will be struck down and perish;*
> *yet one-third will be left in it.*
>
> *This third I will bring into the fire; I will refine*
> *them like silver and test them like gold.*
> *They will call on my name and I will answer them;"*
> Zechariah 13:8-9

In this quotation, the prophet paints an apocalyptic picture of the *end times* and the establishment of the Messiah's Kingdom. This "one-third" will include that last remnant of the Jewish People who recognize Jesus at His Second Coming and convert. As we shall learn, this one-third is also an outstanding attribute of 153. Mathematics mirrors reality.

To explain the preceding, please choose any number you wish. There is only one condition. It must be a multiple of 3 (e.g., 6, 24, 336, etc.). Suppose you pick 1776. Now, apply the Trinity Function to it and to each outcome:

$$1776 \longrightarrow 1^3 + 7^3 + 7^3 + 6^3 = 903 \text{ (1st outcome)}$$
$$903 \longrightarrow 9^3 + 0^3 + 3^3 = 756 \text{ (2nd outcome)}$$
$$756 \longrightarrow 7^3 + 5^3 + 6^3 = 684 \quad .$$
$$684 \longrightarrow 6^3 + 8^3 + 4^3 = 792 \quad .$$
$$792 \longrightarrow 7^3 + 9^3 + 2^3 = 1080 \quad .$$
$$1080 \longrightarrow 1^3 + 0^3 + 8^3 + 0^3 = 513 \quad .$$
$$513 \longrightarrow 5^3 + 1^3 + 3^3 = 153 \text{ (final outcome)}$$

All the preceding can be summarized as,

$$1776 \to 903 \to 756 \to 684 \to 792 \to 1080 \to 513 \to 153.$$

Incredibly, it does not matter how large a number you start with; it could have a trillion digits. The number need only be divisible by 3, and that is "one-third" of all quantities. By continuously reapplying the Trinity Rule to each output, the process quickly ends at 153, the center of the net. So, "one-third" of all numbers do go to 153.

I greatly encourage the reader to use a hand calculator to confirm these unusual statements. Here are a few random examples:

$$99 \to 1458 \to 27 \to 351 \to 153$$
$$1125 \to 135 \to 153$$
$$375 \to 495 \to 189 \to 1242 \to 1080 \to 513 \to 153$$

No other number, be it 666 or whatever, can copy or counterfeit this outstanding property. So totally singular is this characteristic that out of the whole of God's created quantities none can imitate it. This establishes the sacred uniqueness of 153, the most remarkable number in all Holy Scripture.

In the Chapter Notes you will find a proof that every third number eventually ends at exactly 153. Obviously, we cannot check all possible multiples of 3, even with the world's fastest computer. So, we should look for a method to drastically shorten our work. When the Trinity Function transforms any number larger than 2000, something curious occurs. The image (answer) is always smaller than the original number. For example:

2,001 ----> 2x2x2 + 0x0x0 + 0x0x0 + 1x1x1 = 9,
and 9 is smaller than 2,001.

2,899 ----> 2x2x2 + 8x8x8 + 9x9x9 + 9x9x9 = 1,978,
and 1,978 is smaller than 2,899.

99,999 ----> 9x9x9 + 9x9x9 + 9x9x9 + 9x9x9 + 9x9x9 = 3,645,
and 3,645 is smaller than 99,999.

This shows that quantities greater than 2000 will steadily descend — by repeated use of the Trinity Rule — to less than 2000. So, we need test only those that are both smaller than 2000 and multiples of 3. How many numbers fit this description? Unexpectedly, exactly 666. Another link between opposites: i.e., the number (153) formed from a single repetition of the first 3 odd digits, and the number (666) forged from 3 repetitions of the 3rd even digit. Significantly, 2000 is the watershed quantity! Coincidence? Not likely! God creates order, not chaos.

To conclude, the Trinity Function uncovered the following 3 exceptional properties:

- 153 is fixed, constant, and unchangeable.
- One-third of all numbers go to 153 (Jesus).
- All quantities larger than 2000 behave differently than those smaller than 2000, the watershed number.

FIGURE 8.5 on the following page illustrates these three ideas in a unique diagram.

# THE FISHES AND THE NET

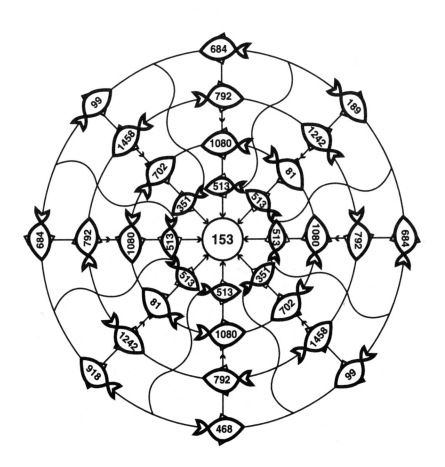

FIGURE 8.5

The constant 153 is at the center of the net. It catches one-third of all numbers. Only multiples of 3 are used, and just quantities below 2000 are shown, or need be.

All the previous properties mark 153 as a most phenomenal quantity. It, as well as 888, will be associated with our Lord Jesus Christ for all eternity. In the phrase "Jesus Christ, Son of God, the Savior," 153 refers to the "Son of God" and 888 to "the Savior."

**153 is Jesus' Celestial Number.**
**888 is Jesus' Earthly Number.**

FIGURE 8.6

# THE GEMATRIA OF THE FISHES

Does the ancient science of gematria cast more light on our wonderful number? Yes it does, in a host of places and passages. Here are a few.

The expression "Sons of God" (Beni Ha-Elohim) occurs in the Old Testament exactly 7 times — the number of completeness. It is fascinating that the Hebrew gematria of this phrase is precisely 153:

$$\begin{array}{ccc} \text{S O N S} & \text{OF} & \text{G O D} \\ \text{ב נ י} & \text{ה א ל ה י מ} \\ 153 = 2\ 50\ 10 & + & 5\ 1\ 30\ 5\ 10\ 40 \end{array}$$

Equal in importance to the previous example, but at a human level, is Romans 8:17 (KJV). It speaks about the "joint heirs with Christ." That is those who suffer because of their witnessing to be with Jesus in the life to come. Numerically, it is *all* those that go to 153, the center of the net. Regard its gematria:

$$\begin{array}{cccccccccccc} \text{J O I N T} & & \text{H E I R S} \\ \sigma & \upsilon & \gamma & \kappa & \lambda & \eta & \rho & o & \nu & o & \mu & o & \iota \\ 200 & 400 & 3 & 20 & 30 & 8 & 100 & 70 & 50 & 70 & 40 & 70 & 10 \end{array} = 1071$$

This quantity equals 7 x 153, or 153 + 153 + . . . + 153.

The miraculous catch of fish in John 21 reveals part of the relationship between 153 and 888. "The net" is a metaphor cast onto the sea of humanity by the Lord Jesus to catch the fishes that live in the abyss of sin. Consider these examples: "the net," "fishes," and "the Lord God."

THE    NET
τ ο   γ ι κ τ υ ο ν
300 70 + 4 10 20 300 400 70 50 = 1224

FISHES
ι χ θ υ ε ς
10 600 9 400 5 200 = 1224

THE  LORD  GOD
Ο Κ υ ρ ι ο ς  Ο  Θ ε ο ς
70 + 20 400 100 10 70 200 + 70 + 9 5 70 200 = 1224

---

**What is so mysterious about 1224?**
**Only the fact that 1224 = 8 x 153.**
**Therefore, it is the chain that binds 8 to 153.**

---

In the same vein, regard the following:

"Fishers of men" has a value of 14 x 153.
"multitudes of fishes" equals 16 x 153.
And "casting a net into the sea" is 20 x 153.

Striking in its consistency and beauty, this rich pattern of words and numbers forever marks this text with the seal of divinity.

We have learned some spectacle properties of Jesus' Celestial Number and the aping arrogance of Lucifer's 666. Despite his diamatic struggles, the Devil only managed to display God's power and greatness. The Trinity Rule uncovered the unique constancy of 153. And one-third of all numbers or persons — as Scripture says — point directly to 153. No atheist, humanist, or non-Christian can deny this. It is not a matter of literary interpretation, but of mathematical certainty. Finally, the gematria of the words and phrases reinforced the relationship between 153 and 888.

Centuries ago, Augustine of Hippo[2] summed up man's condition and the nature of the Fish symbolism in the following manner:

> *You have the Greek word IXΘΥΣ, which means "fish," and the allegorical meaning of the noun is Christ, because he was able to live — that is without sin — in the abyss of our mortal condition, in the depths, as it were, of the sea.*

# CHAPTER — 9

# SATANIC SYMBOLS

*Satan, so call him now, his former name*
*Is heard no more in Heaven; he, of the first,*
*If not the first Arch-Angel.*
John Milton, *Paradise Lost*

## WHO IS SATAN?

S atan is one of the Lord's three created archangels. He is the adversary, the embodiment of evil, and the tempter of mankind. To men and angels, God bestowed the gift of free will. But Lucifer, because of his overpowering pride and conceit, chose to rebel and by that lost his high place in Heaven. When Satan fell (Revelation 12:4), he took *one-third* of the stars (angels) with him. Each archangel led this part of the celestial host: threeness is in Heaven as on earth. (The *one-third* that fell with Satan parallels the *one-third* that will ascend with Jesus.) Our Lord describes the Dark Angel's descent in Luke 10:18:

*I saw Satan fall like lightning from heaven.*

Since the Devil's intelligence is as immense as his actions are evil, this presents many problems. A lesser puzzle is why so clever a being continues to act in such a totally irrational manner. The Dragon knows the Father's plan for the Final Judgment; he is no atheist. The Bible lays out God's will and designs for everyone to see. Yet Lucifer's rebelliousness, conceit, and egoism are of such enormous proportions that he still dreams of scaling the walls of Heaven and stealing the celestial throne. Isaiah 14:12-15 proclaimed his past delusions:

> *How you have fallen from heaven,*
> *O morning star, son of the dawn! . . .*
> *You said in your heart, "I will ascend to heaven.*
> *. . . I will make myself like the Most High."*
> *But you are brought down to the grave,*
> *to the depths of the pit.*

Yes, the Serpent has been cast down to earth. Yet he is still an archangel — though fallen — with all the miraculous abilities and strengths that term implies. You only underestimate Satan's power to your peril. Jesus alludes to the Dragon's might in John 14:30:

> *for the Prince of this world is coming.*

As a share in the original Triangle Creation, God gave Lucifer the triangle number 666 as his heavenly symbol. By applying the Triangle Function to its pre-image, 36, we have the following:

$$36 \; \text{-------->} \; 1 + 2 + 3 + \ldots + 36$$
$$= 666$$

It is interesting that both the pre-image, 36, and the post-image, 666, are triangular.

Lucifer is the angelic name of the creature who, after his fall, became known as Satan. His new name means the adversary; his old meant the bringer of light and had associations with Venus, the Morning Star. Removed from God's love and presence, Satan's celestial losses are incalculable. His number as well as his name have been changed. To mock God, however, he still uses 666 for his henchmen, the Antichrists.

From the Serpent of Genesis to the Dragon of Revelation, the Devil parades by many names. He can be a false figure of light and joy as Paul says in 2 Corinthians 11:14:

> *And no wonder, for Satan himself*
> *masquerades as an angel of light.*

Or he may be a dark being of fright and terror as John Milton writes in his famous epic poem, *Paradise Lost:*

*Black it stood as night,*
*Fierce as ten furies, terrible as hell*
*And shook a dreadful dart; what seem'd his head*
*The likeness of a kingly crown had on.*
*Satan was now at hand.*

The previous paragraphs describe Satan's major attributes as:

- Pride — that which goes before a fall.
- Rebelliousness — Satan's original sin.
- Mockery — the essence of satanic rituals.
- Irrationalism — the actions of a maniacal being.
- Form changes and deception — part of his plan.

These last two characteristics are also the most outstanding features of *his* new number, a quantity better suited than 666 to demonic activities and continual deceptions. Jesus, you will recall, has a divine triangle number of 153 and an earthly Resurrection Number of 888. Long ago Satan chose a worldly quantity — a number not related to life and rebirth but to death and original sin. We will find this second number!

# ORIGINAL SIN

Let's begin at the beginning, when the Bible says:

*Now the serpent was more crafty than any*
*of the wild animals the Lord God had made.*

Immediately, the Great Deceiver enters as a snake to tempt Adam and Eve. And what does he say?

*For God knows that when you eat of it your eyes will be*
*opened, and you will be like God, knowing good and evil.*

Half the Serpent's statement was true: they did learn the difference between good and evil. The first part, however, sounds identical to the present promise of the New Age Movement. This promise, "you will be like God," is as totally false now as it was then, and the source is the same. We all know the outcome of man's first disobedience: it brought death into the world and all our troubles.

Nevertheless, imagine for a happy moment that our original parents had never sinned (acquired sexual knowledge), and therefore the Fall of man had never happened. Then Adam and Eve would not have realized their nakedness. We have every reason to expect they would have lived forever, blissfully enjoying the Garden of Eden and all its treasures. Would they have had children? I think not, because birth is made necessary only by death. And since there would be no death, Eve need never have suffered the pangs of childbirth. Yet it was not to be; their loss is our pain.

Because Adam and Eve had no parents, an unusual question arises. Did they have a navel? If they did, it would imply they had parents. Since this is clearly false, the very presence of a navel would have been a deception, and so could not have come from God. Satan deceives; God does not.

The English writer Sir Thomas Browne, when referring to Adam, said "The man without a navel yet lives in me." Browne was alluding to Adam's original sin (sexual knowledge). Also consider what the Irish author James Joyce wrote about Eve in his novel *Ulysses*: "Heva, naked Eve. She had no navel." Many medieval artists realized the problem concerning the navel. Accordingly, in their paintings of our first parents some properly omitted it. Others hedged their bets by allowing the ample fig leaf to wind up and over the navel as well as the pubic area.

Of course, we know directly from the Bible that Adam had no navel. After all, he was created in the image of God. By definition, the Deity has no predecessors, and therefore no navel. But we, the sons and daughters of Adam, all bear his mark in our nature and on our bodies. The only spiritual difference between humans of today and our first ancestors is original sin. The only physical difference between humans of today and our first ancestors is the navel. *This "birthmark" is just the bodily symbol and reminder of that sin.*

# THE SYMBOL

For thousands of years a single shape has been associated with the Devil. With the rise of murdering Satanic cults, we have seen its bloodstained outline carved on victims' bodies or scrawled on walls. Frequently, the perpetrators have it tattooed on their arms, hands, or even around their navels. Its bold design often contains the face of the carnal sex-driven goat, and its lines always form the five-pointed star, the pentagram.

The upward pointing horns affirm the duality of good and evil, while the bottom point is directed to Hell. Within the star, the goat's head represents Satan as a symbol of lust. This illustration is from *De Occulta de Philosophia* by Agrippa of Nettesheim (1486 - 1535).

FIGURE 9.1

In his classic book *Secret Teachings of All Ages,* Manley P. Hall, an authority in this area, wrote the following. His last reference to Lucifer as "the morning star" harkens back to Isaiah 14:

*When used in black magic, the pentagram is called the sign of the cloven hoof, or the footprint of the Devil. The star with the two points upward is also called the "Goat of Mendes," because the inverted star is the same shape as a goat's head. When the upright star turns and the upper point falls to the bottom, it signifies the fall of the morning star.*[1]

As a symbol of black magic, occultists have known and used the pentagram since at least Babylonian times. "It was a magical charm amongst the people of Babylon," wrote symbolism expert Rudolf Koch[2]. Babylon has been the birthplace for most of the black arts, old and new. Satan has possessed the five-pointed star for millenniums. Its adoption by the New Age Religion is just part of his grandiose scheme to revive Mystery Babylon. Some modern scholars believe the pentagram will be the mark of the Beast mentioned in Revelation 13.

Visit your local secular bookstore. Compare the quantity of Christian to New Age reading materials; you may be surprised. Leaf through one of their gaudy magazines or books, and you will find many pentagrams. It makes one wonder what on earth these people are doing! Don't they know anything about prophecy and Our Age — not the New Age?

The ancient Greeks were very familiar with the pentagram; they often placed it on their coins. The followers of Pythagoras also used it in their secret society as a symbol of recognition. Celtic priests referred to it as the witch's footprint. Goethe, the celebrated German genius, used it in his famous play *Faust*. In the centuries after Rome fell, right up to the modern age, it has always been the preferred satanic symbol. As a mocking blasphemy, present-day Satanists regularly place the letters J-E-S-U-S on the pentagram's five points.

History is a great source of knowledge, but it does not tell us everything. We have learned that the 5-pointed star has been Satan's symbol since ancient times. Yet, just because something has always been done or written about in a certain manner, this alone does not provide a complete explanation. It's just the historical record. Therefore, we still want to know *why the pentagram was chosen to be Satan's symbol?* The next three sections will answer this significant question.

# THE NUMBER AND THE SYMBOL

Consider how closely the figure to the right interrelates the common images of man (in light outline) and Satan (in bold outline). First one dominates and then the other, forever alternating in a symbolic struggle. Man's fall results in Satan's rise, and the descent of Satan allows the ascent of man. This is a small part of the answer for why the pentagram is the Devil's own design.

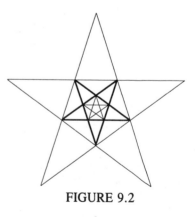

FIGURE 9.2

Since the pentagram can be drawn with a single unbroken line, it is often used to mark off magical enclosures, especially for satanic invocations.

Yet where in the pentagram can we find the complete key to understanding the *symbolic* relationship among man, Satan, and sin? Inside the smaller outline of man (FIGURE 9.2), another bold pentagram of Satan can be sketched, and inside that again man, and so on. Therefore, clearly the size of the figure is unimportant; accordingly, its perimeter and area are of no consideration as well.

Whenever the dimensions of an object are irrelevant, we use ratios. Let me explain. Most people have a gasoline engine at home, such as a lawn mower. You know that whenever fuel is added, the correct amount of oil must also be added. A common ratio is 30 to 1 (fuel to oil). For example, if you add 60 ounces of fuel, then you must also add 2 ounces of oil. This is done to keep the ratio at 30 to 1. Let's investigate the ratios of the lengths in Satan's pentagram.

Consider the ratios of the distances in FIGURE 9.3. In any pentagram there are exactly four different lengths: i.e., AC, AH, AG, and GH. It is remarkable that the ratio of each length to the next larger length equals 1.618 (see proof in Chapter Notes).

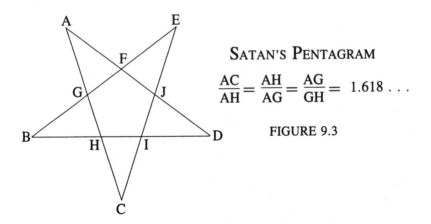

SATAN'S PENTAGRAM

$$\frac{AC}{AH} = \frac{AH}{AG} = \frac{AG}{GH} = 1.618\ldots$$

FIGURE 9.3

The number 1.618 is a rounded value of $(1 + \sqrt{5})/2$, called "Phi" ($\phi$). This name comes from the Greek sculptor and architect **Phi**dias, who used it widely in his pagan temples. Although the ratios in the pentagram are *exactly* $(1 + \sqrt{5})/2$, we will (for convenience) generally use 1.618. An extended decimal version follows:

$$\phi = \frac{1 + \sqrt{5}}{2} = 1.6180339887498948482045868343656 \ldots$$

As you can see by inspecting the decimals, this number has absolutely no pattern. Mathematicians quite properly call such quantities *irrational*. It is singularly amazing that all such ratios in the pentagram are precisely equal to Phi ($\phi$). Truly, Satan's design is just Phi's geometrical illustration: *the number manifested as a symbol*. No other star figure — of however many points — displays this ratio. So, since we know the pentagram is Satan's symbol, then Phi is surely his number.

> *When Lucifer descended to become Satan,*
> *Phi ascended to become his new number.*

# THE THREE FORMS OF SATAN'S NUMBER

As the Apostle Paul said, the Devil is forever changing his form to deceive man, and we should not be ignorant of his devices. It started in the Garden of Eden; it continues to the present moment. He never comes as his true self because to do so would mean instant rejection by any sane person — Christian or not. Goodness, happiness, power, knowledge, wealth, and eternal life fill his tempting mouth; he may appear luminous, wonderful, angelic, or even Christ-like. In contrast, his shape may be serpentine, dragon-like, hideous, monstrous, or bestial, and his voice foul and blasphemous. Whatever his words or shape may be, his essence is the same: rebellious, evil, demented.

If Phi is Satan's new number, then it should somehow reflect his basic characteristics. Remarkably, Phi does *symbolize* Satan's form changes. Here is a list of its three basic variations:

$$\text{Phi} = \phi = 1.618\ldots = \phi \pm 0$$

$$\frac{1}{\text{Phi}} = \frac{1}{\phi} = 0.618\ldots = \phi - 1$$

$$(\text{Phi})^2 = \phi^2 = 2.618\ldots = \phi + 1$$

You will enjoy using a calculator to convince yourself that the reciprocal (1 over Phi) and the square of Phi (Phi x Phi) leave the irrational (decimal) part totally unchanged. No other number — whole or decimal — possesses these unusual features. Although I have again used 1.618 as an approximation for Phi, these strange properties hold true for any number of decimal places. (Turn to the Chapter Notes for a proof.) Transform him as you wish, yet he keeps his essential, demented, maniacal core.

# THE NAVEL AND THE NUMBER

We have learned Adam could not have had a navel, unless the Lord is a deceiver. However, Genesis 3:13 clearly outlines the roles of God and Satan when we read, "The serpent deceived me, and I ate." The Lord created our first parents without sin and with a free will. What most scientists and Christians have long overlooked, painters and writers have consistently recognized. That is, after the Fall and throughout the ages, the symbol of sin has always been *the navel*.

Although secular history gives no compelling reasons for the pentagram's association with Satan, it does, nevertheless, clearly establish it as his symbol. FIGURE 9.4, however, and the following sentences provide some answers. When the Dark Angel plummeted from Heaven with one-third of the stars (angels), he lost both his name, Lucifer, and his triangle number, 666. The symbol of this fallen star is the inverted star — the pentagram. So Phi, the only ratio in the pentagram, became his new number. The inverted star (angel) perfectly represents three of Satan's characteristics:

1. His fall from Heaven.
2. His deceitful form changes.
3. His irrational essence: i.e., 0.61803398874....

The preceding paragraphs and sections lead to the following two conclusions and a crucial new question.

- The navel is the symbol of man's fall.
- The pentagram is the symbol of Lucifer's fall.
- Are these two connected?

Certain events are truly memorable. Discovering the extraordinary connection between Satan's new number, the navel, and the pentagram was such an occasion. Consider the following two famous drawings.

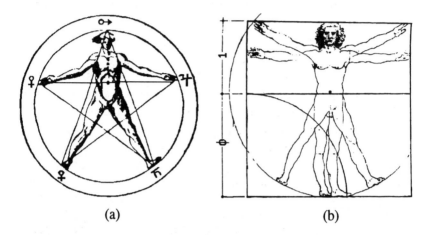

(a)                                      (b)

FIGURE 9.4

FIGURE (a) is the "Man in the Pentagram" from Agrippa's *De Occulta Philosophia*. The well-known drawing on the right is Leonardo da Vinci's *Man as the Measure of All Things*.

On the human figure at the above left, notice that the horizontal line *cuts the body at the navel.* When I saw this drawing, suddenly all the pieces of the puzzle fell perfectly into place. For the first time I understood how the navel, the pentagram, original sin, and Phi were all intertwined in a vast symbolic pattern.

> **In fact, the navel divides the human body
> in the ratio of 1 to Phi.**

First, measure the distance from your head to your navel. Second, measure the distance from your navel to the floor. Now divide the smaller length into the larger, and you get approximately 1.618.... If you divide the larger into the smaller, then you get 0.618..., another form of Satan's number. The Chapter Notes contain a mathematical proof. This implies an astonishingly profound truth about the close relationships among Satan, original sin, the pentagram, and the human body. I urge every reader to confirm this by privately measuring themselves.

Using man's limbs for units of measurement is an ancient practice. The inch was the length from the thumb's knuckle to its tip; the yard went from the king's nose to his outstretched finger. The biblical cubit was from the elbow to the middle finger, while the foot is obvious. All the preceding units are from the body, the body made "in the image of God." However, Phi is from a different body and for a different purpose. It derives from the navel, the symbol of man's fall.

To make man an object of worship, Leonardo designed *Man as the Measure of All Things* (FIGURE 9.4 (b)) at the height of Renaissance Humanism. It also unmistakably shows the navel separating the body in the ratio of 1 to Phi. This number is even written on the drawing's left side. Da Vinci made extensive use of Phi in his geometrical research and his paintings. Shortly we will see where he prominently displayed it in his most famous painting, the *Last Supper*.

At birth, the navel divides the child in half; this central location ensures all body parts are equally nourished. The study of human biometrics (life measurement) reveals that during growth from childhood to adulthood, the navel continually changes its position. Starting from a position beneath Phi, it first moves above and then below and then above again. This alternating continues until about age 25 (see FIGURE 9.7). These fluctuations, however, are always to closer and closer approximations to the Phi point, the final destination. As we shall soon see, this wavering around the irrational spot Phi is perfectly mimicked by an unusual sequence of numbers.

In Chapter 3, I introduced the Triangle of Creation, also known as Pascal's Triangle. Among other things, we learned how it can be used to describe God's Trinity Creation and to find any triangle number. Each entry is generated by adding the two numbers above — both right and left (see FIGURE 9.5). This marvelous arrangement explained much of God's Creation, and it will yet reveal much of The Word's symbolism. So, you might expect to discover Satan's new number in this array. Whether we like it or not, and whether the Devil understands it or not, he plays a pivotal role in God's designs from beginning to end. I take the presence of Phi in the Triangle of Creation as a striking confirmation of this line of reasoning. Let me show you how and where it is cleverly hidden. For convenience I have reproduced the Triangle below. Consider the sums of the numbers on its slanted diagonals.

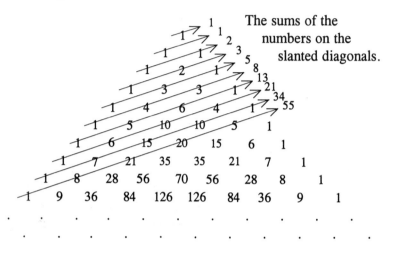

FIGURE 9.5

By adding the quantities on the slanted lines, a strange sequence is formed:

1, 1, 2, 3, 5, 8, 13, 21, 34, 55, 89, 144, . . .

The next term in the sequence can be generated without using FIGURE 9.5 by simply adding the previous two numbers. For example, 5 is the sum of 2 and 3; also 55 is the sum of 21 and 34, and so on. Doesn't this remind you of how we produced Pascal's Triangle? What could be more like Satan than to rebelliously mimic the Triangle of Creation, the Lord's model for His Word and His Works? That is, instead of adding the two numbers above, as in the Triangle, the Devil adds the two in front, as in the sequence.

Usually named after its 13th century Italian discoverer Fibonacci, this sequence is more accurately called Satan's. To reveal its intimate connection with Phi, divide larger and larger adjacent terms of the sequence in the following fashion:

## PHI IN SATAN'S SEQUENCE

| 1. $1/1=1$ | 2. $2/1=2$ | 3. $3/2=1.5$ |
|---|---|---|
| 4. $5/3=1.666...$ | 5. $8/5=1.6$ | 6. $13/8=1.625$ |
| 7. $21/13=1.615...$ | 8. $34/21=1.619...$ | 9. $55/34=1.617...$ |
| 10. $89/55=1.618...$ | . . . . . . | . . . . . . |

FIGURE 9.6

When you divide any two consecutive terms from Satan's sequence, you get an approximation for Phi. The larger the terms you divide, the more accuracy you get. Continued division aims directly at Phi (once again the Chapter Notes have detailed proof).

A graph of the data from the previous table will display the increasing exactness found by dividing ever larger terms. Interestingly, this graph also illustrates the navel's travels from birth to maturity: the fall from childhood innocence to adult sin.

## NAVEL TRAVELS

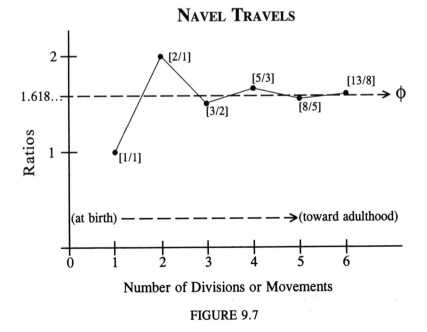

Number of Divisions or Movements

FIGURE 9.7

Incredible isn't it, how the Triangle of Creation, Satan's sequence, the navel, the pentagram, and original sin are all bound together by this number Phi. These are not idle speculations but proven mathematical statements. God's world is a place of pattern and reason. He has the whole world in His mind.

Before we leave this section, let's take one last look at the Garden of Eden. Consider the apple from "the tree of the knowledge of good and evil." If Adam and Eve had not eaten the apple, this life, this drama, and this pain would never have happened. So in countless paintings and cartoons, in earnestness and in jest, all artists have used the apple as the symbol of temptation. Every apple has a most striking property, unknown to almost everyone except Satanists and pagans. Take a knife and slice across the fruit instead of through the stem. The resulting cross-section reveals the core's perfect pentagram — see FIGURE 9.8 (a). Where in all creation could Satan have found an object of greater symbolic meaning?

In addition, the tree that grew the fruit in the middle of the Garden shares in this diamatic arithmetic. Peter S. Stevens in his marvelous book *Patterns in Nature*[3] writes: "The Fibonacci sequence [Satan's] has long served to describe patterns of branching." If you cut across the branches at different stages of growth, you get the terms of Satan's sequence — see FIGURE 9.8 (b). This is particularly true of all fruit trees. So the branches, which bore the fruit hiding the pentagram, also give us the sequence concealing Phi.

### The Apple's Core     The Tree of Knowledge

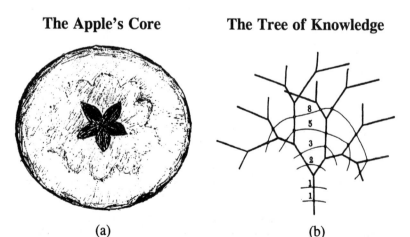

(a)          (b)

FIGURE 9.8

I can hear some alert reader protesting that nowhere in the Bible are we told that the fruit from "the tree of knowledge" was an apple. And the thoughtful reader would be right, but it really does not matter. Surprisingly, every fruit tree with five-petal blossoms conceals a pentagram during some stage of its growth. All varieties of apples and pears have it in their core.

# PYTHAGORAS AND PHI

*All things have a number*
Pythagoras

Born on the island of Samos, and Daniel's contemporary, Pythagoras was the foremost Greek mystic and mathematician of his time. Samos lies off the coast of modern Turkey. It's not far from Patmos, another island, where the Apostle John wrote the immortal Book of Revelation 600 years later.

As all students will recall, Pythagoras is renowned for proving the theorem concerning the relationship among the sides of a right-angled triangle. To this day that remains the single most important idea in all of mathematics. He built up a secret society that dealt with a mixture of mathematics and mysticism. Initiation into this secret society required, among other things, the drawing of a pentagram with a single unbroken line. So great was his fame and influence that the society flourished for several hundred years after his death. Although some of his ideas seem strange to the modern mind, he nevertheless did possess insight into numbers and their symbolic power.

The Pythagoreans especially revered the numbers 1, 2, 3, and 4 as the Holy Tetractys (the Holy Four). They arranged the sum of these (i.e., $10 = 1+2+3+4$) in the triangular pattern shown at the top of the next page. All pagan Greeks falsely believed that nature was ultimately "fourfold." As examples, they cited the four geometrical elements of point, line, surface, and volume, or the first four regular solids. Later Greek philosophers, including Plato, emphasized this further by insisting the material world itself was composed from the four elements of earth, air, fire, and water. Furthermore, they associated each of these with a regular solid. So 10, the fourth triangle number, was considered the ideal quantity to represent their sum.

The Pythagorean oath contains the essence of their religion: "I swear in the great name of the Holy Tetractys which has been bestowed on our soul. The root source of the overflowing nature are contained in it."

These Greeks moved geometry from flatland into the real world of length, width, and breadth. Unfortunately, they

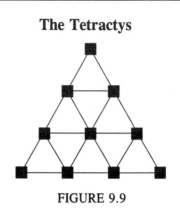

**The Tetractys**

FIGURE 9.9

also applied their knowledge to construct the last of the five regular solids, the dodecahedron (FIGURE 9.10). Present-day Satanists often inscribe each of its 12 five-sided faces with the Devil's bold pentagram (for simplicity only one is shown). Curiously, some modern business-people keep a dodecahedron on their desk as a calendar, each face etched with one of the 12 months. This impressive figure is, in fact, just a 3-dimensional pentagram.

Discovering this fifth regular solid (the cube was the second) disturbed the Greeks' basic fourfold philosophy. Therefore, their "ingenious" thinkers decided this geometrical object represented the form of the universe. So to them, the dodecahedron contained the Holy Tetractys (see Plato's dialogue *Timaeus*). In truth, they elevated Satan's symbol — the illustration of Phi — to represent God's universe.

Even if you removed the 12 pentagrams from the dodecahedron's 12 faces, Phi still cleverly conceals itself here. Consider 3 rectangles with dimensions in the ratio of Phi to 1 (i.e., AB to BC = $\phi$ to 1, as in the figure on the following page). Let them intersect each other at right angles. Incredibly, the 12 corners of these rectangles are the *exact* centers of the 12 faces of a dodecahedron. Accidents do not happen in mathematics.

This property was first mentioned in a book (published 1509) by the Catholic friar Luca Pacioli. Leonardo da Vinci, Pacioli's close friend, drew the text's geometrical illustrations. The friar himself blasphemously called the book *The Divine Proportion*. It lists exactly 13 attributes of Satan's number.

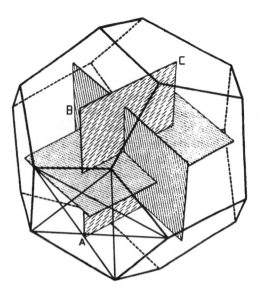

**The Dodecahedron and Phi**
The 12 faces represent power, and the
number Phi shows the nature of that power.

FIGURE 9.10

The modern Dutch artist M. C. Escher arrestingly summarized all this symbolism in his picture *Reptiles* shown on the next page. This is a scene of enticement. Out of the lower world, into the real universe of 3 dimensions crawls a circle of 8 reptiles, images of evil and death. Littered all around are the objects of man's enchantment. In the bottom left corner is a packet of "Job" marijuana rolling papers, while the right corner holds a shot glass and a jug of alcohol. Passing these, the demonic lizards then slither on their counterclockwise journey over a secular zoology book to mount the triangular image of The Trinity. At the drawing's highest point, astride the dodecahedron — the pentagram in three dimensions and the Greek image of the universe — a reptile triumphantly snorts, symbolizing the earthly victory of evil! Continuing its circle over a package of cigarettes, another of man's curses, the creature ends where it began, in the nether world.

***Reptiles*** by M. C. Escher (1943)
The dodecahedron is an ancient symbol of satanic power.

FIGURE 9.11

We have seen the number 12 in association with power — satanic power. However, let us take a short detour to uncover its biblical significance. What does this quantity symbolize in Holy Scripture? A moment's reflection will tell you, how widely the authors used it. Yes, widely used, and always in a context indicating *power and purpose.* Consider the following examples:

- From Seth to Noah there were 12 patriarchs (rulers).
- Israel had 12 tribes from Jacob's 12 sons.
- When Joshua crossed the Jordan river to take his new-found power from the plenty in the Holy Land, he chose 12 stones to commemorate the event (Joshua 4:9).

- The Temple of Solomon — the symbol of God's power — had 12 as a factor in all its measurements. Even the huge bronze ablution tank in front of the Temple rested on the backs of 12 powerful oxen.
- On the 12th night the Magi arrived to recognize Jesus' power. (The Bible does not give the actual number of them, but legend says there were 3.)
- When we next hear of Jesus, He is 12 and in the Temple displaying some of His power.
- Jesus chose 12 Apostles to spread the power of His Word.
- The New Jerusalem, the ruling city of the Millennial Kingdom, is set on 12 foundations.
- This ruling city is to be a perfect cube, 12,000 stadia in length, width, and height. The walls will be 144 (12 x 12) cubits thick (Revelation 21:17).
- It will have 12 gates, with 12 pearls, guarded by 12 chosen angels — all signs of power.

> **In the Bible, the number 12 signifies power given to people, events, or objects chosen for a special purpose. The nature of that power may be judicial or symbolic.**

In the original Hebrew, the famous 23rd Psalm has an outstanding numerical structure. There are 6 perfect triangle verses. More important, the Psalmist directly mentions God exactly 12 times, and 12, of course, equals 6 + 6. The structure of this citing is ABC—CBA (see below and page 91). Part of the power of this Psalm comes from these 12 references, which form an amazing pattern. Consider:

"The Lord"— once (1) in verse one A  
   "He"— twice (2) in verse two B   —Testimony  
   "He" — thrice (3) in verse three C  

  "Thou" — thrice (3) in verse four C  
  "Thou" — twice (2) in verse five B   —Prayer  
"The Lord"— once (1) in verse six A  

Knowledge of this numerical structure only increases the beauty of these immortal verses.

Returning to Pythagoras, we can see by the following quotation attributed to him the extent of his number mysticism:

*Number is the eternal essence; God is number; number is God.*

Whatever the final essence of God may be, we can be certain that Pythagoras had not found it. The frequent occurrence of Phi in the philosopher's work implies the hidden hand of the Dark Angel at work. Throughout the next centuries, until Paul preached Jesus' message, Satan held the Greeks in his unyielding grasp. As we shall see, the signs of his presence were everywhere.

# PHI ON GREEK HUMANISM

Humanism was born on the Greek islands in the 5th century before Christ, but today it flourishes anywhere man does not know God. The foremost ancient humanist was Protagoras (480-410 B.C.) of Abdera. He is responsible for that most notorious saying:

*Man is the measure of all things.*

By this he means all truth is relative to the individual, or there is no truth beyond man. As a result, he implies there is no real truth. Yet, if you deny the existence of an ultimate reality, you also deny the existence of the Creator. God is truth, truth is God. These old Greek teachings sound like the new "situational ethics" taught in our public schools. The Athenians, however, had more moral sense than we do. For even with their pantheon of pagan deities, they banned Protagoras from their city and burned his books!

No detailed knowledge of early Greek society survives — it is lost in history's dust and time. Nonetheless, a few of their writings have come down to us in one form or another. In a single fragmentary manuscript, Pythagoras explicitly mentioned Phi concerning the division of a line segment. But he probably did not realize its occurrence in the pentagram or its generalization in the dodecahedron. Euclid, a later mathematician, summarized all known geometry in his celebrated text *The Elements*. Chapter 6 of his book deals with the study of ratios, and "Proposition 30" is all about Phi.

Euclid was summoned from Athens to head the mathematics department of the new university founded by Ptolemy Soter in Alexandria, Egypt. This first Ptolemy (Cleopatra was a descendant) had been a general under Alexander the Great when he conquered the known world. Daniel 7:6 symbolized this Ptolemy as one of the four heads on the body of the leopard (Alexander). History tells us Ptolemy attended Euclid's classes in the vain hope of quickly learning all geometry. It does not, however, record his reaction when Euclid told him, "There is no royal road to learning."

The preceding paragraphs prove the Greeks knew Phi. They do not show how they used it in their society or religion. Unfortunately, we know very little of the small things from their daily lives. If it were not for the Apostle Paul's immortal letters, we would know even less.

Beyond the writings of Paul and a few others, we have only the ruins of their towns, temples, and theaters to study. Yet, even these ancient structures provide startling insights on the extent of Satan's penetration. Consider their most important pagan temple, the Parthenon. Dedicated to the goddess Athena, supposed protectress of the city, it was then, as now, the showpiece of Greek architecture. Here, if anywhere, we should find Phi.

Built in the 5th century B.C., the Parthenon[4] fits perfectly into a rectangle of height 1 and width **Phi** ($\phi$). The interior housed a 36-foot statue (now lost) of the goddess Athena, gilded in gold and ivory with an immense coiled serpent at her feet. The designer was none other than **Phi**dias, who gave Satan's number its other name.

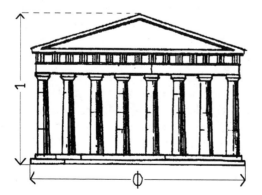

**The Parthenon**

FIGURE 9.12

Of equal importance to their pagan religion was the theater at Epidaurus (FIGURE 9.13), designed by the architect Polyclitus[5]. Today it is a regular tourist attraction. As you can see, a passage (two-thirds up from the stage) runs directly across the amphitheater. This walkway divides the 55 rows of seats into 34 below and 21 above it. Surprisingly, these three numbers are consecutive terms from Satan's sequence. Upon division we get an excellent value for Phi ($34/21 = 1.619...$). Polyclitus knew his pagan proportions well.

The **Greek theater at Epidaurus**, built around 300 B.C.

FIGURE 9.13

Even after 2000 years, Satan still speaks from the rocks of Epidaurus. Perhaps this explains why Paul spent so much of his time traveling and preaching in Greek cities. He addressed many of his letters to their citizens: Corinthians, Ephesians, Philippians, and so on.

Now that we have outlined Phi's march around ancient Greece, we could also follow its tramp through Rome and the Middle Ages. Nevertheless, let's jump ahead to the Renaissance.

# LEONARDO AND PHI

Leonardo da Vinci (1452-1519) is the model for all geniuses, the man who anticipated the modern age. He filled his notebooks with marvelous sketches of airplanes, parachutes, helicopters, bicycles, and hundreds of other mechanical devices, all of this 400 years before any such were built. His gifts as painter, sculptor, architect, inventor, musician, engineer, and scientist are legendary. Of all his magnificent achievements, however, the one that transcends time is the *Last Supper*. To his contemporaries as to us, truly, he seemed beyond all mortal men.

But how did he see himself? We know something of this from an existing introductory letter he wrote to the Prince of Milan in 1482. Among other things, he considered himself an engineer of war and a designer of killing machines. In this letter he numbers his abilities, and the first nine are all about constructing catapults, tanks, battering rams, guns, and mortars. Only in the tenth (and last) does he mention that he can paint as well as any man. The letter ends:

> *And if any of the above-named things seem to any one to be impossible or not feasible, I am most ready to make experiment in your park, or in whatever place may please your excellency — to whom I commend myself with the utmost humility.*[6]

Da Vinci was the world's foremost left-handed person. Furthermore, he could write mirror script as easily as normal script. In his notebooks he purposefully wrote right to left making them unreadable, unless held up to a mirror — a peculiar and secretive habit. To show the difficulty in understanding this left-handed-reflected text, I have written the next sentence as he would have:

He had no children, he never married, and he had no romantic involvements. This was just as well, because his fondness for young men and boys would have doomed any marriage to failure.

The résumé letter Leonardo wrote to the Prince of Milan succeeded. During sixteen years of service to the Prince, he accomplished many of his greatest works, including the *Last Supper*.

At the time Columbus was discovering a new world, da Vinci was creating one. This painting is so familiar (most homes have a copy) one hardly knows what to say by way of something new. Let us examine it, however, from a deomatic and diamatic viewpoint.

Immediately we see that the body of Christ divides the 12 Apostles into two groups of 6, both perfect triangle numbers. These are further huddled into 3s, each a Trinity Number. Mathematically we could say

$$12 = 6 + 6$$
$$= 3+3 + 3+3.$$

Judas, fourth from the left, is physically lowest in the painting, whereas Philip, fourth from the right, is highest. Behind our Lord are exactly 3 windows; the *second* frames His head. All 3 reveal a distant otherworldly landscape and help to give the painting's upper half a great feeling of depth. Significantly, the vanishing point (center of infinity) is precisely in Jesus' mind. (According to some theologians, God and the infinite are so closely connected as to be almost identical.) Yet, the entire picture is not a God's eye view of time and space. It tells of the tension at the moment when Jesus said:

*I tell you the truth, one of you is going to betray me.*

The *Last Supper* by Leonardo da Vinci (1498)
Church of Santa Maria delle Grazie, Milan

FIGURE 9.14

Fearing Jesus has discovered his treachery, Judas draws back and knocks over a salt shaker and by that creates a legend. Despite this, the common fear of having 13 people at a table — lest the first person to leave dies — was not born here. As we shall discover shortly, its origins are older and stranger.

The wisely cautious reader may think I am finding symbols and numbers in Leonardo's masterpiece that the artist never intended. To prove this is not so, consider what the eminent art historian Kenneth Clark has to say on this point. The quotation comes from his splendid book on da Vinci:

> *Very often in reading the description of a picture by*
> *a man of letters we feel that what the writer takes*
> *to be a stroke of dramatic genius is an accident*
> *of which the painter was quite unaware. With Leonardo*
> *this is not the case. We know from his notebooks and*
> *his theoretical writings on art how much thought*
> *he gave to the literary presentation of his subject.*[7]

With Clark's statement in mind, I will go on with an analysis of the painting that is certain to be controversial. You be the judge.

As you can see from the picture itself, the Upper Room of the *Last Supper* has 8 doors, 4 on either side. Now, unless the artist's purpose was purely symbolic, this is an absurd number of entrances for any room. But Leonardo is never absurd, although he is often cunning. Still, why exactly 8 openings, and what do they represent? Previously we proved that the gematria of the name *Jesus* is 888 (see page 51). This quantity, 8, has always been the Number of Resurrection. Christ rose from the dead on a Sunday, the 8th day of the Jewish week. Amazingly, 8 also occurs in all the names and titles of our Lord. For these reasons, the 8 openings symbolize Jesus. It is also curious that the symbol for "the infinite" is an 8 lying on its side: i.e., ∞.

Art experts tell us the present version of the *Last Supper* bears little resemblance to the original. Why? Apparently scores of lesser paint dabblers, in a vain effort at restoration, have overpainted it. These failed attempts are particularly evident in the faces of the Apostles and the background.

Stories surrounding this painting are legion — but only one concerns us here. Leonardo, this keeper of dark secrets, has skilfully woven Satan's number into the painting at least 6 different times. And strikingly he has profanely connected it with 8, Jesus' number of renewal and rebirth. Start with the smallest door on either side:

*Divide its width into the width of the next*
*largest door and you get Phi (1.618...).*
*Now divide the width of the second smallest opening*
*into the next bigger door, and again you get Phi.*
*Continue by dividing the third width into the fourth*
*and last opening. Once again the answer is Phi.*

In other words, the ratio of any two adjacent openings, smaller to larger, is Phi — just like the pentagram and just like Satan's sequence. Due to the many layers of overpainting, this relationship is not so clear today. Nevertheless, some of the peculiarities of the great master have now begun to reveal themselves. The *Last Supper* conceals many secrets.

Could all the preceding be some kind of accident or chance happening? Not likely when you consider that at the very time of the actual painting Leonardo's closest friend was the monk Luca Pacioli. This is the same man, mentioned earlier, who wrote *The Divine Proportion* that da Vinci illustrated. Actually Leonardo did more than draw the figures, he constructed 3-dimensional models of them. Pacioli described 13 strange properties of Phi in 13 chapters with 13 curious titles: "The Incomprehensible Effect," "The Excellent Effect," "The Unutterable Effect," and so forth.

In December 1499, as the century was changing, the French army invaded Milan causing Leonardo to flee at night on horseback.. With him he took only two prized possessions: his painting, the *Mona Lisa*; and his friend, Fra Luca Pacioli. Kenneth Clark says of this flight:

*Like a true humanist he recognised no loyalties* [to the Prince] *and knew no native country but his own genius.*[8]

History, properly viewed, is a continuing conflict between Satan's Destructive Plan for the earth and God's Redemptive Plan through the blood of the Lamb. The Devil advances his schemes whenever he can mock God by manipulating the Lord's symbols in an inverted/perverted manner. We have a classic example of this in Pacioli's book. Let me explain how. Mathematicians are very fond of using Greek letters for special numbers, which normally have no relationship to their original value. For example, π (pi) stands for 3.141..., the ratio of the distance around a circle to its diameter. But for the ancient Greeks, π (pi) meant 80. Similarly, to modern mathematicians Phi always means 1.618.... Yet to the Greeks, φ (phi) was a letter with a value of 500.

The 21st letter of the Greek alphabet is Tau, with a value of 300. Both 21 and 300 are triangle numbers. Since the character T is in the shape of a cross, ancient people used it as a symbol for *the* Cross. For 2000 years, the Tau (also called a Saint Anthony's Cross) has had the form of the capital letter T. Noah's Ark, whose dimensions and design came from God, had a length of 300 (Tau) cubits, a prefiguration of the Tau Cross. In either case, the Lord saved man by the Ark/Cross of wood. The Ark contained the Resurrection Number of human souls: Noah and his wife and his three sons and their wives — 8 in all. See the next chapter for more on "The Ark and the Cross."

So how does all this concern Pacioli and Satan? Simply put, throughout his book *The Divine Proportion* the symbol of the Cross, Tau, is used for Satan's number, Phi! That's equivalent to replacing the sacred Cross with a satanic inverted cross. The Devil must have laughed and danced for days at the foolishness of man. Even today, almost all modern mathematicians still use Tau for Phi.

Since these numbers and their symbols, both ancient and modern, may have been confusing, I have summarized them in the following table:

| Letter Name | Greek Symbol | Ancient Value | Modern Value |
|:---:|:---:|:---:|:---:|
| Pi | π | 80 | 3.141... |
| Phi | φ | 500 | 1.618... |
| Tau | T | 300 | 1.618... |

FIGURE 9.15

So Pacioli and da Vinci used the Devil's sin number in their writings and paintings. Is this so terrible? No one knew Phi symbolized Satan, perhaps not even the author and the painter. How could this number spiritually harm a viewer?

Leonardo's artistic gifts were so extraordinary that the *Last Supper* itself has become a religious shrine. Thousands of Catholics and Protestants pilgrimage each year to the Church of Santa Maria delle Grazie in Milan just to worship for a few minutes in its presence. But the Lord God commanded us in clear language (Exodus 20:4-7) not to have any graven images!

*You shall not make for yourself an idol in the form of anything in heaven above or on the earth beneath or the waters below.*

*You shall not bow down to them or worship them; for I, the Lord your God, am a jealous God.*

Whenever the Old Serpent can snare Christians into breaking one of God's Ten Commandments, then he is gaining power and advancing his schemes. The overwhelming beauty of the *Last Supper* tempts us to worship it, and by that disobey God's Second Commandment about idols and images. This is the Devil's strategy.

> **The numbers are just symbols of intent.**

We know Leonardo was a godless man. His life and philosophy speak boldly on this point. In *The Romance of Leonardo da Vinci*, a biography by the Christian poet and novelist Dmitri Merejkowski, one of the characters says

*Even though he be my brother, and older than I by twenty years, still the Scripture sayeth: Thou shall turn away from a heretic, after a first admonition, and a second. Messer Leonardo is a heretic and a godless man. His mind is darkened by a satanic pride. Through the medium of mathematics and black arts he thinks to penetrate the mysteries of nature.*[9]

With the *Last Supper*, Satan enjoyed enormous success in beguiling believers to commit idolatry. By manipulating the modern Spanish artist Salvador Dali, he repeated that triumph and with the same subject. Consider Dali's painting below. The Spanish master purposefully constructed his canvas in the ratio of 1 unit high to Phi (1.618...) units wide — just like the Parthenon. By measuring the height and width of this figure and dividing, the reader can confirm the presence of this ratio. Dali knew all Leonardo's tricks with Phi; he even dedicated this picture to him.

*The Sacrament of the Last Supper* by Salvador Dali
National Gallery of Art, Washington, DC

FIGURE 9.16

As well as in the dimensions of the painting, Phi is found in the many lines and rectangles of the tablecloth. More important, behind Jesus it looms menacingly in the dodecahedron. This is the same object that Escher used so effectively in *Reptiles* and Pacioli in *The Divine Proportion*. Basically it is a 3-dimensional illustration of Phi. Dali understood perfectly all the symbolism of Satan's number and its many occurrences in this pagan image. Beyond that, Christ's headless body stands in the identical position as Agrippa's *Man in the Pentagram*. How could the imagery be made clearer?

People, who have been to the National Galley in Washington, DC, have told me that it is not uncommon to see believers kneel and pray to this painting. These seemingly pious acts must cause God to shake His head in Heaven at man's folly.

# THE GEMATRIA OF SATAN

Applied to Satan, the ancient science of gematria provides new depths of understanding to the Holy Bible. I plan to find the numerical values of all his names and to look for any obvious patterns. Let's begin with the word "Satan" in both Hebrew and Greek. If we are to learn anything from gematria, then surely his most significant name must give us our most significant clue.

$$S\ A\ T\ A\ N$$
 נ ט ש ה (Old Testament Hebrew)
$$364 = 50\ 9\ 300\ 5$$

And $364 = 13 \times 28$
$$= 13 + 13 + \ldots + 13.$$

$$S\ A\ T\ A\ N$$
Σ α τ α ν ς (New Testament Greek)
$$200\ 1\ 300\ 1\ 50\ 1\ 6 = 559$$

Also $559 = 13 \times 43$
$$= 13 + 13 + \ldots + 13.$$

Surprisingly, both words in both languages are multiples of 13. By a *multiple* of 13, we mean the quantity is composed entirely of 13s. For example, 52 (the number of playing cards in a deck) is such a multiple because $52 = 13 \times 4$ or $13 + 13 + 13 + 13$. In the next few pages we will search Satan's remaining names to see if this pattern of 13s continues. This will be our guide.

Is the fear of this number nothing but a modern superstition? If you believe so, then you have your time-frame reversed. The 13s in the two forms of Satan's name came first; the fear and superstition came second.

Some people think ideas and fears are reborn with each new generation. So, they view history as a disjointed fistful of snapshots rather than a continuous, highly interconnected film. Yet fears, ideas, and words can persist unchanged over vast periods of time. Consider this personal example.

Every summer evening when I was a boy on the farm, my cousin and I would wander out in search of the cows. These warm, placid creatures had to be sheltered in the safety of our barn. Since the farm was heavily forested, they were usually hard to find, even with the help of our faithful dog. So we would call to them in smooth, comforting voices: "Cooo-bos, cooo-bos, cooo-bos." Usually they would answer with deep, lowing sounds, and so tell us where they were. Well, it just so happens that *bos* or *βος* is the ancient Greek word for *cow*. This word had come down through the centuries — to two skinny boys chasing cattle in the darkening hinterland of Ontario — *totally unchanged from the original Greek*. That is the wonderful consistency and endurance of words and ideas. It is the same consistency, since the writing of the Old and New Testaments, that has given 13 the enduring reputation it deserves.

As a student, I thought the reason for 13's bad reputation was simply because it followed 12, the number of power. A dozen is such an easy quantity to work with. You can cut it up in so many different ways, whereas 13 defies all attempts at division. So, I reasoned, it just looked bad in comparison, and there is some truth in that. To avoid even pronouncing the word *thirteen*, many people say *baker's dozen* or, more appropriately, *devil's dozen*. Although earlier societies have often used 12 as their basic unit of measurement, none has ever used 13. Many office and apartment buildings have no 13th floor, and most people avoid a room numbered 13. Franklin D. Roosevelt would hastily invite his private secretary Grace Tully to attend a meal or a meeting just to avoid 13 at the table. Fear of this quantity is so widespread that someone has even coined a tongue twister of a word to describe it: triskaidekaphobia (3 and 10 phobia).

From the founding states to the stripes on Old Glory, Americans surround themselves with reminders of 13. Even the back of a U.S. one-dollar bill is a study in 13s. You can see it in the steps of the pyramid, in the arrows in the eagle's left claw, in the stars above its head, and so on. I leave it as a question for the reader to see how many he can find (I get 7, the number of completeness). "The love of money is the root of all evil" says 1 Timothy 6:10. But even all these 13s prevent no one from trying to get as many dollar bills as possible.

As previously mentioned, many people assume the fear of having 13 people at a table began with the *Last Supper*. As we shall now see, however, its true origins are more deeply buried in history.

The following is a list of Satan's many names. We begin with the "Serpent" of Genesis and end with the "Dragon" of Revelation. The question is, "Are they all multiples of 13?"

1.      S E R P E N T

ף ר שׂ   (Hebrew)

1300 = 800 200 300

And 1300 is 13 x 100, or 13 emphasized. The word itself is from the root "to burn." The Serpent has six names; this is one.

2.      S E R P E N T

Ο φ ι ς   (Greek)

70 500 10 200 = 780 = 13 x 60

= 13 + 13 + . . . + 13

3.      S O N   OF   M O R N I N G

ר ח שׂ  –  נ ב

364 = 4 8 300    50 2

And 364 = 13 x 28 = 13 + 13 + . . . + 13.

This comes from Isaiah 14:12, which referred to the Devil as the Fallen Angel (star). Remarkably, this sum, 364, is identical to the Hebrew value for "Satan."

4.      T E M P T E R   (Matthew 4:3)

π ε ι ρ α ζ ω ν

80 5 10 100 1 7 800 50 = 1053 = 13 x 81

= 13 + 13 + . . . + 13

5.      B E L I A L

Β ε λ ι α λ

2 5 30 10 1 30 = 78 = 13 x 6

Paul uses this name for Satan in 2 Corinthians 6:15: "What harmony is there between Christ and Belial?"

6.        M U R D E R E R    (John 8:44)
α  ν  θ  ρ  ω  π  ο  κ  τ  ο  ν  ο  ς
1  50  9  100  800  80  70  20  300  70  50  70  200  = 1820

And 1820 = 13 x 140.

This is the longest Greek word whose gematria we will find and the only one with 13 letters. Interestingly, the 13th letter of the Hebrew alphabet is M (mem), and even today M still holds the 13th position in the English alphabet.

7.        B Y    B E E L Z E B U B
ε ν    B ε ε λ ζ ε β ο υ λ
5  50  +  2  5  5  30  7  5  2  70  400  30  = 61

And 611 = 13 x 47. This expression for Satan occurs in Luke 11:15-19 and always in this form.

8.        D E V I L
Δ  ι  α  β  β  ο  λ  ο  ς    (original spelling)
4  10  1  2  2  70  30  70  6  = 195 = 13 x 15

9. Many entire sentences and phrases referring to Satan have a revealing gematria. Consider the following example from Revelation 12:9 (KJV). Here, John mentions him exactly 3 times and triple 13s result.

"That old serpent, called the Devil, and Satan" which equals 2197 or 13 x 13 x 13.

10.        D R A G O N
Δ  ρ  α  κ  ω  ν
4  100  1  20  800  50  = 975 = 13 x 75
= 13 + 13 + . . . + 13

Besides this sum, it is also noteworthy that the word *Dragon* is found only in the Book of Revelation and then only 13 times. Yet the number, as such, does not occur anywhere in the New Testament.

Other important examples abound. On page 98 we discovered that "Sons of God" (Job 2:1) has a gematria of 153, the Fish Number. Now consider the full sentence "Sons of God and Satan was among them." Like the words themselves, the astonishing numerical value of this sentence implies both Jesus and Satan, Christ and Antichrist. This value is 1989 — a multiple of both 153 and 13.

$$1989 = 153 \times 13$$
$$= [153 + 153] + [351] + [666 + 666]$$
$$\quad\quad \textbf{Christ} \quad\quad \textbf{reverse} \quad\quad \textbf{Antichrist}$$
$$= \textbf{all triangle numbers}$$

By neglecting the gematria of "Lucifer," perhaps the reader feels I have committed an error of omission. This name, however, cannot be found anywhere in the Bible. It first appeared in St. Jerome's Latin translation of the Old Testament (the Vulgate). He used it for the title "morning star" or "son of morning" (see Isaiah 14:12 and NIV note). Nevertheless, let's find the Latin gematria value of "Lvcifer," as it was originally written:

$$\text{L \quad V \quad C \quad I \quad F \quad E \quad R}$$
$$\text{50 \quad 5 \quad 100 \quad 1 \quad 0 \quad 0 \quad 0}\ = 156 = 13 \times 12$$
$$= 13 + 13 + \ldots + 13$$

By referring to page 48, the interested reader can confirm this sum. Everyone knows, who has seen old Latin texts or monument script, that the Romans always wrote "U" as "V."

At this point it seems natural to ask if the numerical values of *Antichrist, Beast, etc.,* show the same abundance of 13s. The answer is yes they do, and we shall uncover all of them in Chapter 14. In his *Number in Scripture*, E. W. Bullinger produces an extensive list of satanic references — all multiples of 13: *Deceiver; that crooked serpent; the dragon that is in the sea; the Lion; Fowler; that old serpent, even Satan;* and so on.[10]

Summary: Counting the name *Satan* in Hebrew and Greek, the list of 10, the quotations, all Bullinger's examples, the Antichrist instances that I will give later, we have 30 or more cases. Therefore, the Bible has emphatically answered the original question.

> **Yes, all the names and titles of Satan are multiples of 13!**

This is just the short list of the abundant instances where the number 13 is directly bound to Satan. These results seem inconceivable; the odds against this happening by chance only are truly astronomical. If you randomly choose any number/word, then there exists 1 chance in 13 that this number/word is a multiple of 13. If you choose any two numbers/words, then there is 1 chance in 169 (= 13 x 13) both are multiples of 13. If you pick any three, the probability is 1 in 2197 (= 13 x 13 x 13), and so on. To be very conservative, we will choose just Satan's 10 names from our itemized list. Now, calculate the likelihood that all 10 could be multiples of 13 by accident alone. After doing the arithmetic (i.e., 13 x 13 x ... x 13 or ten 13s) we find the probability to be

> **1 in 137,858,491,849.**

or approximately 1 chance in 137 billion. That is the same as choosing 1 particular second out of the last 4370 years. This gigantic number is larger than all the years of seconds since Abraham's birth.

Only a madman would deduce that pure chance was operating here. As with the superabundant triangle numbers in the Lord's Word and Works, so it is with 13 in Satan's many names. Both provide undeniable proof that over hundreds of years The Holy Spirit inspired all the authors of the Bible. No other book contains any mathematical patterns remotely similar. Truly, the Bible is the very breath of God.

I do not wish to assail the reader with large and possibly meaningless numbers. Sadly, some writers of biblical commentaries have done this, no doubt with the very best of intentions. To ease my conscience over this matter, I urge you to actively do the trials described in the next two paragraphs.

To illustrate what this probability really means, we will do a simple experiment. Begin by assigning numbers to the letters of our alphabet (see below). You can do this in countless ways. However, let us do it identically to the ancient Jews and Greeks. Incidentally, present military and business establishments have already done this. Why? So they can send coded messages of highly classified information — just like the Apostle John in Revelation 13:18.

## THE ENGLISH ALPHABET

| UNITS | TENS | HUNDREDS |
|:---:|:---:|:---:|
| A = 1 | J = 10 | S = 100 |
| B = 2 | K = 20 | T = 200 |
| C = 3 | L = 30 | U = 300 |
| D = 4 | M = 40 | V = 400 |
| E = 5 | N = 50 | W = 500 |
| F = 6 | O = 60 | X = 600 |
| G = 7 | P = 70 | Y = 700 |
| H = 8 | Q = 80 | Z = 800 |
| I = 9 | R = 90 | |

FIGURE 9.17

Pick any book, magazine, or article you wish, other than the Bible; now randomly or otherwise choose 10 words from it. They could be the first 10, the last 10, or the names of 10 characters, or — but you get the idea. Next, find the number value of the whole word by adding up individual letter values (use FIGURE 9.17, or make your own system). We will pause while you do the necessary arithmetic.

. . . . . . . . . . . . . . . . . . . . . . . . . . . . . . . . . . . .

Are any of your choices divisible by 13 (i.e., multiples of 13)? Perhaps 1, maybe 2, but almost certainly not 5. And no one got 10, not even if every man and woman on earth did the experiment. To repeat, the probability of this happening by just chance is less than 1 in 137 billion.

Challenge a humanist, an apostate, or an atheist to account for these numerical patterns. If they cannot, then they must reexamine their philosophy, or religion, or lack of it. In world evangelism these patterns and probabilities can be a great first step in opening the door to the Gospel.

Just by being able to read, educated people of the ancient Hebrew-Greek world knew some gematria: it was a natural result of their letter-numbers. They interchanged words and numbers quickly and easily in a fashion completely foreign to us. After that, it was a small step to notice that all the names of Satan are multiples of 13. So, the association of the Dark Angel with this number, through the medium of gematria, became a source of fear.

> **The fear of 13 originated in the numerical value of Satan's many names.**

Up to this point, we have uncovered the root fear of 13 in Satan's various names. Still, that is only half the story. The other part is "Why 13 and not say 23, or some other number?" God could have arranged these sums to be anything He wished. Why 13? The answer has two parts: one involves the nature of the number system, the other the nature of Satan.

Our system is based on 10. We think and compute in groups of 10, and our practice beautifully shows that. For example, when we write Jesus' Celestial Number, 153, we mean

$$
\begin{array}{rcr}
\text{1 group of ten tens} &=& 100 \\
\text{5 groups of ten} &=& 50 \\
\text{Trinity Number} &=+& 3 \\
\hline
&& 153
\end{array}
$$

Your car's odometer also shows this system when the digits run from 1, 2, 3, 4, 5, 6, 7, 8, 9, to 0 (really 10). After these ten digits the whole cycle starts again with 1. The great biblical scholar E. W. Bullinger says the following about the number 10:

> *Completeness of order, marking the entire round of anything,
> is, therefore, the ever-present signification of the number ten.
> It implies that nothing is wanting; that the number and order
> are perfect; that the whole cycle is complete.*[11]

As already stated, one of Satan's major weapons is mocking
mimicry, which is really a form of rebellion. Born in pride and nursed
in sin, rebellion is the true essence of Lucifer. In the last three and
one-half years of the coming Tribulation, he will use the Antichrist to
mock The Holy Trinity and mimic the Resurrection. In that terrible
time, he will also put together an inverted or anti-trinity composed of
the following:

**Antichrist**
(first Beast as
a false Christ)

**False Prophet**
(second Beast as a
mock Holy Ghost)

**Satan**
(who would be God)

## THE ANTI-TRINITY

During the *last days*, the Apostle John foretells (Revelation 13:3)
how the Devil will even parody our Lord's Resurrection. This passage
reveals that the Antichrist will receive a fatal head wound yet recover
— by Satan's help — to the wonderment and praise of the entire
world. Therefore, the ideas of the previous paragraphs tell us:

- 10 represents a complete cycle of numbers.
- The Devil continually ridicules The Holy Trinity.

With these two thoughts in mind, few actions could be more certain than for Satan to mimic the Trinity Number, 3. And what is the nearest possible quantity with which to do this? It is 13: *the next 3 in the next cycle*. After all, the very word *thirteen* (three-ten) means 3 and 10. These two quantities, the Trinity Number 3 and the complete cycle number 10, are both triangular. For all eternity, and for all to see, The Holy Spirit has recorded Satan's choice in the Holy Scriptures. For these reasons

> **13 is the False Trinity Number of Rebellion.**

The Bible's very first mention of 13 associates it directly with rebellion. Occurring notably early in God's Word (Genesis 14:4, KJV), it says:

> *For twelve years they served Chedorlaomer,*
> *and in the thirteenth year they rebelled.*

So, we have tracked 13's origin to its lair in rebellion, the antechamber to sin. Rebellion implies sin.

In this age, Christians know the horror and pain that rebellion brings, especially in the family. The near total revolt of today's youth against God's moral truths tears at almost every home. Coincidentally, rebellion usually starts in the first teenage year, the 13th. As the commonplace expression says, the more things change, the more they remain the same.

The medieval writer Dante (1265-1321), in his famous epic poem *The Inferno*, also understood rebellion to be at the very heart of sin. The entire poem is organized around the author's imaginary journey through Hell. Its inner structure builds on an elaborate use of the symbolic numbers 3, 7, and 10. As you descend through the circles of *The Inferno*, the sins of the damned become more and more horrendous. In the central circle of the pit lie all the arch-rebels of history. Lucifer has 3 faces and 3 mouths with a sinner in each — a grotesque parody of The Trinity. Dante says:

> *In every mouth he worked a broken sinner*
> *between his rake-like teeth. Thus he kept three*
> *in eternal pain at his eternal dinner.*

*For the one in the front the biting seemed to play*
*no part at all compared to the ripping: at times*
*the whole skin of his back was flayed away.*

*"That soul that suffers most," explained my guide,*
*"is Judas Iscariot, he who kicks his legs*
*on the fiery chin and has his head inside.*

*Of the other two, who have their heads thrust forward,*
*the one who dangles down from the black face*
*is Brutus: note how he writhes without a word.*
*And there, with huge and sinewy arms, is Cassius."* [12]

Dante's symbolism for sin is perfectly consistent: all those in Hell eternal have earned their sentence by rebelling. Lucifer and Judas we know. You may also recall Brutus and Cassius, who did the ultimate rebellious act by assassinating their leader Julius Caesar. We, of course, might not have put these last two in Hell, but a poet uses the images and ideas from his own time and place.

# DIAMATICS AND THE DEVIL

Diamatics is the mathematics surrounding Satan. With the addition of 13, we now have an unholy trinity of numbers relating directly to the Devil:

- **666, LUCIFER'S TRIANGLE NUMBER:**
  After rebelling in Heaven, Lucifer was stripped of this number. However, he always rewards the Antichrists with his former triple 6.

- **Phi, 1.618..., SATAN'S SIN NUMBER:**
  The number connected to original sin, the navel, the satanic pentagram, and paganism in every age.

- **13, the DEVIL'S FALSE TRINITY NUMBER:**
  The quantity associated with fear, phobias, and rebellion. Also, the Devil's number in God's Holy Word.

These three numbers are intimately linked with Satan and his rebellion in Heaven (666), on earth (1.618...), and in the Bible (13). So their relationship to the Dark Angel is evident, but what unites them with each other? On the surface they appear totally different: 666 is even and large, 1.618... is a decimal and small, while 13 is middle sized and odd. Nevertheless, all three numbers are tightly interwoven in a fantastic structure. Let's investigate.

Earlier in this chapter, I wrote about Satan's sequence and how it hides in one of God's greatest patterns, the Triangle of Creation. You may recall how each new entry in the Triangle was generated by adding the two numbers directly above (see FIGURE 9.5). Similarly, Satan produces his sequence by adding the two numbers directly in front. Of course, this method for producing the sequence just mimics the method for producing the Triangle.

We will start a second satanic sequence, beginning not with 1 and 1, but with 13 and 666. The method for finding new terms will be the same as before, just add the previous two. Here are the first few:

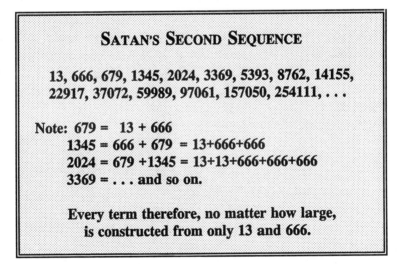

**SATAN'S SECOND SEQUENCE**

13, 666, 679, 1345, 2024, 3369, 5393, 8762, 14155, 22917, 37072, 59989, 97061, 157050, 254111, . . .

Note: 679 =  13 + 666
1345 = 666 + 679  = 13+666+666
2024 = 679 +1345 = 13+13+666+666+666
3369 = . . . and so on.

**Every term therefore, no matter how large, is constructed from only 13 and 666.**

As with Satan's first sequence, divide consecutive terms and observe what happenss (see FIGURE 9.18 on the next page). Even by the eleventh division, 1.618... has oozed out. It seems miraculous to have caught Phi hidden away in this second satanic sequence constructed from just 13 and 666. As this sequence grows, the target of all these divisions is exactly Phi. Unquestionably, Satan's numbers form an intertwined unholy trinity.

## SATAN'S NUMBERS

| | | | |
|---|---|---|---|
| 1. | **666/13** = 51.23... | 2. | 679/666 = 1.019... |
| 3. | 1345/679 = 1.980... | 4. | 2024/1345 = 1.504... |
| 5. | 3369/2024 = 1.664... | 6. | 5393/3369 = 1.600... |
| 7. | 8762/5393 = 1.624... | 8. | 14155/8762 = 1.615... |
| 9. | 22917/14155 = 1.619... | 10. | 37072/22917 = 1.617... |
| 11. | 59989/37072 = **1.618...** | | . . . . . . |

FIGURE 9.18

So 13, 666, and Phi coil together in a second satanic sequence. Phi is associated with everything godless and pagan; 13 marks rebellion in the Bible. And 666 is the number of the first rebel, Lucifer, and will be of the last rebel, the Antichrist. Still other deep connections exist among these numbers and, unexpectedly, 153. For example, apply the Trinity Function to 666:

$$666 \; \text{-------}> \quad 6^3 \;\; + \;\; 6^3 \;\; + \;\; 6^3$$
$$= 6\text{x}6\text{x}6 + 6\text{x}6\text{x}6 + 6\text{x}6\text{x}6$$
$$= \;\; 216 \;\; + \;\; 216 \;\; + \;\; 216$$
$$= 648$$

Nothing unusual yet. Now, however, apply this rule to 648 and each new image until something exceptional happens.

$$666 \; \text{---}> \; 648 \; \text{---}> \; 792 \; \text{---}> \; 1080 \; \text{---}> \; 153$$
$$[1] \qquad\quad [2] \qquad\quad [3] \qquad\quad\;\; [4] \qquad\quad [5]$$

Remember, 153 is unalterable and the home point for one-third of all numbers. As with all multiples of three, 666 transforms into Jesus' Celestial Number. In fact, they span 5 terms.

Could Satan approach Jesus, as the Trinity Function implies? Approach, yes, when he was the archangel Lucifer; touch, no. Although, even after his rebellion Satan did come near our Lord during the Temptation. Yet, Jesus, armed only with the power of His Father's Word, met and defeated the Devil and his 3 deceptions. After which He commanded,

*Away from me Satan.*

Now use the Trinity Function on 13:

$$13 \text{ --------> } 1^3 + 3^3$$
$$= 1x1x1 + 3x3x3$$
$$= 1 + 27$$
$$= 28$$

Surprisingly, 13 converts into the second perfect number. Perhaps this shows Lucifer's original position as the first archangel referred to by this chapter's opening quotation from Milton's *Paradise Lost*. Or perhaps it alludes to the Hebrew gematria of *Satan,* which is a multiple of both 28 and 13, a mixture of arch-angel and fallen-angel.

Whatever his high beginnings, he ends in the central circle of Hell, in the center of the pit. Repeated applications of the Trinity Rule strikingly symbolize this:

13 --->28-->520--->133--->55--->250---> 133

Here we have something quite unforeseen. Repeated use of this rule propels 13 into an infinite cycle of 3 quantities whirling around in endless circles. Remarkably, 133 is very like 13. Also, it's almost as if the False Trinity Number were trying to imitate 153, by ending where it began. To clarify, let's fully diagram this sequence.

## THE CIRCLES OF HELL

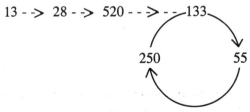

FIGURE 9.19

The sum of the numbers $13 + 28 + 520 + 133 + 55 + 250$ is exactly 999. The final chapter will explain the significance of this sum in particular and 9 in general.

This wheel (FIGURE 9.19) includes **1**, **5**, and **3**, yet it never reaches 153 or 13, however close it may approach. Symbolically speaking, it moves condemned to unending steps from 133 to 55 to 250 to 133 again. Clearly, 13 never touches our Lord or itself. Just like Dante's circles, Satan's number tumbles and swirls forever through an endless triad. Scripturally, this figure parallels John 14:30 when Jesus, referring to Satan, said:

*He has no hold on me.*

In the final years of the Tribulation, the mark of the Antichrist will be Lucifer's triangle quantity, 666 — a grotesque insult to The Holy Trinity. Previously I expressed this number as a trinity of triangles:

$$666 = \quad 15 \quad + \quad 300 \quad + \quad 351$$
$$\text{truncated 153} \quad \text{Tau Cross} \quad \text{153 reversed}$$

You may verify the triangularity of these numbers from FIGURE 3.2. Beneath each I have shown some of the irreligious symbolism.

The False Trinity Number of Rebellion also has an interesting expression as the sum of three triangles — just 5 short of $6 + 6 + 6$.

$$13 = 6 + 6 + 1$$

Several pages back, I wrote about the other satanic reason for using 13. It is the next 3 in the next cycle of 10 — both triangle numbers.

$$13 = 10 + 3$$

Before leaving this section on diamatics, observe two final striking associations: one between Christ and Antichrist, the other between 153 and 13. In the language of the New Testament, the holy name *Christ* is written as

$$\begin{array}{ccccccc}
\text{CH} & \text{R} & \text{I} & \text{S} & \text{T} & \text{O} & \text{S} \\
\text{X} & \rho & \iota & \sigma & \tau & \text{o} & \varsigma \\
600 & & + & & 200 & = & \mathbf{800}
\end{array}$$

As stated previously, early Christians used the first and last letters, Xς (800), of *Christos* as a shorthand for the entire name. Like the sign of the fish ( ), these letters served as cryptic symbols for our faith and emphasize rebirth and renewal. On the other hand, scholars have for centuries pointed out the disturbing similarity between these two letters and the number Xξς (666). To put it bluntly, the symbols for Christ, Xς, with the addition of the serpent number, ξ, are the symbols for the Antichrist, Xξς. Yet I find this a magnificent piece of number and literary imagery. Consider. Like the word *Anti-Christ* itself, the letters X-ξ-ς symbolize Satan's opposition to Christ.

(The previous paragraph leads to an interesting aside. All those who object to the "X" in "X-mas" should weigh that this is the original and proper first letter for *Christ*.)

The relationship between 153 and 13 is like that just mentioned, but the opposite happens. Something is subtracted, not added. Markedly, taking the 5 out of 153, leaves 13. In other words Satan is deficient, wanting, or incomplete — by the Trinity Function's 5 steps from Antichrist (666) to Christ (153) as shown on page 142.

| Christ ---> Antichrist | and | Jesus ---> Satan |
|---|---|---|
| Xς ---> Xξς | | 153 ---> 13 |

When we see a red scarf, a cardinal, or a red sunset, we are experiencing the sensation of color. Although to a scientist, we are just encountering electromagnetic radiation from 6300 to 7600 angstrom units. This is one difference between subjective reality (experiencing red) and objective reality (measuring red wavelengths). What is true for the Lord's Works is also true for His Word. When you enjoy and live in the light of God's Word, you are having a personal relationship with Jesus. Nevertheless, behind the subjective reality of experience always lies the other universe of mathematics.

## SATANISM IN AMERICA

*Woe to those who call evil good and good evil,*
*who put darkness for light and light for darkness.*
Isaiah 5:20

*The spirit clearly says that in later times*
*some will abandon the faith and follow deceiving*
*spirits and things taught by demons.*
Paul, 1 Timothy 4:1

Thirty years ago even the title of this section would have been absurd. Times change, people change. We are now experiencing a godlessness and an apostasy that all the nightmares of our past could not have dreamed up. To doubt the existence of Satan, as humanists and secularists do, takes a special kind of blindness to the evidence all around us. In the next few pages, we will explore this final rise of Satanism and its many activities.

On Walpurgis Night, 30 April 1966, Anton Szandor LaVey, former lion tamer, shaved his head in the tradition of medieval executioners. Later that same night he founded the Church of Satan, declaring it to be "Year One, Anno Satanas," the first year of the Satanic Age. In hindsight, his prophecy seems correct.

LaVey, often called the Black Pope, is one of the chief instruments furthering Satan's Plan for the return of the Antichrist. Toward that end he has been "inspired" to write *The Satanic Bible* and *The Satanic Rituals*. Believers often read them against a background of heavy-metal music. The entire LaVey family of father, mother, and daughters involves itself in his "ministry." They even maintain a listing in the San Francisco yellow pages under the heading "Churches — Satanic."

Presently, U.S. sales of *The Satanic Bible* have surpassed one million copies. Beyond these huge sales figures, research finds that approximately three people read each book. Also, by retaining at least a single copy, public libraries provide further circulation. And, regrettably, on college campuses in the U.S.A. and Canada, LaVey's "Bible" outsells God's.

The groups of rebels that follow **ANT**on Sz**A**ndor LaVey — his name is an anagram for Satan — call themselves grottos. They exist throughout America from mega-city to micro-village. Their names scream out demonic intent: the Beasts, the Demons, Black Nights, Lucifer Rising, the Pentagrams, the Antichrists, and so forth.

Michael A. Aquino, lieutenant colonel U.S. Army and Vietnam War veteran, was a former national commander of the Eagle Scout Honor Society. Michael A. Aquino, private citizen and author of *The Coming Forth by Night*, is the satanic chief priest of the Temple of Set. With his high priestess wife Lilith, they also have their headquarters in San Francisco. Formerly a member of the Church of Satan, Aquino quarreled so frequently with LaVey that the two bloated egotists separated. Later Aquino founded his own "church."

Aquino refers to himself as the Great Beast from Revelation, and makes no attempt to hide his detestable practices from authorities. Amazingly, the U.S. Army officially recognizes Satanism as a religion and even allows Aquino to lecture on it.

LaVey has a copyright, no less, on the title "Church of Satan." So for his "church," Aquino chose the name of a supposedly different malevolent god called Set. In Egypt, Set was one-third of an ancient unholy trinity. (Repeatedly history shows us, go to God's sacred triangle symbol and there you will always find Satan's sacrilege.) By the title Mulge he was considered the heart of Babylonian magic and the central figure in their demonic systems. The Bible knows him as Baal, but he is the Devil by whatever name you call him. The San Francisco telephone directory also lists the Temple of Set.

# THE STARS AND THE SATANIST

Hollywood's fascination with Satanism is part of the Devil's Plan to provide twisted role models for today's youth. In the past, those involved hid their names and activities fearing a public boycott of their films or concerts. Nevertheless, the rumors and stories of Hollywood Devil worshipers wiggled their way out to the frenzied media and the adoring public. That was then, this is now. Today, many openly seek converts for Satan.

Among the most blatant practitioners was the late Sammy Davis Jr., who during his stage performances always wore a satanic neck medallion. By setting up meetings between LaVey and other Hollywood stars and personalities, Davis actively recruited for their "church." Singer Barbara McNair and old-time actor Keenan Wynn have been members; LaVey even awarded Wynn an honorary priesthood. There are many others.

**Davis and Satanist LaVey embrace.**

A book by Arthur Lyons, called *Satan Wants You* tells of Jayne Mansfield's deep involvement with this cult. As mentioned, most stars did not want their union with LaVey known, but Jayne relished it. Lyons writes of the sex symbol:

> *Mansfield showed up at the church in 1966 with a request that the High Priest put a curse on her second husband, Matt Cimber with whom she was engaged in a child custody battle. After she won a favorable court ruling, she became an ardent Devil's disciple. When her young son, Zoltan, was later critically mauled by a lion at Jungleland Wild Animal Park, the actress called LaVey for help. The High Priest drove to the top of Mount Tamalpais, near San Francisco, and in the middle of a torrential rainstorm summoned all his magical powers while bellowing out a soliloquy to Satan. Mansfield credited the boy's miraculous recovery to Satanic intervention and swore undying loyalty to LaVey and the Prince of Darkness.*[13]

Later, Mansfield's new boyfriend Sam Brody took a dislike to LaVey and tried to stop Jayne from seeing him. Apparently he was jealous. LaVey reacted by putting a curse on Brody, who shortly afterward severely broke his leg in an auto accident. Undeterred, the boyfriend continued to threaten LaVey who retaliated with yet another and much stronger curse. The High Priest warned Jayne to avoid Brody, but she ignored his advice. On 29 June 1967, in the outskirts New Orleans, the car in which they were driving ran under the tailgate of a truck. Both died instantly, but Jayne was decapitated.

The figure to the right shows Jayne Mansfield and Anton LaVey at her Hollywood home called the Pink Palace. She owned the chalice in her hands and the skulls on the table. During the year before the tragic accident, she habitually used them in satanic rituals.

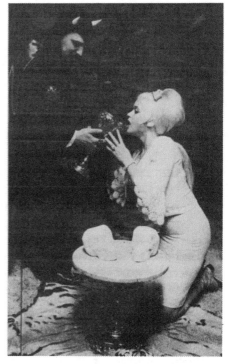

**Mansfield and LaVey**
at the Pink Palace

Hollywood stars were not the only Americans LaVey influenced, or who joined in satanic rites. Arthur Lyons, quoted earlier, says on page 107 of his *Satan Wants You*:

*In 1967, the Church received national press coverage when LaVey performed a Satanic wedding of socialite Judith Case and radical journalist John Raymond. In May of that year, it made news again when LaVey performed a Satanic baptism of the LaVey's three-year-old daughter, Zeena, and in December, he created another media event when he performed Satanic last rites for a sailor member, complete with full naval color guard. With the publicity came a flood of would-be initiates to the church.*

The Mansfield story has a bizarre postscript. LaVey claims that while clipping a newspaper article about himself he noticed that Jayne's photograph was on the back, and he had accidentally cut her head off. Within the hour he received a telephone call saying she had been killed.

# HEAVY-METAL SATANISM

LaVey's grottos, although very influential, are like a gentle summer breeze compared to the full satanic blast of heavy-metal music. New members of Devil worshiping cults are invariably teenagers or young adults whose main preoccupation is shock-rock. The lyrics of their songs screeeeeech about violence, drugs, sex, cruelty, hatred, suicide, and death! The bands have telltale names like Black Sabbath, KISS, Venom, AC/DC, Mercyval Fate, Slayer, and Judas Priest. You would have to be a complete liberal jackass not to realize the overpowering satanic influence of this tidal wave of sonic garbage!

During the week of 12 March 1990, New York City's John Cardinal O'Connor spoke out against the horror of heavy-metal music. O'Connor warned of "diabolically instigated violence" and added "heavy-metal rock music can trap youth into dabbling in Satanist practices." In particular, he denounced lead singer Ozzy Osbourne's song "Suicide Solution" for its lyrics:

*Suicide is the only way out. Don't you know what it's really about.*

The Cardinal received support from Protestants and Catholics alike. Everyone recognizes a common enemy. Father Richard Rento of Clifton New Jersey, an expert on Satanism, said of heavy-metal music: "It is one of the factors helping to create a climate in which the hitherto unthinkable becomes the thinkable."

Anyone with teenage children at home should be aware of what they are listening to. Check out the covers of their record albums or compact discs. Only someone totally blind to all satanic handiwork will fail to recognize the presence of demonic symbols. Undoubtedly, your son or daughter occasionally listens with a walkman. Pick it up, put it on, turn it on, and attentively listen to the lyrics. The wholly evil character of the words may stun you. Also, be alert to your child's preferences in movies and rock-videos. All these influences and pressures could be molding your son or daughter into a lifetime of depravity.

Many authorities believe heavy-metal music is part of a satanic conspiracy to gain control over our youth. For instance, the name of the leading band KISS is rumored to be an acronym for Kids In Satan's Service. King Diamond of Mercyval Fate openly parades his Satanism. And Black Sabbath's influence is phenomenal: even in the seventies this group sold over 7 million records. Each gets played hundreds of times, and sales for all such groups have skyrocketed ever since. Presently, every major band has sold millions of albums. Like their record sales, their fans too are legion. Ozzy Osbourne, lead singer of Black Sabbath, bites the heads off live bats and spits the pieces at his hordes of squealing fans. What is left to shock parents?

The influence of these groups is overpowering and hypnotic; they totally assault the spiritual side of devotees. For days after a concert the participants appear glassy-eyed, emotionally dead, and physically deaf.

Watch for satanic graffiti in shopping malls and supermarkets. Visit local junior and senior high schools, and check them out for Satan's symbols. Have unexplained dead cats, rats, dogs, or other animals been found in your neighborhood? Have they been mutilated? Virtually every teenager or young adult convicted of a ritualistic crime involving Devil worship has been a heavy-metal addict. Be aware! Be concerned!

What could be more natural (unnatural) than for Satan to put hidden messages into his altar music, heavy-metal? How could this be done? If we follow past clues, one of his chief blasphemies was to do sacred Christian acts in reverse. Often his followers accomplish this by inverting a religious sign, object, or number. For example, reading the Lord's Prayer backwards, inverting the Cross, or reversing Jesus' number, 153, to 351 (i.e., 13 x 27).

A similar device exists in much of rock music, not just heavy-metal: experts call it backward-masking. Evidently, by playing certain records in reverse, you can hear hidden messages such as "I live for Satan" and "Satan is God." Just how many groups have back-masked is uncertain, but any short list would include Styx, ELO, The Cars, Led Zeppelin, and Twisted Sister.

To clearly warn consumers which records contain backward-masked words and phrases, responsible legislators and groups have been calling for labeling laws for the music industry. One such group, the Parents' Music Resource Center (PMRC) of Arlington Virginia, is taking this and other heavy-metal horrors very seriously. Two important members are Tipper Gore, wife of Vice-President Al Gore, and Susan Baker, wife of former secretary of state James Baker. By lobbying the music industry to rate concerts and records, they hope for basic ethical standards from singers, musicians, and the recording companies. Some have proposed the following labeling system:

"R" for records with backward-masked messages.
"X" for albums containing profanity or lyrics about suicide.
"O" on records with occult lyrics or intentions.
"G" for gangster rap records or compact discs.

It's a beginning.

When in public, teenage Satanists regularly speak certain words backwards so the public will not be alerted. For instance, if you overheard the word *lived*, you would be unconcerned. But depending on the context, and the frequency with which they used this word, you might begin to suspect they were discussing the Devil. Similarly, when reversed, *live* is *evil* and *Natas* is *Satan*.

So, not only must the reader be aware of satanic symbols, but the listener must also be alert for satanic sounds. Too frequently, the symbols and sounds of our time are Satan's handiwork.

In the past it was the Devil's policy to persuade us that he did not exist. By a cover of supposed non-being, he thought to more easily carry out his malevolent acts. But with the *time of the end* approaching he has blown any such pretense and now boldly struts the earth for followers and fools.

# SATANIC SYMBOLS

Young cult members rarely understand the full meaning or the ancient origin of satanic symbols. They merely copy and imitate. Sadly, most Christians are equally uninformed. However, to defeat the enemy you begin by recognizing his presence. To remedy this lack of information, we shall investigate and expose the essence of every major diabolical design. There are *exactly* 5.

## THE PENTAGRAM

The main satanic symbol is the two horns-up pentagram denoting the Devil, not the single point-up showing man. All demon worshiping ceremonies or ritual criminal acts feature this design. The figure's true meaning and its intriguing structure were explained earlier. Any two consecutive lengths are in the ratio 1 to Phi, the same ratio in which the navel

**Satan's Star**

divides the human body. The only physical difference between us and Adam, *the navel*, symbolizes the only spiritual difference between us and Adam, *original sin*. Satan's sin number, Phi, and its presence in the pentagram signify the fall of man. That's why when you invert man's outline, Satan's pentagram rises. In addition, Devil worshipers frequently impale our Savior's name on the pentagram's horns and always in the counterclockwise direction.

## THE NUMBER OF THE BEAST

**Lucifer's Triangle**

Among teenagers, this mark predominates. Interestingly, they usually group the digits as shown in the figure to the left, and they often invert the entire triangle. By this formation they unknowingly imply the triangularity that forms the basis of this book. This arrangement creates a double taunt at The Trinity: both number and form are triangular.

Although all members of demonic cults are aware of this number's connection to Satan, few comprehend its past or future significance. Christians, on the other hand, know the future of 666 from Revelation 13:16-17:

*He also forced everyone, small and great, rich and poor, free and slave, to receive a mark on his right hand or on his forehead, so that no one could buy or sell unless he had the mark, which is the name of the beast or the number [666] of his name.*

By "the number of his name" John implied gematria.

In the distant past, before Lucifer's rebellion in Heaven, 666 was his shining triad number. Then, he and it were part of God's original Trinity Creation. His was the number of Heaven's first rebel and will be the number of earth's last.

## THE SIGN OF THE HORNS

By extending the first and little fingers of your left hand, while using the thumb to hold down the middle two, you can easily make this hand gesture. Often it serves as a quick recognition signal among cult members. At heavy-metal rock concerts and rallies, it is a sign of approval — a salute to Satan. This hand signal also shows three 6s: the two downturned fingers and the upturned thumb form the bottom curl of each 6.

**Horned Hand**

Horns are the traditional headdress of the Devil or Goat, symbolizing sexual excess and perversion. Even the slang word *horny* derives from this source.

Teenagers give **"the sign of the horns"** at a Slayer concert.

## THE INVERTED CROSS

What more sacrilegious act could the Devil do than invert Christendom's most beloved symbol, the Holy Cross? Unfortunately, that is not the only desecration here. By recalling the many crosses you have

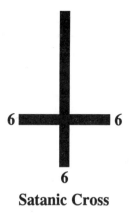

6 **6**

6

**Satanic Cross**

seen, the lengths in this figure should appear abnormal. Let the level bar be 1 unit long, then the upright height is 1.618... (Phi) units. So, Satan's earthly number and all its torrent of pagan symbolism have been cleverly hidden here. If on some album jacket or in a book you see the profane satanic cross, measure it to confirm the presence of this ratio. However, the crosses scrawled by know-nothing youths or occult dabblers could have any dimensions. In contrast, the vertical shaft of the sacred, Holy Cross reaches up twice and preferably three times the length of the horizontal crossbar. As a final insolence, Satanists often put 6s or phallic designs on the three downturned ends forming an inverted triangle.

## THE PITCHFORK OR TRIDENT

**Pitchfork**

To mock The Trinity, Satan's pitchfork invariably has exactly 3 upturned prongs. Each prong symbolizes an erect penis, and each is for an open orifice in the harlot or triple goddess: oral, anal, vaginal. To further emphasize its evil intent, an inverted cross is often placed on the shaft. As the trident it was the preferred weapon of Poseidon (Neptune), the pagan god of the undersea world.

All Christians should know and understand these 5 satanic marks. Teenagers or young cult devotees do not begin to comprehend their full meaning, but

*God does, Satan does, and we should.*

Nevertheless, a symbol is just what the name says: a symptom, not the disease. These signs are not evil in and of themselves, but of what they represent. The real malignancy is rebellion from God and hence separation from Jesus' truth.

# THE SABBATS OF SATAN

Every night when the moon is full, pagans and Satanists all across America celebrate the Black Sabbat (Latin for Sabbath). To parody Jesus and the 12 Apostles, each unhallowed gathering includes a Black Master and 12 coven members for a total of 13. And the year has precisely 13 such occasions, one every 28 days because 28 x 13 = 364. Besides these 13 full-moon rituals, there are 8 high Black Sabbats of utmost importance making 21 in all — the 6th triangle number. In light of our previous research, the reasons for the 13 are clear, but why would Satan use 8?

As we know, the Bible uses 8 as a symbol for resurrection and rebirth. Christ rose from the dead on the 8th day, a Sunday. Near the beginning of the Book of Revelation, John even refers to this 8th day as the "Lord's Day." Moreover, the startling gematria of "Jesus," 888, should make the point perfectly clear to every doubting Thomas. Also, by the Father's majestic time-scale, the genesis of man and his life on earth reflect this quantity. Let me explain. At the end of the Millennial Reign, 7000 years will have passed since the creation of man. God tells us through His servant John (Revelation 21:1):

*Then I saw a new heaven and a new earth,*
*for the first heaven and the first earth had passed away.*

Consequently, the 8th millennium will start with a completely new genesis of Heaven and earth, the beginning of eternity itself. So, for the Lord God, "8" symbolizes — after the completeness of 7 — a celebration of new life and new beginnings.

Inevitably and profanely, the Devil has twisted this quantity into a ceremony of death. That is the reason the exact number of high demonic rituals is always 8 when followers must offer sacrifices to Satan. Here is a list of these supreme Black Sabbats:

1. February 2: Candlemas day — festival of winter purification for Catholics, but a rite of putrefaction for Satanists.
2. March 21: Spring equinox — equal hours of night and day and a time of wild pagan sexual rites.
3. April 30: Walpurgis Night — for demons and witches.
4. June 21: Summer solstice — longest day of the year.

5. August 1: Lammas day — pagan rite of first fruits, especially those with a pentagonal core.
6. September 21: Fall equinox — equal day and night again.
7. October 31: All Hallow's Eve (Halloween) — another night for demons and witches.
8. December 21: Winter solstice and the shortest day of the year — a ritual night of infanticide to mock our Lord's nativity on the 25th.

To protect themselves from Satan's insanities, some deny his authorship or the reality of these horrific deeds. They feel the crimes are too frightful to exist. The presence of evil also causes many to flee to a world of drugs and alcohol and others to the sensuality of food and sex. Still others hide in the comfortable pew of a bloodless Christianity that neither Paul nor any of the Apostles knew. To live for Christ — then as now — is to be a rock submerged in a torrent of depravity. The effluent flows and boils around and over your being, while you stand anchored on the bedrock of your faith!

*Anyone who says there is no Devil*
*will before long say there is no God.*

# CHRISTIANS AND SATANISM

*Let no one be found among you who sacrifices his son*
*or daughter in a fire, who practices divination or sorcery,*
*interprets omens, engages in witchcraft, or casts spells,*
*or who is a medium or a spiritualist or who consults the dead.*
*Anyone who does these things is detestable to the Lord.*
Deuteronomy 18:9-12.

A satanic cancer grows in the bowels of America. As the final decade of this millennium stumbles to its end, western society has belched up the most evil personalities of all times. What then should a follower of Jesus do? First, do not be like those with their hands over their eyes or their fingers in their ears, neither seeing nor hearing evil. The solution to any difficulty begins by a full recognition of its power and extent.

Secondly, know how widespread Satanism has become. Read up on the issues. Since these cults are far less secretive than formerly, note the names of the covens, grottos, or pylons in your area. Some of the largest are the Illuminati, the Stygians, the Babylonians, the Beasts, and the Antichrists. Warn friends, educators, and authorities of their presence. As the Apostle Paul said, we are the sons of light and should not be surprised by the signs of the *end times*.

Thirdly, understand every satanic symbol; know Satan's presence and his place. Recognize certain special words when spoken backward. Watch for LaVey's *Satanic Bible* and his *Satanic Rituals*. Be alert to any heavy-metal rock records in your home or concerts in your city.

Assuming you recognize the problem, its extent, and all its signs, what else must you do? Initially, take heart, encourage one another. For 40 days Jesus resisted Satan's worldly temptations armed only with God's invincible Word. And remember, our Lord was victorious on the Cross. We are the winning team. Submit yourself to the Lord and His will; ask His forgiveness of your sins; pray for strength, wisdom, and faith to combat the Devil. If you know someone in Satan's service, pray The Holy Spirit may come into their life and lead them to Christ Jesus. Remember Isaiah 54:17 and grow strong:

*No weapon forged against you will prevail.*

Although I have not emphasized the connection between the New Age Movement and Devil worship, the thoughtful reader must have recognized their relationship. Satanism is the tip of the New Age spear taking deadly aim at the heart of every Christian. To protect yourself from both, read God's Word and flourish in your faith — wrap yourself in the invincible armor of truth:

*Submit yourself to God. Resist the devil, and he will flee from you.*
James 4:7-10

If we trust in the Lord and His ways, we shall find joy and eternal happiness in the magnificence of His Holy Presence. Then, truly, we can say with Jesus and for all eternity:

*Get thee behind me, Satan.*

# CHAPTER — 10

# THE ARK AND THE CROSS

*In it* [the Ark] *only a few people, 8 in all, were saved through water, and this water symbolizes baptism that now saves you also. . . . It saves you by the resurrection of Jesus Christ.*
1 Peter 3:20-21

In the continuing fiery debate between evolutionary theorists and scientific creationists, the combatants stake out totally opposite positions in their interpretation of Noah's Flood. The evolutionists maintain it is just a fossilized myth of something that neither was nor ever could be. In the other camp, the creationists say the Deluge was an actual historical event for which we have a great deal of evidence. Regarding the reality of the Flood, I am in complete agreement with the creationists. Yet, they have missed at least half the meaning of this narrative epic, while the Darwinians have lost everything. The account of the Deluge portrays events not only historical but also symbolic, eternal, and religious. It is the substance and nature of these figurative truths that we will explore in this chapter.

More than sixteen centuries ago in his famous *City of God*, the great Christian writer and theologian St. Augustine had some thoughts on this topic. He said:

*No one ought to imagine, however, that this account* [of the flood] *was written for no purpose, or that we are to look here solely for a reliable historical record without any allegorical meaning, or, conversely, that those events are entirely, unhistorical, and the language purely symbolical, or that, whatever may be the nature of the story it has no connection with prophecy about the Church. Surely it is only a twisted mind that would maintain that books which have been so scrupulously preserved for thousands*

> *of years, which have been safeguarded by such a*
> *concern for so well-ordered a transmission, that such*
> *books were written without serious purpose, or that*
> *we should consult them simply for historical facts?* [1]

In the account of the Deluge, it is surprising how many different numbers Genesis uses and how often it repeats them. We are told Noah's age, his generations, the dimensions of the Ark, exact dates, the numbers of the animals, and so on. If quantities were not important, why were they continually used?

The Ark's incredible variety of life forms — from insect to elephant — compelled the building of an immense structure. But why was it necessary to load 7 of every clean animal rather than the 2 of every unclean? The builder could have preserved the different "kinds" in pairs and so allowed the Ark to be much smaller. On the other hand, why bother with any of this? God had the power to produce a second creation without Noah and the Ark. For that matter, without anything except His Word. Surely this implies that everything about the patriarch's epic adventure symbolizes deeper meanings. Let's try to discover these meanings by using our three levels of interpretation discussed in Chapter 4: The Rule of Three. These were as follows:

Level 1. References to quantities, times, measurements,
        and the number of occurrences of important
        words, phrases, and events.
Level 2. The gematria of the words.
Level 3. The triangle form of God's Word as revealed
        by the Triad Rules.

In the Bible, the period from Adam to Noah spans 10 generations. As in everyday life, 10 represents completeness of a cycle, not a one-time list. And whether for good or evil, the old is finished, and the new is about to begin. In Genesis 6:9 (KJV) the Lord tells us Noah's generations are perfect (complete at 10):

> *These are the generations of Noah: Noah was a just man*
> *and perfect in his generations, and Noah walked with God.*

At that time man's wickedness had covered the earth, and, except Noah and his family, evil controlled every person. Satan had been very busy.

The Lord commanded Noah to build the Ark and gave him *exact* specifications on its size, material, construction, and cargo. Genesis 6:14-15 (KJV) declares:

> *Make thee an ark of gopher* [cypress] *wood;*
> *rooms shalt thou make in the ark, and shalt*
> *pitch it within and without with pitch.*
>
> *And this is the fashion thou shalt make it of:*
> *The length of the ark shall be 300 cubits, the breadth*
> *of it 50 cubits, and the height of it 30 cubits.*

The figurative importance of these dimensions is profound. When I first realized that 300 was a triangle number, it was a revelation. Shortly afterward the entire symbolism of the Ark-Cross became clear. We begin our explorations by considering the *pre-image* of 300. Recall from page 32 how this is done:

$$
\begin{aligned}
&(\text{pre-image}) \\
&24 \; \text{-------}> \; 1 + 2 + 3 + \ldots + 24 \\
&\qquad\qquad\quad = 300 \; (\text{image}) \\
&\qquad\qquad\quad = \text{a triangle number}
\end{aligned}
$$

So 300 is the 24th triangle number, and $24 = 8 + 8 + 8$. This gematria value could be a reference to *Jesus* and His Resurrection Number. Remarkably, 300 is also — the reader may anticipate this next statement — the number of the Cross, the Tau Cross. Obviously, even to a confirmed literalist, these verses have additional meanings. In point of fact, the wooden Ark was a prefiguration of the wooden Cross. Both saved humanity from certain destruction.

If this were all the symbolism, we would be fully satisfied, but it's only the beginning. Regard the dimensions of the Ark as ratios and compare them to the human body. Consider a man lying on his back, like the Ark on the deep. If you measured him, his length (head to toe) would be 6 times his width (shoulder to shoulder). His length would also be 10 times his depth (chest to floor). Or simply stated, man's ratio of height to width to depth is identical to the Ark's ratio of length to width to depth.

**Height to Width to Depth   =   300 to 50 to 30**
**[Man's proportions]        [Ark's proportions]**
**Therefore, the Ark was built on the proportions of man.**

**The Ark on the Flood**

FIGURE 10.1

An accident? Not likely when you consider who gave these dimensions to Noah or, more importantly, who created man. The NIV scholars translated the length of the Ark as 450 feet, not the original 300 cubits. Changing the unit obscures the symbolism of the Ark-Cross. Yet the ratios are all the same, whether in the NIV, the KJV, or the Hebrew Pentateuch.

When Noah had finished the great three story structure, he loaded all the animals by 2s and 7s. Humanity, however, boarded in one group of 8: the builder, his wife, their sons (Shem, Ham, and Japeth), and their wives. To start the human race a second time, after the cataclysm of the Flood, God selected 8 souls, the Number of Resurrection and Rebirth. Of all life forms on the Ark, only Noah's family contained 8 — *man is different from every other living thing:*

*And spared not the old world, but saved Noah*
*the 8th person, a preacher of righteousness,*
*bringing in the flood upon the world of the ungodly.*
2 Peter 2:5 (KJV)

The symbolism continues with the volume of the Ark (the total amount of space inside), found by multiplying all the dimensions:

$$
\begin{aligned}
\text{Volume} &= \text{length x width x depth} \\
&= 300 \ \ \text{x} \ \ 50 \ \ \text{x} \ \ 30 \\
&= 450{,}000 \\
&= 45 \ \text{x} \ 10000 \ \text{cubic cubits}
\end{aligned}
$$

Emphasized by additional zeros, this intriguing result is Adam's (mankind's) number (45). What could be more appropriate? The space that saves man, and is built on man's proportions, also symbolizes man.

This imagery extends unbroken through the levels of gematria and triangularity. Consider the name *Noah*. Not only does it have an interesting value of 58 (see page 169), but also it can be expressed as the sum of 3 triangle numbers:

$$
58 = \ \ 3 \ \ + \ \ 10 \ \ + \ \ 45
$$

Trinity   cycle   Adam

This triplet of triangles connects the outstanding events in Noah's life and God's great purpose in using him.

Gathering all these pieces together, any reasonable person could conclude that the Ark was the pre-image of both the Cross and our Savior. To make these comparisons easier to understand, I have arranged them in the following chart:

| ARK | JESUS and the CROSS |
|---|---|
| The Ark had a length of 300 cubits. | The triangle number of the Tau Cross is 300. |
| Its dimensions were in man's proportions. | Jesus was God as man. (God in man's proportions.) |
| Constructed of cypress wood. | The Cross was made of wood. |
| The 24th triangle number is 300. | $24 = 8 + 8 + 8$ |
| The volume equals Adam's number. | Jesus was the second Adam. |
| Saves 8 souls. | "JESUS" = 888 |
| The door in the Ark's side was its only opening. | Jesus had only a single wound that was also in His side. |
| The Ark saved mankind for a second creation. | Jesus saved mankind for eternity. |

To see the Flood simply as an historical event is to miss the mind-enriching symbolism outlined above.

# MAN IN OUR IMAGE

*I praise you because I am fearfully and wonderfully made.*
Psalm 139:14

God created man in His image, and, appropriately, man has always used the human body for units of measurement. The biblical cubit[2] used by Noah was the distance from your elbow to the tip of your middle finger (approximately 21 inches). Ancient people subdivided this into 7 palms, and each of these equaled 4 fingers. More familiar units like the foot have an obvious source. The yard originated as the distance from your nose to your furthest outstretched finger. Other units like inch, hand, and fathom have a similar origin.

Considering this, what could be more natural than for God to command Noah to build the Ark in the proportions of the human body?

You will remember another number that also derives from man's body. In the Garden of Eden our first parents did not have a navel. No sin meant no death. No death meant no birth. No birth meant no navel. So, Phi (1.618...) could not be found on man's body before the Fall. Now, like sin itself, it is everywhere in our culture. Yet no matter where it is hidden — whether in art, architecture, or satanic symbols — you can always sense its presence by the absence of good and the entrance of evil.

# THE WINDOWS OF HEAVEN

*Noah was 600 years old when the flood waters came on the earth.*
Genesis 7:6

By telling us Noah's age, Genesis implies its importance. Everything written in the Bible has a function and a meaning. Here it emphasizes both the length of the Ark and the number of the Cross since $600 = 300 + 300$.

As God commanded, Noah entered the cavernous Ark for his great epic voyage. All the animals, birds, and the creeping things of the earth, as well as his family, were aboard. Then the master builder closed the huge door in the vessel's side. After this, God allowed him 7 more days to completely arrange everything before:

*The windows of heaven were opened.*
*And the rain was upon the earth 40 days and 40 nights.*
Genesis 7:11-12 (KJV)

People everywhere have recognized the number 40 for its association with probation, trial, punishment, and mourning. All religious groups appreciate its symbolic meaning. At the death of Iran's fanatical leader Ayatollah Khomeini, their Islamic government legislated 40 days of official mourning. Other examples abound: the 40 days of quarantine for disease, the 40 days of Lent before Easter, and so forth.

Triangle numbers give a good explanation of why 40 was used by The Holy Spirit (and now by man) for such intervals:

$$40 = \quad 6 \quad + \quad 6 \quad + \quad 28$$
1st perfect   1st perfect   2nd perfect

As we know, 6 and 28 are both triangular and perfect. So, 40 equals two creation periods plus one average cycle of the moon (from full phase to full phase). This quantity may also refer to years. For example, the 40 years the Israelites wandered in the wilderness or the three 40-year divisions in Moses' life. Nevertheless, whether for days or years, the number of trial or mourning is always 40. The Bible records many such periods:

- The 40 days and 40 nights of rain (Genesis 7:4).
- After the tops of the mountains were showing, Noah waited 40 more days and then opened the window of the Ark (Genesis 8:6).
- To receive the Ten Commandments, Moses was on the mount 40 days and 40 nights (Exodus 24:18).
- After the sin of the golden calf, Moses was again on Sinai for 40 days and 40 nights (Deuteronomy 9:25).
- The 40 days of the spies (Numbers 13:25) and the 40 years wandering in the wilderness, one year for each day (Numbers 14:34).
- For 40 days Goliath came forth each morning and evening and confronted the Israelites (1 Samuel 17:16).
- Elijah traveled 40 days and 40 nights to reach Horeb (Sinai), the mountain of God (1 Kings 19:8).
- The Lord was angry with the Israelites for 40 years after they refused to undertake the conquest of Canaan (Psalm 95:10).
- Ezekiel lay on his right side 40 days to symbolize the 40 years of Judah's transgression (Ezekiel 4:6).
- The 40 days to overthrow Nineveh (Jonah 3:4).
- For 40 days and 40 nights Jesus fasted before being tempted by Satan (Matthew 4:2).
- After the Resurrection and before the Ascension, Jesus spent 40 more days on earth (Acts 1:3).

During the 40 days of torrential rain, the Ark floated upwards until water covered the entire earth. This colossal ship, like an enormous whale, withstood the elemental forces of wind and wave that must have occasionally driven it beneath the surface. For 150 days in this watery wilderness, above the total destruction of a corrupted world, Jesus protected the Ark. The terrified souls on board experienced the most cataclysmic events since the 6 Days of Creation. What a fantastic sense of joy and relief Noah's family must have felt when the Ark finally lurched to a halt on Mount Ararat!

The Deluge brought judgment to a wicked world; it also gave deliverance and a new beginning to the human family in the Ark. Without it they would have been corrupted by sin, the universal disease raging in antediluvian times — the same epidemic sweeping our world today.

# 17 AND SECURITY

God's Word, like His World, resembles a triple-layered cake. We have merely tasted the icing and the first layer; two deeper levels remain to be savored and enjoyed.

Significantly, the Lord tells us the Flood began on precisely the 17th day of the second month, 7 days after Noah entered the Ark. Also, the Ark touched land exactly five biblical months (150 days) later, on the 17th day of the seventh month. The question arises then, "Why the emphasis on 17?"

When the two numbers representing different forms of completeness are added (i.e., $7 + 10 = 17$), the idea of fullness expands. This new quantity is also the 7th prime number (2, 3, 5, 7, 11, 13, 17). Taken together, these points give a threefold enhancement of completeness and abundance. Consequently, the Bible associates 17 with a special kind of fullness. A fullness that provides a reassuring message for mankind.

Henry M. Morris in his *Many Infallible Proofs* comments perceptively on 17:

> *The theme of security and eternal life is stressed in Romans 8:35-39, where there are 17 entities — ". . . tribulation, distress, . . . height, nor depth, nor any other creature" listed —*

*all of which are "unable to separate us from the love of God
which is in Christ Jesus our Lord." Psalm 23, perhaps the
greatest chapter on the believer's security in the Old
Testament, contains 17 personal references to the believer
(i.e., "my shepherd," " all the days of my life," etc.).*[3]

Moving to the deepest level, let's find the 17th triangle number
and see if it has any symbolic meaning for the Flood.

$$\text{(pre-image)}$$
$$17 \text{ --------> } 1 + 2 + 3 + \ldots + 17$$
$$= 153 \text{ (image)}$$
$$= \text{a triangle number}$$

Now the meaning of the dates is clear: 17 is the pre-image of the
**Fish Number**, Jesus' triangle quantity. From the Flood's first to its
last day, Jesus was with them. To preserve the Ark on the waters of
the deep, the Father sent His Son — just as He would in the future —
to save drowning humanity. During this time, we can safely assume
Satan was also at work desperately trying to sink the Ark and destroy
all its precious cargo. Therefore, supernatural guidance and safeguards
were necessary to successfully carry out God's will.

(Lucifer's number and 17 have some unusual mocking connections. Interested readers should see the Chapter Notes.)

The 7th month of the Jewish civil year later became the first
month of their religious year (Exodus 12:2). Rabbis always slay the
Passover Lamb on the 14th day of the month (Exodus 12:6). Christ ate
His last supper with the disciples on this day, and the Romans
crucified Him the next.

So, Jesus rose from the dead on the 17th day of the month (of
Nisan, Jewish calendar) the exact day of the Ark's landing! Both
events speak of deliverance and new life. Their occurrence on the same
date is wonderfully symbolic.

After a 40-day waiting period, Noah released a raven and a dove
from the Ark's window. The raven, because of its wild nature, flew
about and would not return as the dove did. He waited 7 more days,
and again let the dove — a symbol of The Holy Spirit — out on the
surface of the waters. It returned with a freshly picked olive branch.
Once more Noah waited 7 days before releasing the dove a third time.
When it failed to return, he knew it had found dry land.

God remembered the Ark's epic voyagers. His Son protected them on the cruel seas, and His Holy Spirit told them when the waters had disappeared. Ever since those times, our rainbow of 7 colors has been the image of a complete covenant between God and man: never again would water cover the earth.

# THE SECOND SON

After landing and starting a new life in this second Eden, one of Noah's sons did something that really should not surprise us: he sinned! We might have expected this since the patriarch's family contained the seeds of the original Fall. All were born and so all had a navel, the mark of rebellion. Man and beast were not the Ark's only cargo.

Let's investigate the gematria of *Noah* and his sons *Shem*, *Ham*, and *Japeth* — the only names The Holy Spirit gave us. As mentioned previously, the father's name has a value of 58. Here are all four:

$$
\begin{array}{c}
\textbf{N O A H} \\
\textbf{נ ח} \\
58 \; = \quad \text{8} \quad \text{50} \\
\\
\textbf{S H E M} \\
\textbf{ש מ} \\
340 \; = \quad \text{40} \quad \text{300} \\
\\
\textbf{H A M} \\
\textbf{ח מ} \\
48 \; = \quad \text{40} \quad \text{8} \\
\\
\textbf{J A P E T H} \\
\textbf{י פ ת} \\
\underline{+490} \; = \quad \text{400} \quad \text{80} \quad \text{10} \\
936
\end{array}
$$

And **936** = 13 x 72 or **13 + 13 + . . . + 13**.

So, the total gematria of the family is a multiple of 13, Satan's False Trinity Number and the quantity the Bible associates with rebellion. Accordingly, the progenitors of the races of man concealed at least a single seed of revolt. History has provided many fertile fields for that seed.

After the Flood, the first rebellion occurred when Ham, the second son, sinned against his father (Genesis 9:22-25). Strikingly, if you consider the gematria of the family without him, the difference is uniquely instructive:

$$936 - 48 = 888$$

Family    Ham    Jesus

**Without the second son, the total of the remaining three is exactly Jesus' Resurrection Number, 888.**

CHAPTER — 11

# THE LAMB AND THE STARS

*Then I looked, and there before me was the Lamb,
standing on Mount Zion, and with him 144,000 who had
his name and his Father's name written on their foreheads.*
Revelation 14:1

C hristians have wondered, speculated, and written about the
famous 144,000 for nearly two millenniums. So it seems
almost immodest for me to suggest I can add anything new to
this discussion. However, no one, as far as I am aware, has ever
looked at the Word of God as a magnificent triangular structure. This
point of view has served us well so far; therefore, we have no reason
to abandon it now. By the end of this chapter you will have:

• Learned who the 144,000 will be.
• Gained a complete understanding of this number.
• Discovered the meaning of the seals of the Lamb
  and the Father.
• Learned the number of the chosen.
• Found out why King David's name and symbol
  are closely connected with the 144,000.
• Uncovered the gematria of *Jerusalem, the elect,
  the saints,* and so forth.
• Discovered how gematria connects The Holy Spirit,
  the dove, and Jesus.

The opening verse, quoted above, comes immediately after
Revelation 13:18, the verse concerning the Antichrist and his number
666. Evidently, John wanted to contrast these passages: the first has
the mark of the Antichrist, and the second has the seals of the Lamb
and God. What two things could be greater opposites? The Antichrist

and Satan extract everlasting punishment and pain; the Lamb and God give eternal life and security.

In Revelation 14:3, the 144,000 are mentioned again:

> *And they sang a new song before the throne and before the four living creatures and the elders. No one could learn the song except the 144,000 who had been redeemed from the earth.*

Some biblical scholars believe the 144,000 comprise the total number of those saved during the last years of the Tribulation. To put an exact quota on the saved, however, implies man has no free will. If that were true, then he could not be judged morally fit or unfit by his actions: sinner and saint would be equal. Consequently, this idea rightly offends most Christians, as it must also offend God. In any case, John clearly told us in Revelation 7:3-4 who these 144,000 will be:

> *"Do not harm the land or the sea or the trees until we put a seal on the foreheads of the servants of our God."*
> *Then I heard the number of those who were sealed:*
> *144,000 from all the tribes of Israel.*

In the verses following this one, the author actually names the 12 tribes, saying each will contribute 12,000 to the final total. This does not mean no other Jews will recognize Jesus as Christ and be saved. It does mean these 144,000 are very special, and no one, neither man nor dark angel, can harm them until Jesus returns. The popular writer Hal Lindsey says the following in *The Late Great Planet Earth*:

> *After the Christians are gone* [raptured] *God is going to reveal Himself in a special way to 144,000 physical, literal Jews who are going to believe with a vengeance that Jesus is the Messiah. They are going to be 144,000 Jewish Billy Grahams turned loose on the earth — the earth will never know a period of evangelism like this period. These Jewish people are going to make up for lost time. They are going to have the greatest number of converts in all history. Revelation 7:9-14 says they bring so many to Christ that they can't be numbered.*[1]

# THE CHOSEN

The Son of God has the power to do whatever He pleases. He could have picked any number of men to be His Apostles or none at all. Out of all creation He *chose* exactly 12.

When Satan gained Judas Iscariot to his host of the damned, the 12 became 11. Yet, since the original number possessed such great symbolic importance, the first deed of the Apostles was to select a new member (Acts 1:26). By lot they voted for Matthias to fill Judas' place and so keep the total at exactly 12. Note, Matthias was not added to the 12 to produce 13, but he replaced the traitor. As Peter said (Acts 1:20), "May another take his place." People sometimes call 13 the Devil's dozen; we have encountered it in the gematria of all Satan's names.

Jacob's 12 sons were the progenitors of Israel's 12 tribes — the Chosen People. In the great miracle of the fishes and the loaves, the disciples had only 2 fishes and 5 loaves for the thousands of followers: 7 items in all. Nevertheless, after the blessing and the meal, they gathered 12 large basketfuls of fish and bread. From the multitudes scattered in the fields, the 12 basketfuls have always symbolized the *chosen*. We still choose 12 good people for our juries. For over 4000 years this number has maintained an unbroken history of prominence.

Previously I mentioned 12 concerning judicial and governmental power. Now we can expand this to mean the power of those *chosen* for a set purpose. See pages 118-119 for more 12s in the Bible.

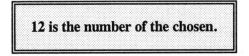

**12 is the number of the chosen.**

A few simple patterns will show the symbolic reason for using 12 as the quantity of the chosen. In two dimensions it is possible to surround 1 circle with exactly 6 others so they all touch. Try this with some pennies, and you will arrive at the figure to the right. The diagram also shows how these 7 form a centered hexagonal number. We will see this pattern again.

Now consider our real world of three dimensions. Imagine you have a white sphere and you wish to know how many other spheres can touch the white one simultaneously. It is just like our problem with the pennies, only one dimension higher. In 1694 Sir Isaac Newton argued with Oxford astronomer David Gregory about this mystery. Gregory said 13, Newton declared 12.

**The symbolism of the 12 and Jesus**

FIGURE 11.1

One hundred and eighty years passed before mathematicians proved Sir Isaac was correct (see FIGURE 11.1 for the solution). You will notice in this diagram, unlike the pennies, that the outer spheres do not touch each other: this is what makes the problem difficult. The *combined* extra space between them is more than enough to fit in a 13th sphere. Many thought you needed only to shift the 12 around and perhaps deform them slightly to do this. But, as was proven in 1874, it cannot be done. With Newton's immense knowledge of the Bible and mathematics, it is no surprise he was right.

Similar to the pennies, each sphere centers on one corner of a regular figure. This time it is an icosahedron, a perfect shape like the hexagon or cube but with *triangular* faces. The 12 outer spheres symbolize the chosen Apostles. Each touches Jesus, the white one at the center, and gains inspiration from history's most extraordinary being. Although there exists enough extra space, no amount of juggling or rearranging will allow another sphere to touch the center. There is no 13th Apostle.

Earlier we learned that the dodecahedron, a figure with 12 *pentagonal* faces, was the pagan icon of the universe. In secular and sacred paintings, artists have always used it to signify evil. Both objects are outlined below: one the image of our Lord and the 12 Apostles, the other of Satan and his 12 mocking pentagrams.

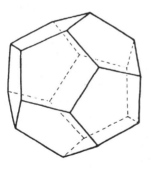

**Dodecahedron**        **Icosahedron**

FIGURE 11.2

By comparing these two forms an extraordinary property appears. A property so striking that it shows how these shapes can be total opposites yet still be related. Merely cut off every corner on the dodecahedron, and you create an icosahedron. Similarly, cut off every corner on the icosahedron, and you produce a dodecahedron. Mathematicians call these dual figures.

Observe this duality for yourself in the figure below. See how the icosahedron with its *triangular* faces encloses the *pentagonal* faces of its dual. The corners of one are the faces of the other — triangle versus pentagram or Trinity versus Phi. Clearly these figures are direct opposites like day and night, good and evil, Christ and Antichrist. As we have previously seen, the pentagonal faces of the dodecahedron have an intimate relationship with Phi, the Devil's number. In fact, this entire figure is nothing but Phi's compound symbol with 12 mocking pentagrams, one for each Apostle.

# THE NUMBER OF THE STARS

Most people know $144 = 12 \times 12$
$$= 12 + 12 + \ldots + 12 \text{ (12 times).}$$

So 144 symbolizes an intensification of being chosen or special, and 144,000 is an enlargement even on that. To be in that number places you among the very elect of God. It is the quantity of the redeemed Jews of the *end times*, part of the Bride of the Lamb.

Our earliest copies of the New Testament were written on papyrus. This is a kind of paper made from a bulrush that grows along the banks of the Nile river. (These are the same rushes that formed Moses' floating cradle.) Artisans sliced the reed into long thin pieces and interweaved them into a thick mat. After this they rolled and beat the mat. This allowed the plant's natural glue to bond the strips into a strong thin sheet of paper. Some first, second, and third century biblical papyrus documents survive. Among these are the most priceless written records we have: the Gospels, Paul's letters, and other books of the New Testament.

In Dublin, Ireland, exists the oldest known copy of the Book of Revelation, the Chester Beatty manuscript[2]. It dates from somewhere between 200 and 300 A.D. Naturally, all the numbers are written as letters of the Greek alphabet, otherwise gematria would not exist. For example, 12 is ιβ and 144 is ρμδ. On the other hand, this ancient text does not show 144,000 in quite this manner because the Greeks had no symbol for (or idea of) 0, zero. They wrote this quantity as ρμδ χειλαδες (144 thousand) where the second Greek word meant *thousands*.

So far in our symbolic study of the chosen, we have considered only Level One. Now let's examine the next depth, the gematria. The study of this subject, although hardly known today, has a long, rich biblical tradition.

In form and content, the Bible is like a grand jigsaw puzzle. Force a piece into place here and this causes other pieces to be out of place there. Everything from Genesis to Revelation must fit and harmonize. The Scriptures contain more patterns and symbols than anyone on earth will ever discover or understand. Perhaps in Heaven we will comprehend its fullness and majesty. Here on earth we must let the great code of the Bible speak for itself.

And it says the 144,000 will be among the Tribulation saints, the elect of God. This is supported by the gematria of all the important words concerning "the elect" and those who have been redeemed. Why? Because they are all exact multiples of 144. Here are a few examples:

$$\begin{array}{ccc} \text{T H E} & \text{E L E C T} & \text{(Romans 11:7)} \\ \eta & \text{E κ λ ο γ η} & \\ 8 \quad + & 5 \ 20 \ 30 \ 70 \ 3 \ 8 = 144 & \end{array}$$

$$\begin{array}{ll} \text{B E L I E V E R S} & \text{(1 Timothy 4:12)} \\ \pi \ \iota \ \sigma \ \tau \ \omega \ \nu & \\ 80 \ 10 \ 200 \ 300 \ 800 \ 50 = 1440 = 144 \times 10 \\ \qquad\qquad\qquad\quad = 144 + 144 + \ldots + 144 \end{array}$$

A most significant word in John's Apocalypse is "saints."

$$\begin{array}{ll} \text{S A I N T S} & \text{(Revelation 8:3)} \\ \text{A } \gamma \ \iota \ \omega \ \nu & \\ 1 \quad 3 \ 10 \ 800 \ 50 = 144 \times 6 \end{array}$$

Of course the saints are those who keep "the faith":

T H E       F A I T H       (Revelation 14:12 (KJV))
τ η ν     π ι σ τ ι ν
300 8 50 + 80 10 200 300 10 50 = 144 x 7

The saints are also those who come out of the Tribulation, that incredible 1260 (= 12 x 105) days of horror. They will have survived when the Antichrist ruled the "kingdoms of the world":

K I N G D O M S        OF THE  W O R L D   (Luke 4:5)
β α σ ι λ ε ι α ς      ο ι κ ο υ μ ε ν η ς
2  1 200 10 30 5 10 1 200 + 70 10 20 70 400 40 5 50 8 200 = 666 x 2

The saints and the redeemed will dwell with Jesus in "Jerusalem" for the 1000 year Millennial Reign:

J E R U S A L E M      (Revelation 3:12)
Ι ε ρ ο υ σ α λ η μ
10  5 100  70 400 200 1  30  8  40 = 144 x 6

In eternity, they and all the saved will live under Jesus' rule in the "Kingdom of Heaven":

K I N G D O M       OF       H E A V E N  (Matthew 3:2)
Β α σ ι λ ε ι α    τ ω ν    Ο υ ρ α ν ω ν
2  1 200 10 30 5 10 1 + 300 800 50 + 70 400 100 1 50 800 50 = 144 x 20

Matthew 14:20 (KJV) speaks about the miraculous multiplication of the fishes and the loaves. Believers have always interpreted the 12 basketfuls of collected food, "the fragments," as symbols of the chosen, saved, or redeemed:

T H E       F R A G M E N T S
τ ω ν      κ λ α σ μ α τ ω ν
300 800 50 + 20 30 1 200 40 1 300 800 50 = 144 x 18

I have shown only a few of the many cases that overwhelmingly confirm 12 and 144 as the numbers of the chosen or redeemed.

Hundreds exist. I should not leave this section, however, without quoting one of the Bible's most famous verses. Everyone knows it; everyone loves it; Christians accept it as the essential statement of their faith. I am referring to John 3:16 (KJV) which tells us *how to be saved*:

> *For God so loved the world, that He gave His only*
> *begotten Son, that whosoever believeth in Him*
> *should not perish, but have everlasting life.*

This immortal passage has a value of 12 + 12 + . . . + 12 or 144 x 95.

# THE SPIRIT AND THE DOVE

> *I baptize you with water,*
> *but he will baptize you with the Holy Spirit.*
> Mark 1:8

> *Now the Lord is the Spirit, and where*
> *the Spirit of the Lord is, there is freedom.*
> 2 Corinthians 3:17

Wherever you discover The Holy Spirit, there you will also discover God. With our limited vision, we find it more difficult to distinguish between the Father and The Holy Spirit than between the Father and the Son. This is no accident. It is part of The Trinity Mystery.

The concordance of any Bible lists many entries under *spirit* and even more under *holy*. Yet when the writers of the Scriptures wished to denote the Third Person in The Trinity, they always used the definite article "the" and wrote "The Holy Spirit." Regard the wonderful gematria of this title:

```
T H E   H O L Y      S P I R I T
T o   A γ ι ο ν    Π ν ε υ μ α
300 70 + 1  3 10 70 50 + 80 50 5 400 40 1 = 1080
```

FIGURE 11.3

# THE NUMBERS OF THE TRINITY

The first number, $1^3 = 1\text{x}1\text{x}1 = 1$, symbolizes
the First Person of The Trinity, God the Father.

The second number, $2^3 = 2\text{x}2\text{x}2 = 8$, symbolizes
the Second Person of The Trinity, God the Son.

The third number, $3^3 = 3\text{x}3\text{x}3 = 27$, symbolizes
the Third Person of The Trinity, God The Holy Spirit.

This last connection is affirmed by the gematria of "The Holy Spirit":

$$1080 = 27 \times 40$$
$$= 27 + 27 + \ldots + 27$$

If you want to know God, then you must approach Him through
Jesus under the inSPIRation of The Holy Spirit. This word *spirit* or
*pneuma* ($\pi\nu\epsilon\upsilon\mu\alpha$) meant *breath*, *soul*, or *spirit*. Some of that meaning
survives today in words like *pneumatic* and *pneumonia*.

The Fishes and The Net (FIGURE 8.5) dramatically points out
that the path to 153/Jesus is only through 1080/The Holy Spirit. All
the numbers in the third circle symbolize the Third Person. They are
either 1080 or multiples of 27.

Yet, it is probably by chance that the average number of breaths
a person takes in an hour is 1080 (test yourself). Regardless, this
quantity has abundant connections with the physical world. However,
the relationships we are seeking are in The Word, not the world. The
following famous passage from Mark 1:10-11 (KJV) forever unites The
Holy Spirit with the image of the dove. The Father speaks, the Son is
baptized, and The Holy Spirit descends:

> *And straightway coming up out of the water, he saw*
> *the heavens opened, and the Spirit like a dove descending*
> *on him. And there came a voice from heaven, saying,*
> *Thou art my beloved Son, in whom I am well pleased.*

And what is the value of "dove" in the original Greek?

**D O V E**

π ε ρ ι σ τ ε ρ α

80   5  100  10  200  300  5  100   1   = **801**

FIGURE 11.4

Is 801 related to 1080 or to Jesus? In Revelation 1:10-11 (KJV) our Lord refers to Himself in a most revealing way. John speaks first:

*I was in the spirit on the Lord's day, and heard*
*behind me a great voice, as of a trumpet, Saying,*
*"I am the Alpha and Omega, the first and the last."*

Among many things, Jesus is declaring He is the same at the beginning as the end. This is just like the reversible Hebrew and Greek poetic forms used throughout the Bible (pages 303 to 305). Furthermore, alpha (α) equals 1, and omega (ω) equals 800 for a total of 801. By this, Christ appears to be affirming His identity with the dove/The Holy Spirit.

As with the written Word, so it is with the gematria. If you view **0801** (with an initial "ghost" zero) from the right side and look to the left, then you see **1080**. Chance again? Not likely when you realize, **0801** is precisely the same number as **801**. Strangely, the Greeks could not have known this since they had no 0 (zero).

This practice of reading words and numbers backward must seem unusual to English readers. Yet, since Hebrew was and is (always) read right to left, it was a completely normal practice for ancient Jews — like the Apostle John — writing in Greek. So Jesus, the dove, and The Holy Spirit are all intimately linked through gematria. Although the text of the Bible already implies this relationship, the gematria offers a striking and harmonious confirmation.

Having considered some of the vast gematria of the Lamb and the Stars, we will now enter Level Three, the triangular form.

> *And if anyone does not have the Spirit*
> *of Christ, he does not belong to Christ.*
> Romans 8:9

Paul is saying, you must first pass through (be possessed by) The Holy Spirit if you are to know Jesus. The above quotation beautifully reflects the path results of the Trinity Function. By "path results," I mean all the numbers from the initial pre-image to that ultimate triangle image, 153. To illustrate, use this rule on 12 and 144,000:

$$12 \text{ -------> } 1^3 + 2^3$$
$$= 1x1x1 + 2x2x2$$
$$= 1 + 8$$
$$= 9$$

$$144,000 \text{ ---> } 1^3 + 4^3 + 4^3 + 0^3 + 0^3 + 0^3$$
$$= 1x1x1 + 4x4x4 + 4x4x4 + 0x0x0 + 0x0x0 + 0x0x0$$
$$= 1 + 64 + 64 + 0 + 0 + 0$$
$$= 129$$

When applying the Trinity Function to the digits 1 and 2, the order does not matter, both 12 and 21 have the same image. Of course, the addition of any number of zeros also leaves the outcome unchanged. So, I normally list the digits from smallest to largest. As in previous chapters, we now use the rule on each image until we arrive at the heart of 144,000: the Fish/153. For "the sealed" their path is symbolically long and torturous, but their destination is security, love, and eternal life.

$$12 \text{ --> } 9 \text{ --> } 279 \text{ --> } 1080 \text{ --> } 153$$

144,000 -> 129 -> 378 -> 288 -> 132 -> 36 -> 243 -> 99 -> 1458 -> 027 -> 153
(pre-image)                                                                    (image)

Clearly, on the narrow path to Jesus you must go by way of 27 or 1080, The Holy Spirit. To dramatically see this crucial point, look again at FIGURE 8.5, The Fishes and The Net. There you will see how Jesus/153 has two sources: 27 and 1080. Since 1080 is also a multiple of 27, the two are really one.

As another indication of the Trinity Rule's revelatory nature, notice how it immediately links The Holy Spirit and the dove:

$$1080 \; ---> \; 513 \; ---> \; 153$$

$$801 \; ---> \; 513 \; ---> \; 153$$

The Third Person in The Trinity is not some disembodied ghost floating around in space seeking a human body to possess. Quite properly, the New International Version Bible replaced the old King James' *Ghost* with *Spirit*. The word *ghost* conjures up negative thoughts of the occult, witches, and black magic. Those interested should read Luke 24:37-39 where the word *ghost* is used twice in this modern sense. Our Spirit is not a ghost, but a blessed activity in the soul leading to true knowledge of our Lord and Savior.

The Bible contains many mysteries, the greatest being the Tri-Unity. Yes, picturing The Trinity as a perfect triangle is helpful because you can see that the 3 distinct pieces form a whole. Yet, it is only a symbol for the Triune Mystery we scarcely comprehend. Without complete understanding we must, nonetheless, accept this three-in-one-ness. It is irrational and even irreverent to ask for what cannot be known — a natural limitation of being human.

Consider again the opening quotation for this section (2 Corinthians 3:17): "Now the Lord is Spirit." For this and the reasons expressed above, we seldom think of The Holy Spirit's number by itself. All this implies that invariably 1080 is associated with God the Father. So, it's natural to consider them together:

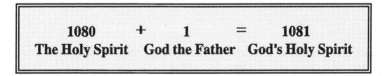

| 1080 | + | 1 | = | 1081 |
|------|---|---|---|------|
| The Holy Spirit | | God the Father | | God's Holy Spirit |

# THE STARS

This result is truly extraordinary, because **1081** will explain everything meaningful about the 144,000. First, 1081 is a triangle number, a building block in the Trinity Creation of The Word. Recall the Triangle Rule from page 32:

$$46 \text{ --------> } 1 + 2 + 3 + \ldots + 46$$
$$= 1081$$

With diagrams, this means you can arrange 1081 people, pennies, or points into a triangle. A design like this has perfect symmetry.

Secondly, there is something unusual about 1081, something uniquely distinct: it is a member of an infinite family of similar triangle numbers. Here are some others:

| An Infinite Triangle Family | |
|---|---|
| 1080 | The Holy Spirit |
| 1081 | The Holy Spirit /Father |
| 108811 | The Holy Spirit /Jesus /Father |
| 10888111 | .    .    . |
| 1088881111 | .    .    . |
| . . . . . . . . . | .    .    . |

When the extra 1s and 8s are added — the numbers of the Father and the Son respectively — the triangularity remains. Of all the quantities in the Lord's Creation, only 1080/The Holy Spirit has an expansion into an eternity of triangle numbers. The Holy Spirit and Its number are alike: both are infinite in extension and identical in form. With this new number and its family in mind, let's return to the Jewish Tribulation saints.

Some religious groups and cults have developed very peculiar doctrines concerning the 144,000. The Jehovah Witnesses are a prime example. Evidently they believe only 144,000 saints will go to Heaven, while the remaining faithful will live on earth and never die.

Another such group is the Seventh Day Adventists, one of the world's fastest growing religious sects with over 4 million members. Because 85 percent of their followers are found outside North America, they are not well known here. Their charismatic prophetess Ellen Gould White, with her husband James, founded the Adventist movement around 1850. Professing divine authority for her many writings, Mrs. White would often fall into a trance from which she would later awake with "great" religious revelations. In one of her early visions she claims to have seen the 144,000 saints standing on a sea of glass arrayed in "a perfect square."

Unfortunately for Mrs. White, it is impossible for 144,000 people to arrange themselves into a perfect square. Why? Because only numbers with exact square roots may be grouped into squares, and the square root of 144,000 is far from exact. In fact,

$$\sqrt{144,000} = 379.473 \ldots .$$

This must cast grave doubts on either the source of her visions or her honesty. Certainly, someone had a problem with their arithmetic. Note that 9, 16, and 25 people could group themselves into squares since they have exact square roots (3, 4, and 5 respectively):

$\sqrt{9} = 3$
□□□
□□□
□□□

$\sqrt{16} = 4$
□□□□
□□□□
□□□□
□□□□

$\sqrt{25} = 5$
□□□□□
□□□□□
□□□□□
□□□□□
□□□□□

Anyhow, it is just nonsensical to suggest a square formation for the Jewish Tribulation saints. Most readers, given a few moments, could think of the perfect geometrical figure for the Jews. Really, only one symbol will do! It must be the Star of David.

Zionists officially adopted the 6-pointed star in the last century, although Jews have known and used it since ancient times. In the present century, it has become the design on the Israeli flag and the symbol for Jews everywhere. During the Medieval Ages scholars called it the hexagram or the hexalpha. The latter name derives because many people saw this figure as 6 overlapping letter "A"s. Traditionally, the two interwoven triangles represented the faithful (△) and the apostate (▽) tendencies of the 12 tribes of Israel. The noble associations of this figure have always clashed with the demonic aspects of Satan's pentagram or pentalpha (5 overlapping "A"s).

As a child, you probably enjoyed the game called Chinese checkers. You may even remember the playing board had 121 positions in the form of David's Star.

**Star of David**

Naturally we call quantities arranged in this shape "star numbers." You will find a general formula for producing them in the Chapter Notes. In the following diagrams of the first four star numbers, triangles are also evident.

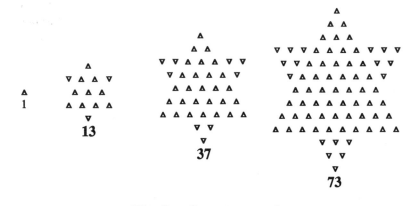

**The first four star numbers**

FIGURE 11.5

DaviD's two-triangle star, one pointing up and the other down, accurately reflects the contradictions in his own life and that of the Jewish people. He was the boy who slew the giant Goliath with 5 smooth stones from a stream. He was the man who founded the capital city of Jerusalem and became the national hero of Israel. He was the author who wrote the most beautiful Psalms in the Bible. He was also the adulterer with Bathsheba and the murderer of her husband Uriah the Hittite and a frequent apostate.

But to DaviD belongs the singular honor of being the first and last human mentioned in the entire New Testament. The overlapping triangles that form his star have a marvelous connection with his name and perhaps even with his New Testament distinction. In Greek, DaviD appears as $\Delta\alpha\beta\iota\Delta$, with triangles (deltas) first and last. Although

| **D** | **A** | **V** | **I** | **D** | |
|---|---|---|---|---|---|
| **Δ** | **α** | **β** | **ι** | **Δ** | |
| 4 | 1 | 2 | 10 | 4 | **= 21** |

the Greek name for DaviD, may be spelled in one other way (see page 228), the deltas (Δ) are always first and last. DaviD has an additional distinction. The gematria of this name is the triangle number 21, another foundation stone in God's Holy Word.

Between David's triangle number and the 7th star number there exists a curious and exceptional relationship. Take 21 (David's gematria) and add it up 12 times (once for each tribe of Israel). To this add God the Father, and you get 253, the 7th star. In a further out-of-the-way twist, 253 is also the 22nd triangle quantity. And 22 is the number of *different* letters in the Hebrew alphabet. Numbers simultaneously triangular and star are exceedingly rare. Because of its connection to David, the 12 tribes, the Hebrew alphabet, and God, I think of this quantity as the Flag of Israel Number. Like the people themselves, this number is similar to, yet removed from, 153/Jesus.

---

### FLAG OF ISRAEL NUMBER

| 253 | = | 21 + 21 + ... + 21 | + | 1 |
|-----|---|-----|---|---|
| The 7th star and the 22nd triangle | | David's gematria for each of Israel's 12 tribes | | God the Father |

---

Shortly, we will see the connection between the Star of David and the Jewish Tribulation saints. First we must take a short detour to answer an important question. At the heart of this entire discussion exists an unspoken problem: "Why will 144,000 Jews, after two thousand years of uninterrupted denial, suddenly recognize Jesus as the Messiah?"

The ancient Hebrews had always expected a Messiah — the Old Testament declares this. Recall Isaiah 9:6 (KJV):

*For unto us a child is born, unto us a son is given:*
*and the government shall be upon his shoulder:*
*and his name shall be called Wonderful Counsellor,*
*The mighty God, The everlasting Father, The Prince of Peace.*

Amazingly, after hundreds of years of predicting His arrival, the Jewish people did not recognize Jesus when He did come. They still don't: no man is a prophet in his own land. They wanted a Conquering Messiah; they received a Suffering One. Most regarded Him as a teacher or rabbi. To the Romans He was just a common rabble-rouser. Other sects caused His Crucifixion by accusing Him of disloyalty to the emperor and labeling Him the "King of the Jews."

Some scholars say that during His 33 years on earth, Jesus fulfilled exactly 300 ancient prophecies — the number of the Tau Cross. These prophecies ranged from His birth in Bethlehem of David's line (Micah 5:2) to His burial in a rich man's tomb (Joseph of Arimathea). The prediction concerning the burial is found in Isaiah 53:9, the fulfilment, in Matthew 27:57-60. None of this, however, convinced Jesus' contemporaries.

In a particularly dramatic Gospel scene (Matthew 16:15-16), Jesus turned directly to face Peter and said:

> *"But what about you?" he asked.*
> *"Who do you say I am?"*
>
> *Simon Peter answered, "You are the*
> *Christ, the Son of the living God."*

This confirmation of Jesus as "the Christ" must have overwhelmed Peter even as he spoke the words. Still, Thomas the doubting would not affirm the Resurrection until he had plunged his hand into the wound in Jesus' side. Yet, these sometime believers and followers were few and powerless. The vast majority of Jews simply rejected Jesus as the Christ. Matthew 27:20-22 compellingly makes this point:

> *But the chief priests and the elders persuaded the crowd*
> *to ask for Barabbas and to have Jesus executed.*
>
> *"Which of the two do you want me to release to you?"*
> *asked the governor. "Barabbas," they answered.*
>
> *"What shall I do then, with Jesus who is called Christ?"*
> *Pilate asked. They all answered, "Crucify him!"*

The Jews continue to reject Jesus — right up to the present moment. Because of this history, "Why will 144,000 of them suddenly accept Jesus and become called-out evangelists?" It seems extremely unlikely! But such an event is easy for God. Unquestionably, He wants to save every soul possible before His Son returns as the Conquering Messiah. His grace saves us, and His Holy Spirit gives this freely so that we may come to know His Son, Jesus. Accordingly, the only imaginable way these Jews will convert is when God fills them with

His Holy Spirit. Hal Lindsey said: "God is going to reveal Himself in a special way to 144,000 physical, literal Jews who are going to believe with a vengeance that Jesus is the Messiah." This implies you must add God's Holy Spirit/1081 to the 144,000 to transform them into the Tribulation saints. Symbolically, we have the following:

| 144,000 | + | 1081 | = | 145,081 |
|---|---|---|---|---|
| Tribulation Saints | | God's Holy Spirit | | David's Star |

FIGURE 11.6

It is a magnificent example of the Master's handiwork that **145,081 is an exact star number**. By that I mean, 145,081 can be arranged precisely into David's Star with no left over or missing parts. This is the first of two new discoveries concerning the 144,000. The Chapter Notes contain a proof of this.

A star of this magnitude is too large to draw. However, in the scaled-down model below, I have shown its outstanding features: the Lord at the precise center and the 12 inspired tribes each forming a perfect triangle. When filled with God's Holy Spirit, the 144,000 will be evangelizing "Jewish Billy Grahams."

**A Model for the inspired 144,000**

FIGURE 11.7

To symbolize the equal distribution of The Holy Spirit among the 12 tribes, place 90 in each group (90 x 12 = 1080). This further emphasizes the triangularity because 90 + 1 is a triangle number paralleling the 1080 + 1, The Holy Spirit and God we saw earlier.

If these were all the patterns in David's Star, it would be a truly wondrous figure, but there exists at least two more. The 12,000 in each triangle plus the 90 of The Holy Spirit form yet another threefold quantity. Secondly, consider our immense living star as two overlapping triangles — like the design on page 85. Then either of the larger ones (up or down) contains 108811 parts, the second member in The Holy Spirit's family of triangle numbers.

Let's summarize these results:

> **1080 = The Holy Spirit.**
> **90 + 1 = 91 is a triangle number.**
> **1080 + 1 = 1081, a triangle number.**
> **108810 + 1 = 108811, a triangle number.**
> **12,000 + 90 = 12,090, a triangle number.**
> **144,000 + 1081 = 145,081, David's Star.**

To check any of these startling patterns, see the notes for this chapter.

# THE SEALS AND THE STARS

*He anointed us, set his seal of ownership on us, and put his Spirit in our hearts as a deposit, guaranteeing what is to come.*
2 Corinthians 1:22

*God himself made all he made according to a pattern.*
*He made nothing of which he had not perceived the form.*
John Donne, *Sermon to the King* (1628)

The KJV rendering of Revelation 14:1 says, ". . . having his Father's name written in their foreheads." These translators gave no mention of the Lamb's seal. The definitive NIV says, ". . . who had his name (the Lamb's) and his Father's name written on their foreheads." All the other modern translations interpret this passage in the same manner as the NIV. A reference to the Greek texts confirms that John mentions both parts of the Godhead. Recall that because of gematria a *name* is also a *number*.

Throughout the centuries, a legion of men has penned a host of books and articles on 666. I am also guilty of adding to this pile. Man seems fascinated more with wickedness and evil than holiness and good. Revelation 13:18, the verse about 666, immediately precedes 14:1, the verse concerning the 144,000 and the seals of the Lamb and the Father. John is contrasting these passages, and he wishes us to do the same.

History has researched the number of the Beast; we will investigate the numbers on the seals. It is reasonable to expect them to connect the 144,000 with the Lamb and the Father. After all, John cites both in the same sentence. Recall that wonderful expression "Jesus Christ, Son of God, the Savior" which implies both of the Lord's numbers. The famous triangle number 153 represents Jesus' heavenly quantity as the "Son of God," while 888 stands for the gematria of His earthly name as "the Savior." Also, in the mystery of The Trinity, we find the Father is 1 or 3 persons in different verses. Like all God's Word and Works this awesome enigma is essentially mathematical. This leads us to the meaningful question: "How are the numbers/names/seals of the Lamb and the Father found among the Tribulation Stars?"

When I tried using my computer to express 144,000 in terms of triads, I received an immense surprise. There are 536 triangle numbers smaller than 144,000. These can be chosen in pairs in over a quarter of a million different ways. Nevertheless, only a *single pair* has a sum precisely equal to 144,000. They are:

| 144,000 | = | 13,695 | + | 130,305 |
|---|---|---|---|---|
| Tribulation Saints | | Triangle Number | | Triangle Number |

FIGURE 11.8

These two quantities are exact triangle numbers! Out of all God's creation no other pair exists that has a sum of 144,000. Prove the triangularity for yourself by our previous techniques, or read the Chapter Notes. Even beyond this, both quantities are hexagonal as well as multiples of the Trinity Number 3. This is the second discovery on the number of the Jewish Tribulation saints.

What else, if anything, do these quantities symbolize? What images do they conceal? Surely their uniqueness implies their importance. Yet, by themselves they are perhaps too long to be physically written on the saints' foreheads.

In earlier chapters we discussed the different levels of interpretation. In the Third (and deepest) Level, the three functions uncovered hidden meanings and forms. We have already applied the first, the Triangle Function; so let's now employ the remaining two. Recall our old friend, the Trinity Rule.

When we use it on the two triangles, identical paths and images result. Both numbers transform to The Holy Spirit/1080 and then to Jesus/153:

---

### THE SEAL OF THE LAMB

13,695  - - -> 1080  - - -> 153

### THE SEAL OF THE FATHER

130,305  - - -> 1080  - - -> 153

---

FIGURE 11.9

Now apply the Digital Root Function (just add up the numbers):

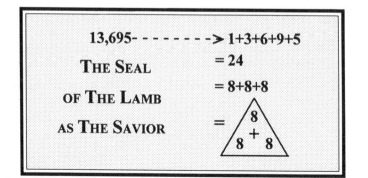

FIGURE 11.10

Clearly, 13,695 represents the pre-image of the Lamb's Resurrection Number. Definitely $8+8+8$ must be one of the great seals — the mark of eternal life — on the foreheads of the Tribulation saints. For our other and larger triangle number apply the Digit Root Function twice:

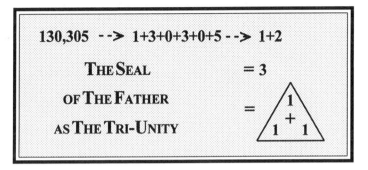

FIGURE 11.11

The image of this quantity declares itself as God the Tri-Unity. This is the other great seal protecting the saints from death and dark angels. These two triangles, unlike the two in David's Star, will not be symbols for the faithful and the apostate, but icons for the faithful and the saved.

John did not completely mark his chapters and verses. Yet it seems extraordinary that the number of the Beast is given in chapter 13 and verse 18 [= $6+6+6$]. While the next verse, 14:1, implies the Lamb [= $8+8+8$] and God [= $1+1+1$].

What a beautiful form Solomon's Seal presents with its many relationships of stars and triangles. More patterns exist within this figure than I have been privileged to find. It is exhilarating, however, to see that the Bible's mathematics harmonizes with the triangular structure and the triumphant prophecies of the *end times*. Truly, God is the Greatest Mathematician.

These numbers and symbols are a crucial part of God's design even if, like the air itself, they are at first invisible. Mathematical design is no more blatantly apparent in the Bible than in the natural world, and yet, it is the hidden structure of both. When these patterns proved to be correct, I offered thanks to The Holy Spirit for the inspiration. My feelings were a mixture of gratitude and humility. The numbers had dovetailed and said, this is part of, a key to, the structure of the Bible itself.

*You shall not make for yourself an idol in the form of anything in heaven above or on the earth beneath or in the waters below. You shall not bow down to them or worship them; for I, the Lord your God, am a jealous God.*
Exodus 20:4-5

God's Second Commandment is transparently clear. It allows no room for the worship of golden calves, plaster figurines, shrouds, or any other so-called "holy" relics. Neither money, sex, power, rock stars, movie stars, marble statues, nor religious paintings should be given sacred reverence. If you give any form whatsoever to God, you effectively limit Him in some way. Therefore, God has no visible form.

## THE TABERNACLE

During the 40 years the Israelites wandered in the Sinai wilderness, they worshiped in a portable temple called the Tabernacle. God gave Moses (Exodus 25) its exact dimensions and construction, right down to the furniture and the lampstands. Several times the Lord cautioned Moses to follow His design instructions precisely:

> *Make this tabernacle and all its furnishings exactly like the pattern I will show you.*
> Exodus 25:9

> *See that you make them according to the pattern shown you on the mountain.*
> Exodus 25:40

Below is a sketch of the Tabernacle. As you can see, a curtain divides the covered area into two parts: a rectangular Holy Place and a square Most Holy Place or Holy of Holies. The NIV study note at Exodus 26:31-35 gives further details on this:

*A curtain was to divide the tabernacle into two rooms, the Holy Place and the Most Holy Place, with the former twice as large as the latter. The Most Holy Place probably formed a perfect cube, 15 feet by 15 feet by 15 feet* [10 cubits by 10 cubits by 10 cubits].

## THE TABERNACLE

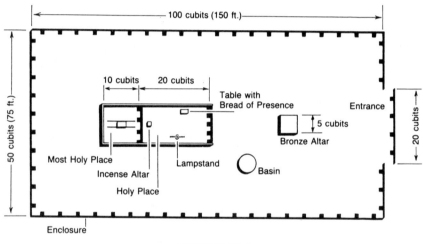

FIGURE 12.1

The Ark of the Covenant rested in the Holy of Holies and symbolically served as the Lord's footstool — but never as an idol. A 7-branched candlestick lighted the outer court, but only the presence of God, the Shekinah Glory, illuminated the innermost.

For these nomadic Jews, the Tabernacle's most important feature was its portability. For us, its significance lies in the fact that all later temples were modeled on this first one, whose design came directly from God.

# KING SOLOMON'S TEMPLE

*Thou* [God] *hast ordered all things in measure and number.*
The Wisdom of Solomon 11:20, Old Testament Apocrypha

Eventually the Jewish people left the wilderness, conquered the Promised Land, and became farmers. Much later, after David had chosen Jerusalem as his capital city, the country was ready for a permanent temple. David's son Solomon constructed this first, great monument to the Lord.

Solomon was 7 years completing the Lord's House, but 13 in building his own (1 Kings 6:38 and 7:1). (Secular and sacred history alike record that his palace was full of idol worship, apostasy, and prostitution.) As you can see in the diagram below, this Temple had two main parts and a portico. The design follows the Lord's original ratios as revealed to Moses on Sinai.

## SOLOMON'S TEMPLE

### 960-586 B.C.

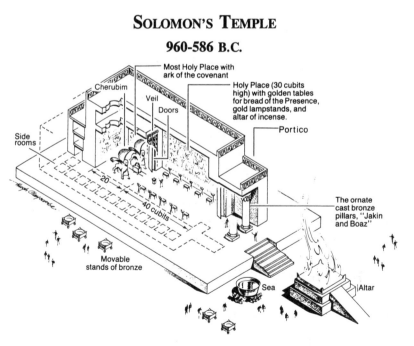

FIGURE 12.2

1 Kings 6:20 reveals the exact dimensions of the Most Holy Place, confirming it was a perfect cube:

*The inner sanctuary was 20 cubits long, 20 cubits wide and 20 high.*

Recall that the cube in the Tabernacle was 10 cubits per side. Doubling every length increases the volume by a factor of 8:

Volume of the Most Holy Place
in the Tabernacle = 10 x 10 x 10
= 1,000 cubic cubits.

Volume of the Most Holy Place
in the Temple = 20 x 20 x 20
= 8,000 cubic cubits.

Similar volume ratios exist between the Holy Places of both sacred structures (i.e., 1 to 8). In addition, 1 Kings 6:2 gives the dimensions of the whole Temple. Like the volume of Noah's Ark, it too is an amplified triangle number.

Volume of the entire Temple = 60 x 20 x 30
= 36,000
= 36 x 1,000 cubic cubits.

So sacred was the Holy of Holies that only the high priest could enter it. And tradition allowed this entry only on the most important day of the Jewish year, Yom Kippur, the Day of Atonement.

The Jews began the construction of Solomon's Temple twelve generations after Exodus and dedicated it in 960 B.C. It became the center of their spiritual life and remained so until Nebuchadnezzar's armies demolished it on 14 August 586 B.C.

# THE SEA

It would take us too far afield to comment widely on the dimensions and design of Solomon's Temple. The literature on this topic is vast. Sir Isaac Newton wrote volumes on it. Nevertheless, we will explore a single, outstanding point.

A famous controversy surrounds "the sea," a huge bronze reservoir standing just outside the Temple shown in FIGURE 12.2. It rested on the backs of a dozen oxen. The craftsmen arranged these beasts in 3s with each group facing a major compass point. Atheists and humanists charge that the reservoir's dimensions from 1 Kings 7:23 (quoted below) are internally contradictory. This implies, they assert, that *the Bible is flawed* and therefore cannot be God's Word:

> *He* [Huram of Tyre] *made the sea of cast metal, circular in shape, measuring 10 cubits from rim to rim and 5 cubits high. It took a line of 30 cubits to measure around it.*

The supposed error lies in the circumference being 30 cubits when the diameter is 10. The distance around any circular object is the product of its diameter and $\pi$ (pi = 3.1415926... has no pattern at all).

Every person must judge the accuracy needed in their answer and round off accordingly. Even the hardware on the Apollo moon rockets required only four decimal places. For "the sea" let's use two. So the circumference would be 3.14 x 10 or 31.4 cubits. This is 1.4 cubits (2½ feet) larger than the Bible gives — longer than your forearm.

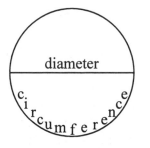

Pi x diameter = circumference
3.14 x 10      = 31.4 cubits

It is unfortunate for atheists and humanists that the error was not much smaller. Let me explain. The 2½ feet is far too large to result from a sloppy measurement, however bad. Usually a mistake of this type is a matter of inches or less, but rarely a foot, and never 2 feet. So there must be another explanation. The NIV text note for 1 Kings 7:23 provides two alternatives.

It suggests this is either a rounded measurement or the circumference came from the inside of the reservoir. That is, the diameter was taken from the larger outer circle, and the circumference from the smaller inner circle. With this, the 10 cubit diameter and the 30 cubit circumference would agree. This implies the basin was approximately 5 inches thick — a reasonable result. No true problem exists here. Unbelievers grasping at such straws to find "errors" in God's Holy Word, reveal deeper motives.

Although pi (3.1415...) is a totally lawless decimal, triangle numbers can tame it. As unlikely as it may seem, these triads provide the necessary building blocks for finding pi to an infinite number of decimal places. Again, see the Chapter Notes.

## EZEKIEL'S DREAM TEMPLE

After Jerusalem's destruction and during the Babylonian exile, the Lord gave to Ezekiel the celebrated vision of the rebuilt Temple. The dream's specifications for God's House are so precise that some scholars have drawn blueprints from it.

For an example of its architectural detail consider the following. The prophet is speaking about the steps in his vision Temple: *Seven led into the outer court* (40:22), *and eight led from the outer to the inner* (40:31). Or as Bullinger interprets this on page 198 of his *Number in Scripture*, "the seven from labour to rest, and the eight from rest to worship."

As before, the Temple has two main parts: the rectangular Holy Place and the cubical Most Holy Place. This consistent cubical shape for the Holy of Holies — from the desert Tabernacle to Solomon's Temple to Ezekiel's vision — is its most striking feature. We shall learn that this form continued in subsequent temples. What is more important, we will discover the transcendent truth symbolized by this shape.

## THE SECOND TEMPLE

*Nebuchadnezzar king of Babylon came to Jerusalem and besieged it. And the Lord delivered Jehoiakim king of Judah into his hand, along with some of the articles from the temple of God.*
Daniel 1:1

The year was 606 or 605 B.C. when the Babylonians first triumphed over the city. Yet, they did not totally plunder it. The Temple itself escaped real damage. However, the victors did take thousands of influential and wealthy

Jews captive to Babylon — and Daniel was among them. While Jeremiah remained to prophesy at home, Daniel rose to great prominence in the king's court. We will deal with Daniel's astonishing predictions and numbers later; the other prophet concerns us now.

The militarily inferior Jews foolishly revolted against the occupying Babylonians and the inevitable happened: Nebuchadnezzar's armies returned. They recaptured Jerusalem in 586, demolished the city walls, and burned the Temple. Most biblical scholars believe it was during these tragic days that the Cherubim and the Ark of the Covenant were lost forever (?).

Without the Temple the Jewish people are like an eagle without wings. They can flutter but they cannot fly. Despair tethers their bodies to the earth while their spirits long for the freedom of the skies. Culturally, the focus of their life was, and is, the Temple — even if it is only a Wailing Wall. Until a new Temple rises from the original site, the modern state of Israel will not be spiritually whole. For the exiles in Babylon, as for modern Israelis, their undying passion was, and is, to rebuild the Temple. History tells us that neither destruction of the Lord's House nor exile from His country is permanent. Kings live and die, empires come and go, but man's longing for God endures forever.

After Cyrus ascended to the Persian (Iranian) throne and conquered the Babylonian (Iraqi) Empire, history took an unusual twist. The last verses of 2 Chronicles tell us this new monarch was different from all previous ones: he treated the Jews humanely. The author ends this book with the following joyous pronouncement:

> *In the first year of Cyrus king of Persia, in order to fulfill the word of the Lord spoken by Jeremiah, the Lord moved the heart of Cyrus king of Persia to make a proclamation throughout his realm and to put it in writing: This is what Cyrus king of Persia says: "The Lord, the God of heaven, has given me all the kingdoms of the earth and he has appointed me to build a temple for him at Jerusalem in Judah. Anyone of his people among you — may the Lord his God be with him, and let him go up [to Jerusalem]. "*

Almost 50,000 Jews took advantage of Cyrus' generous proclamation of 536 B.C. In what would be one of history's most renowned journeys, they trekked home through the Fertile Crescent.

Upon arriving, plans for rebuilding the Lord's House began almost immediately under Zerubbabel's leadership. Using the existing primary foundation stones of Solomon's Temple and the dimensions of 1 Kings 6, the Second Temple was finished and dedicated in 516 B.C. Like the first, it was completed in 7 years[1]. This new building lacked the grandeur of Solomon's, but it served the people well, and hostile armies never destroyed it.

However, the Ark of the Covenant and the Cherubim were missing; so the cubical Most Holy Place was, as Josephus said, "completely empty." No other shrine on earth is totally without religious objects in its holy of holies.

Jeremiah prophesied (29:10) the length of the Jewish exile from God and Temple. His predictions startle the unknowing reader with their accuracy:

> *This is what the Lord says: "When 70 years are completed for Babylon, I will come to you and fulfill my gracious promise to bring you back to this place* [Temple].*"*

| Temple | 70 YEARS | New Temple |
|---|---|---|
| destroyed | ----------------> | dedicated |
| 586 B.C. | | 516 B.C. |

Jeremiah also predicted (25:11) the duration of the Jewish captivity in Babylon. Their initial removal to that city began in 605 B.C. when Nebuchadnezzar first conquered Jerusalem. From that time to Cyrus' decree is again 70 years if you count from the beginning of 605 (anyhow, some texts say 606). The following verse of the woeful prophet refers directly to this time period:

> *This whole country will be a desolate wasteland, and these nations will serve the king of Babylon 70 years.*

| Beginning | 70 YEARS | Cyrus' |
|---|---|---|
| of | ----------------> | decree |
| 605 B.C. | | 536 B.C. |

Since 7 is the number of completeness, 70 stands for the same thing intensified. The Babylonian hostages did complete their period of separation from home, country, Temple, and God. This exile or captivity was the second of many the Hebrew people would endure: the Egyptian was the first. Six centuries into the future, a Roman general would destroy an entirely renovated Second Temple (the Herodian) and scatter the Jews worldwide.

Similar to 153, the number 70, or 7, possesses an extraordinary property that only the Trinity Function reveals:

$$70 \ \text{-------->} \ \ 7^3 \ + \ \ 0^3$$
$$= 7\text{x}7\text{x}7 \ + \ 0\text{x}0\text{x}0$$
$$= \ \ 343 \ \ + \ \ 0$$
$$= 343$$

Nothing unusual yet, except you should notice that the extra 0 does not affect the total of 343. To understand the phenomenal attributes of 70, continuously apply our rule to each new image:

$$70 \ \text{--->}343\text{--->}118\text{--->}514\text{--->}190\text{--->}730\text{--->} 370$$

It is easy to prove the image stops at 370.

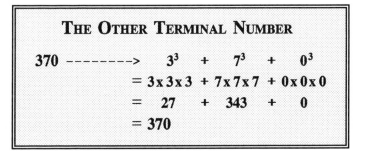

**THE OTHER TERMINAL NUMBER**

$$370 \ \text{--------->} \ \ \ 3^3 \ + \ \ 7^3 \ + \ \ 0^3$$
$$= 3\text{x}3\text{x}3 + 7\text{x}7\text{x}7 + 0\text{x}0\text{x}0$$
$$= \ \ 27 \ \ + \ \ 343 \ + \ \ 0$$
$$= 370$$

FIGURE 12.3

Consequently, 370 resurrects itself with each new application of the Trinity Function, just like 153. As we know, one-third of all quantities lead to Jesus' Fish Number. This is not so with 370 or 37. Those numbers that reach this second terminal point are much less common, but we shall find several. So, ultimately 7 or 70 transforms to 37 or 370: the final face behind this mask. Before this chapter ends the reader may think — with good reason — *that 37 is the most phenomenal number in the entire Holy Bible.*

Can 70 be expressed as a threefold sum of triangle numbers? Yes, it can, and with appealing results:

$$70 = 6 + 28 + 36$$

| 1st perfect number | 2nd perfect number | 1st perfect squared |

We know 6 and 28 are perfect and triangular, and 36 is 6 x 6. Thus, 70 is the sum of perfect quantities or their product. Biblically this symbolizes an important period for a judgment. We will see more of this in Daniel's "70 weeks of years."

The numbers 7 and 10 connect different aspects of completeness: the first with a list, and the second with a cycle. Of course 70 also equals 7 x 10. From this viewpoint, it implies the completion of a list of cycles or a cycle of lists. That is, 7 repetitions of 10, or 10 repetitions of 7 (see NIV text note at Genesis 10:2). The Bible uses this number for the *completion of judgment*. On the other hand, it has so many connections with Zion that we might also call it Jerusalem's Number. In this regard the most outstanding instance is Rome's annihilation of the city and the Temple in 70 A.D.

The following is a selection of 70s, both sacred and secular:

- Jacob's (Israel's) children numbered 70 when they left Canaan to go into Egypt (Exodus 1:5). Ahab also had 70 sons (2 Kings 10:1).
- God established 70 original nations as shown by adding up the names in Genesis 10, "The Table of Nations." Moses further revealed the significance of this in Deuteronomy 32:8:

  *When the Most High gave the nations their inheritance, when he divided all mankind, he set up boundaries for the peoples according to the number of the sons of Israel.*

- The Book of Numbers (11:16) records how the Lord spoke to Moses concerning the quantity 70:

  *The Lord said to Moses: "Bring me 70 of Israel's elders who are known to you as leaders and officials among the people."*

- The 70 member Sanhedrin court of judgment was modeled on the 70 elders called out by God to help Moses.
- Isaiah 23:15-17 implies the relationship of this number to judgment:

> *At that time Tyre will be forgotten*
> *for 70 years, the span of a king's life.*
> . . . . . . . . . . . . . . . . . . . . . . . .
> *At the end of 70 years, the Lord will deal with Tyre.*

- We have already discussed how Jerusalem's citizens suffered through 70 years of Babylonian exile and 70 years of separation from God and the Temple.
- Daniel used this quantity in his famous and prophetic "70 sevens."
- Zechariah 1:12 provides another link among judgment, Jerusalem, and 70:

> *Lord Almighty, how long will you withhold mercy from*
> *Jerusalem and from the towns of Judah, which you have*
> *been angry with these 70 years? So the Lord spoke kind*
> *and comforting words to the angel who talked with me.*

- Jesus sent 70 disciples into the world, "as lambs among wolves" (Luke 10:1-3, KJV — yet the NIV says 72).
- The ancients understood the extra-mathematical meaning of 70. It was part of their culture. Consider the actions of the Assyrian king Sennacherib (705-681 B.C.). During a difficult, but successful, campaign to take Babylon, his army suffered such huge losses that he declared the city should remain devastated for 70 years.

To complete the Septuagint (Latin for 70) translation of the Old Testament, tradition says that 70 scholars labored for 70 days. This is the version Paul used. And finally, a biblical life span has always been three score and ten — time for the completion of our judgment.

# HEROD'S TEMPLE

In a vain effort to win the Jews' support, Herod totally rebuilt the Second Temple (Zerubbabel's) into a grand structure of fifteen stories. Despite this major overhaul, Jews still referred to it as the Second Temple. From the drawing below the reader can see the extra ceiling constructed over the Most Holy Place to preserve its historic cubical shape.

## HEROD'S TEMPLE
### 20 B.C — 70 A.D.

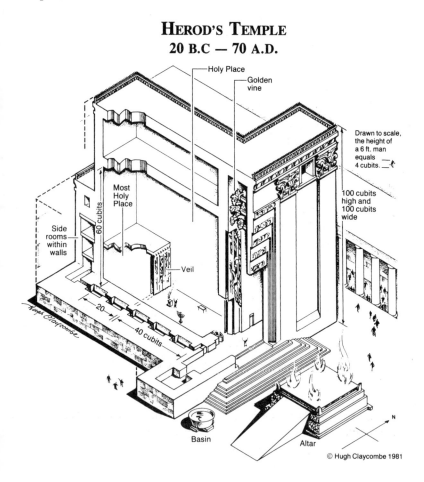

FIGURE 12.4

The Bible establishes its authority in many ways, not the least of which is by the power and truth of its prophecies. Predictions not about trivial matters concerning movie stars or prime ministers or even presidents, but revelations of the highest order: the destruction of God's Temple, the fate of a people, the events of the Apocalypse. In Matthew 24:1-2, our Lord precisely foretold the destruction of Herod's Temple:

*Jesus left the temple and was walking away when his disciples came up to him to call his attention to its buildings. "Do you see all these things?" he asked. "I tell you the truth, not one stone here will be left on another; every one will be thrown down."*

History fulfilled this prophecy on the 9th of Av, 70 A.D. On that portentous day, the Romans, under Titus, completely demolished Jerusalem and all her Temple buildings. Titus had ordered his legions not to harm the Lord's House, but in the chaos of battle they torched it. After the holocaust, the looting soldiers even pried and chiseled the mortar from between the building blocks. This was to collect the gold leaf that had melted from the Temple's roof. Truly, no stone was left on another.

The present Western (or Wailing) Wall formed no part of the Lord's House. Then, as now, it was merely a retaining structure for the Temple Mount.

In his great history *The Jewish Wars*, Josephus tells us the destruction of the Second Temple occurred on the same day and in the same month as the First[2]. Josephus also relates that, as the Temple burned, Titus hurriedly looked behind the sacred curtain into the cubical Most Holy Place. Observing nothing, and apparently unharmed, he quickly left the devastation. To the Jews of that day there existed no greater act of desecration. Only one other gentile ever penetrated the Most Holy Place: the Roman general Pompey in 64 B.C.

Whether for their sacrilege or for other reasons, both men afterward suffered extreme bad luck. The next few years of Pompey's life were as unfortunate as the previous 42 had been blessed. While battling with Julius Caesar (a bad choice in opponents), Pompey fled to Egypt where one of his own centurions beheaded him. So terrible was his change of fortune that stories and legends have grown around it. Titus fared no better. In his first year as emperor, Rome had a

3-day fire that consumed the pagan Temples of Jupiter, Juno, and Minerva. Long dormant Mount Vesuvius erupted, burying the cities of Pompeii and Herculaneum. In the following year, the worst plague in Rome's history struck the city. At the early age of 41, after only 28 months as emperor, Titus died in the same farmhouse as his father Vespasian. The Jews attributed the terrible fate of both men to their defilement of the Cube. Others ascribe it to coincidence. You be the judge.

History is not just our past; it is often a reminder of our present fears and prejudices. In a strange way, a remembrance of the destruction of Jerusalem and her Temple still lives in our language. Consider the well-known cheer "hip, hip, hurrah" which is a variation of "hep, hep, hurrah." Its origin lies deep in our past — all the way back to 70 A.D. The Romans were so overjoyed at demolishing Jerusalem and exterminating the Jews that at banquets the common toast was "Hierosolyma Est Perdita," meaning "Jerusalem Is Destroyed." The guests immediately respond with "hurrah." H, E, and P are the first letters of each Latin word. To this day only one person says HEP, then the rest join in the shout that greets it. This ancient anti-Semitism must make the Devil smile!

# THE KAABA

Other peoples of the ancient Middle East have also felt the power of the Cube — the Holy of Holies. Consider, for example, the Arabic nations. They claim descent from Ibrahim (Abraham) by way of Hagar and her son Ishmael. It is more than a passing accident that Islam's most holy place, the Kaaba, is cubical as well. Five times each day Moslems turn toward their cube in Mecca and pray. Arabic tradition says this earthly shrine sits directly beneath its heavenly equivalent. In their language, even the word *Kaaba* means *cube*.

At least once during a lifetime, every Moslem must hadj (journey) to the cubical rock. After arriving, the hadji (pilgrim) is to walk around the Kaaba exactly 7 times in a counterclockwise direction. Fellow hadji carry those disabled by time or events. Failure to do exactly 7 cycles renders the entire hadj incomplete. Any infidel (Christian) found in or near Mecca, not to mention their holy of holies, is killed — historically by inverted crucifixion.

Curiously, the Arabs have reversed the basic symbolism of the Cube. Instead of this shape enclosing only empty space — as with the Jews — theirs is solid black Meccan granite.

# THE NEW TEMPLE

We have seen the Tabernacle and the Temples of the past. Now we will look to the future:

> *In that day will I raise up the tabernacle of David that is fallen, and close up the breaches thereof; and I will raise up his ruins, and I will build it as in the days of old:*
> Amos 9:11 (KJV)

Although Amos was writing for a different time and audience, his words seem strangely compelling for our generation.

Daniel's famous and still future prophecy, given below, clearly implies the Temple in Jerusalem is standing. Otherwise, the entire passage is meaningless. And obviously the desecrating Antichrist can be stopped only if he has already begun:

> *He will confirm a covenant with many for one 'seven'* [years]. *In the middle of the 'seven' he* [the Antichrist] *will put an end to sacrifice and offering. And on a wing of the temple he will set up an abomination that causes desolation,* [a statue of himself] *until the end that is decreed is poured out on him.*
> Daniel 9:27

Knowing that the Temple will be rebuilt, Jesus recalls Daniel's prediction of the Antichrist's heresies:

> *So when you see standing in the holy place "the abomination that causes desolation," spoken of through the prophet Daniel — let the reader understand —*
> Matthew 24:15

Paul, in 2 Thessalonians 2:4, also speaks of the Temple:

> *He* [the Antichrist] *will oppose and will exalt himself over everything that is called God or is worshiped, so that he sets himself up in God's temple, proclaiming himself to be God.*

It is all very simple, either the Jews rebuild the Temple, or Jesus, Daniel, and Paul prophesied falsely.

"Time for a New Temple?" questions the headline of a 16 October 1988 *Time* magazine article. The piece opens with the following Jewish prayer, recited three times daily:

> *May it be Thy will that the Temple be speedily rebuilt in our days.*

So, religious Jews have absolutely no doubts concerning rebuilding. Before the brilliant victory of the 6-Day War (June 1967), when Israel finally took possession of David's City, this was not even a possibility. On that singular day, after the paratroops had stormed the Temple Mount, Chief Rabbi Shlomo Goren raced directly to the Western Wall of the Second Temple. He blew the shofar to announce to the world, *we are home and we are free.* Two thousand years of exile were over!

The main obstacle to rebuilding remains the presence of Islam's third most holy place, the Dome of the Rock. When the Moslems built the Dome of the Rock in A.D. 691, the Temple Mount had already been abandoned for centuries. Legend says this mosque rests directly over the site of the original Temples and, of course, the Holy of Holies. Any hint of demolishing this structure would outrage Moslems and positively result in a jihad (holy war)!

But legends, like history, may be mistaken. As the years pass, the land rises due to falling dust and the debris of human habitation. This is why archaeologists must dig for a living. In 691, after centuries of accumulation, it is extremely unlikely the Arabs — without knowledge of archaeology — could have even located the Holy of Holies.

Recently, Dr. Asher S. Kaufman from Hebrew University uncovered parts of the foundation of the First and Second Temples. The respected journal *Biblical Archaeological Review* (March/April 1983) published an excellent article by Dr. Kaufman concerning this.

FIGURE 12.5 on the next page shows the superimposed outline of the First Temple's true position from Dr. Kaufman's article.

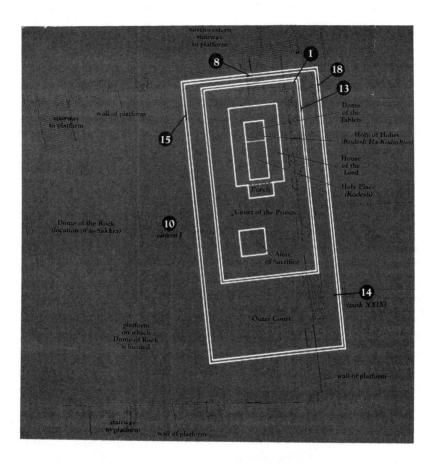

**Plan of the First Temple superimposed
on the Temple Mount platform**

FIGURE 12.5

On the first page, he states the major result of his research:

*One of the most surprising conclusions from this evidence is that the golden Dome of the Rock in the middle of the Temple Mount was not on the site of the Temple but to the south of it. The original Temple site is approximately 330 feet (100 meters) to the northwest of the Dome of the Rock.*

He ends the article with the following strong declaration:

*The archaeological finds on the site interlock precisely in a consistent manner in the plans of both Temples and with the ancient literary sources. The result* [the Temple locations] *precludes any other interpretation.*

Other excavations, involving tunnels — yards beneath the surface of the Mount — also place the cubical Holy of Holies north of the mosque. Rabbi Goren and others believe this confirms that the Israelis could rebuild the Temple without unduly disturbing Moslem sensibilities. The rabbi declares:

*I cannot leave this world without assuring that Jews will once again pray on the Mount.*[3]

Within a few hundred yards of the Mount, two Talmudic schools have taught almost 200 students the elaborate particulars of Temple service. Skilled modern craftsmen have constructed most of the ancient ritual implements. These are a popular exhibit attracting thousands of visitors. Even the priestly vestments, carefully hand-spun from flax into 6-stranded threads, are ready. As yet, no stockpiling of marble or limestone has been done. However, with modern techniques and equipment, dedicated workers could build the Third Temple in a few weeks. Great preparations have been made; great expectations are at hand.

To delight and attract tourists, owners of Jerusalem's Holyland Hotel display an elaborate scale model of the Lord's House. The Temple Institute has blueprints for a more elaborate prototype costing over $1 million. This group's leader, Rabbi Israel Ariel, was one of the first paratroopers to reach the Mount in 1967.

Many intellectual and religious leaders in Israel and elsewhere are lobbying the Knesset (Jewish parliament) to begin the construction. Historian David Solomon maintains that a Third Temple is indispensable:

> *It was the essence of our Jewish being, the unifying force of our people. Every day's delay is a stain on the nation.*[4]

Putting aside all arguments about the true location of the Temple and its rebuilding, who actually owns the Temple Mount? History records only one person: David, the son of Jesse. The last verses of 2 Samuel tell how David bought the threshing floor of Araunah the Jebusite who wished to give it to him:

> *But the king replied to Araunah, "No, I insist on paying you for it. I will not sacrifice to the Lord my God burnt offerings that cost me nothing." So David purchased the threshing floor and the oxen.*

# The New Jerusalem

> *I saw the Holy City, the new Jerusalem, coming down out of heaven from God, prepared as a bride.*
> Revelation 21:2

Man's Third Temple will be his last. God's New Jerusalem will be His first and last. In lyrical language John sings about the Sacred City. The song says it does not have a Temple because now the whole city is the Lord's House (Revelation 21:22).

> *I did not see a temple in the city, because the Lord God Almighty and the Lamb are its temple.*

If the entire New Jerusalem is the Lord's Chamber, what shape should it be? In 21:16 the Apostle chants out the form of the Temple-City.

> *The city was laid out like a square, as long as it was wide. He measured the city with the rod and found it to be 12,000 stadia in length, and as wide and high as it is long.*

(A stadium is 616 feet, and 12,000 stadia equal 1400 miles.) Significantly the New Jerusalem will be a perfect cube, like the Most Holy Place in the Tabernacle and all previous temples. Therefore, the transcendent question becomes

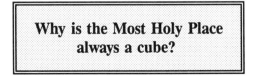

**Why is the Most Holy Place always a cube?**

According to the famous astronomer Johannes Kepler, our world's 3 dimensions reflect The Holy Trinity's 3 parts. The cube is the simplest and most stable object with 3 equal dimensions, like the 3 coequal parts of the Godhead itself. This is a beginning toward a complete understanding of the cube's deep enigma.

Before fully answering this intriguing problem, however, let's first seek the solution to an easier question. "Does the gematria of the Bible lend support to a kinship among holy objects, sacred places, and cubes?"

## THE GEMATRIA OF THE CITY

*I asked, "Where are you going?" He answered me, "To measure Jerusalem, to find out how wide and how long it is."*
Zechariah 2:1-2

*I was given a reed like a measuring rod and was told, "Go and measure the temple of God and the altar, and count the worshipers there."*
Revelation 11:1

The above passages unquestionably imply that the mathematics of the Temple contains spiritual knowledge. The Lord is instructing us to measure the Temple, the altar, and Jerusalem, and that is exactly what we shall do:

THE          ALTAR          (Revelation 8:3)
To    θ υ σ ι α σ τ η ρ ι ο ν
300 70 + 9 400 200 10  1 200 300 8 100 10 70 50 = 1728

Since 1728 equals 12 x 12 x 12, this number is an exact cube.

Continuing with the Temple-City itself, the volume is found by multiplying its length, width, and height:

The volume = 12,000 x 12,000 x 12,000
            = 1,728,000,000,000 cubic stadia

So both the altar and the New Jerusalem, the heart and the whole, are the perfect cube 1728.

Next we will encounter a series of amazing gematria sums of the essential words revolving around the Temple, its place, and its people. The significance of these examples and their relationship to 1728 will be explained afterward. For the present, recall the value of "Jerusalem" and "saints" (pages 177-178):

JERUSALEM          (Revelation 3:12)
I ε ρ ο υ σ α λ η μ
10 5 100 70 400 200 1 30 8 40 = 864 (= 12 x 72)

SAINTS          (Revelation 8:3)
A γ ι ω ν
1  3 10 800 50 = 864 (= 12 x 72)

The New Jerusalem will be the House of the Lord God Almighty and the Lamb (Revelation 21:22). Thus, consider the gematria of "God's Temple":

GOD'S  TEMPLE
Θ ε ω ν
9 5 800 50 = 864

Through His beloved disciple John, the Lord revealed the City of Revelation to be a perfect cube, 12,000 stadia on each side. So the area of a single face is 12,000 x 12,000 square stadia. The total surface area consists of 4 walls plus the ceiling and the floor (6 surfaces):

$$\text{Total surface area} = \text{(area of one face)} \times \text{(6 surfaces)}$$
$$= (12{,}000 \times 12{,}000) \times 6$$
$$= 864{,}000{,}000 \text{ square stadia}$$

To convert Greek stadia to feet, meters, or miles is unwise because it destroys the symbolic intent of the original unit.

I found many notable words and phrases whose value was 864. Gradually a simple pattern emerged. Most referred to the same thing: the faithful people. Here are seven:

God's flock                                         864 x 1
1 Peter 5:2

the wedding of the Lamb and his bride    864 x 4
Revelation 19:7

Many will come from the east
and the west and sit at the table
with Abraham, Isaac, and Jacob
in the kingdom of heaven.                     864 x 10
Jesus, Matthew 8:11

Don't you know that you are God's temple
and that God's spirit lives in you?          864 x 4
Paul, 1 Corinthians 3:16

redeemed his people                            864 x 5
Luke 1:68

the seed of the faith                            864 x 4
Romans 4:16 (KJV)

After life's banquet, however grand or mean, God will gather up 12 basketfuls of the faithful, the broken pieces, "the fragments":

the fragments                                     864 x 3
Matthew 14:20 (KJV)

All these results mark out a striking set of relationships. Still, I need to explain why 864 is special and what connects it to the Cube. The next two points should provide clear, strong answers to these questions.

- **The Image of the Cube**:

Apply the Trinity Function to 1728 (12 x 12 x 12), the perfect cube of the altar and the Temple:

(the cube)

$$1728 \longrightarrow \begin{aligned} & 1^3 + 7^3 + 2^3 + 8^3 \\ = & 1x1x1 + 7x7x7 + 2x2x2 + 8x8x8 \\ = & 1 + 343 + 8 + 512 \\ = & 864 \text{ (the image)} \end{aligned}$$

Therefore, the cube transfigures directly to 864.

- **The Cube of the Image**:

Surprisingly, 864 is also exactly one-half of our altar cube:

$$\frac{\text{altar}}{2} = \frac{1728}{2} = 864$$

Just as 864 is half a cube, "the fragments" are part of a fish. And we, the broken pieces, fulfill only a fraction of God's Commandments and know only a portion of the Cube's truth.

The earlier quotation from Revelation 11:1, "a reed like a measuring rod," referred to an actual measuring device:

A REED LIKE A MEASURING ROD

κ α λ α μ ο ς    ο μ ο ι ο ς    ρ α β δ ω

20 1 30 1 40 70 200 + 70 40 70 10 70 200 + 100 1 2 4 800 = 1729

This quantity has several unique properties; the most important are the following:

$$\begin{aligned} 1729 & = 1728 + 1 \\ & = 12 \times 12 \times 12 + 1 \times 1 \times 1 \\ & = 12^3 + 1^3 \end{aligned}$$

or

$$\begin{aligned} 1729 & = 1000 + 729 \\ & = 10 \times 10 \times 10 + 9 \times 9 \times 9 \\ & = 10^3 + 9^3 \end{aligned}$$

In other words, 1729 is a *double cube* in two different ways. Probably these double cubes follow from the two instruments: the reed and the rod.

Since the entire structure of the New Jerusalem is the Most Holy Place, then the "body of Jesus" is the Temple:

$$\begin{array}{lll} \text{B O D Y} & \text{of} & \text{J E S U S} \quad \text{(John 19:38)} \\ \Sigma \ \omega \ \mu \ \alpha & & \text{I} \ \eta \ \sigma \ o \ \upsilon \\ \text{200 800 40 1} & + & \text{10 8 200 70 400} = 1729 \end{array}$$

Remarkably, this is also 1729, our rare double cube. Possibly the twin cubes here stand for the two aspects of Jesus: man and God. The Trinity Rule transforms this immediately to God's Holy Spirit:

(Body of Jesus)

$$\begin{aligned} 1729 \ \text{---------}\!\!> \quad & 1^3 \ + \ 7^3 \ + \ 2^3 \ + \ 9^3 \\ = \ & 1{\times}1{\times}1 \ + \ 7{\times}7{\times}7 \ + \ 2{\times}2{\times}2 \ + \ 8{\times}8{\times}8 \\ = \ & 1 \ + \ 343 \ + \ 8 \ + \ 729 \\ = \ & 1081 \ \text{(God's Holy Spirit)} \end{aligned}$$

The point has been strongly shown: the Bible abounds with cubes. These are found not only in the Temple but also in the gematria of its most meaningful words involving holy places, objects, and people.

# GOD IS SPIRIT

While peering trillions of miles into deep outer space, why haven't astronomers actually found God? If not there, then perhaps the laboratory's electron microscope can detect Him in the molecules, atoms, or quarks. Silly questions? Man has not always thought so. (Be certain I am not writing about the Lord's handiwork in nature, which is everywhere apparent.) Unquestionably, many have hoped to prove His existence by discovery. Today, however, man no longer believes he can find the Deity in the stars or the elements. There is no God particle. Isaiah 45:15 states:

> *Truly you are a God who hides himself,*
> *O God and Savior of Israel.*

Nevertheless, as the *last days* approach, knowledge about God and His true being are increasing. A full explanation of the cubical structure in the Lord's holy places involves the ultimate nature of God *as revealed to man*. We shall discover how the Cube provides penetrating new insights into this final reality.

Whenever I want answers, I consult the Bible. In John 4:24, Jesus tells us a great truth about the Lord:

*God is spirit, and his worshipers must worship in spirit and in truth.*

So, attempting to see God in the material universe is foolishness. This implies He must exist in another dimension — hardly a novel thought. Many artists and several leading Protestant theologians have maintained similar ideas for decades, notably the religious thinker Karl Heim, and the painter Salvador Dali.

Using the shape the Lord gave Moses for the Most Holy Place as our guide, I plan to take the reader on a journey into the Cube's symbolism and other dimensions. First we will visit the world of flatland or 2 dimensions and then jump to the higher space of 4. It promises to be exciting, but more importantly we will learn wonderful new things about God and His Holy Scriptures. These will be facts and ideas to share with fellow Christians, casual or committed, to strengthen or confirm their faith.

# A POINT OF VIEW

Consider the three figures at the top of the next page. Drawing (a) is obviously a cube, and (c) is clearly a hexagon, but what is the middle sketch? Imagine cube (a) were sitting in front of you. Now shift your point of view to cause part of line AB to be in front of line CD. What would you see? After reflecting a few moments, I am sure you will agree it would be the middle figure. Again change your perspective so that only point A covers point D. Interestingly, you now have sketch (c). So the 3-dimensional cube *is* the 2-dimensional hexagon. Consequently, these are all the same figure. What you see depends on your point of view. That is as true in life as it is in geometry.

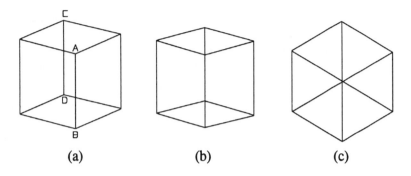

Three views of the same cube

FIGURE 12.6

These drawings have an optical illusive quality, intensified by staring. For most people they appear to randomly shift back and forth from 2 to 3 dimensions.

So, the cube can be pictured as a flat hexagon. Convince yourself of this. Pick up something cubical in your home; manipulate it until you can see its 6-sided profile. As you know, triangle numbers and the triad structure of the Bible are the bases of this book. Are triangles and hexagons related? The answer is yes, and the connection is beautifully simple. When you take any triangle and cut off its corners, you create a hexagon — implying these two forms relate like parent and child. The following diagrams illustrate the first four. The edges of each related cube have been darkened.

**Hexagonal Numbers**

FIGURE 12.7

In the diagram on the right, 37 appears again, but this time as the fourth hexagonal number. If you have a 4 x 4 x 4 cube, then the most you can ever see of it — in one view — are three sides made up from 37 smaller cubes (see FIGURE 12.15).

Return now to the gematria of the "Body of Jesus" and "a reed like a measuring rod." Both have a value of 1729, and both equal $12^3 + 1^3$ and $10^3 + 9^3$. Since we now know about 6-sided quantities, an even more interesting representation is possible. Surprisingly, this notable number is the product of two hexagonal quantities or the sum of identical triangles/hexagons. See the Chapter Notes for a detailed list of hexagonals, but examine the following for an immediate explanation:

$$1729 = \quad 19 \quad x \quad 91$$
$$\text{hexagonal} \quad \text{hexagonal}$$
$$= \quad 91 + 91 + \ldots + 91$$
$$\text{all triangle/hexagonal numbers}$$

As so often occurs with numbers involving Jesus and the Bible, 19 x 91 is the same whether read forward or backward. This curious and prevalent symmetry originated in Hebrew and Greek poetic forms and writing techniques. Even the digital root of our double cube is 19:

$$1729 \text{----------} > 1 + 7 + 2 + 9$$
$$= 19$$

Triangles are the basic units. Add 3 small ones to each side and a star is born; cut 3 from each corner and a hexagon is formed. Therefore, stars and hexagons are variations on the triangular theme. The diagrams below show this.

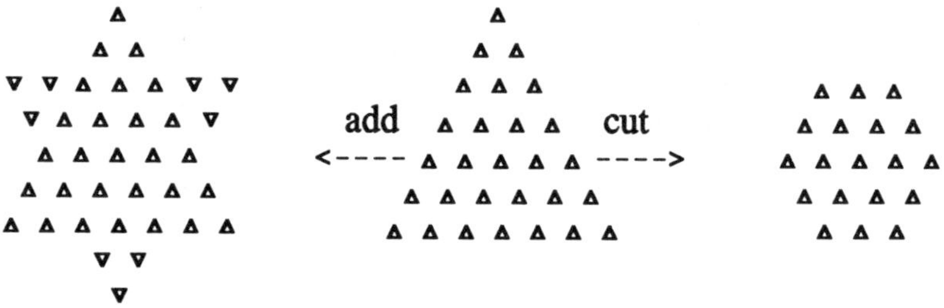

FIGURE 12.8

The following examples emphasize the intimate connection between cubic and hexagonal numbers:

$$\text{All hexagons} = \begin{bmatrix} 1 + 7 = 8 = 2 \times 2 \times 2 \\ 1 + 7 + 19 = 27 = 3 \times 3 \times 3 \\ 1 + 7 + 19 + 37 = 64 = 4 \times 4 \times 4 \end{bmatrix} = \text{All cubes}$$

Accordingly, by adding hexagonal numbers you always produce a perfect cube — an unexpected result. Just as unusual is the fact that the difference between two cubes is a hexagon. For instance, 64 (4x4x4) minus 27 (3x3x3) equals 37. This points out the close fraternity among these numbers (see Chapter Notes). In the next section you will discover the immense symbolic and spiritual meaning of this kinship.

Often during my research on the Cube something would occur to remarkably confirm the ideas. This happened with such regularity that I almost came to expect it; the following was one instance.

Jewish history gives the hexagon unusual reverence, a respect unexplained and unaccounted for. A version of it, the Star of David, has even become the national symbol for Israel and the universal image for all Jews. Beyond this, rabbinical tradition says the sacred Ark of the Covenant held precisely 3 holy objects: the Mosaic Tablets with the Ten Commandments, the Torah with the first five books, and a scroll with a drawing of the hexagon[5]. No reasonable explanation has ever been given for the presence of this last object. But, as the image of the Holy of Holies (the Cube), it seems only right that the hexagon should be the third in a trinity of consecrated objects. Notably, each item is associated with one part of the Godhead:

*The Ten Commandments came from the Father.*
*The Torah, from the inspiration of The Holy Spirit.*
*The cube or hexagon, as we shall see, from Jesus.*

# JESUS AND THE CUBE

*He* [Jesus] *is the image of the invisible God.*
Colossians 1:15

We have arrived at the high point in this book. Contemplate the complete gematria of the most majestic name in the universe, **Jesus Christ**:

| JESUS | CHRIST |
|---|---|
| Ι η σ ο υ ς | Χ ρ ι σ τ ο ς |
| 10 8 200 70 400 200 = **888** | 600 100 10 200 300 70 200 = **1480** |

Total = **888** + **1480** = **2368**

FIGURE 12.9

Earlier we learned how 8 symbolized resurrection and renewal. Of course repeating it three times just adds greater emphasis. Biblical scholars generally agree that exactly 8 different authors wrote the New Testament. In Revelation 21:5 (KJV), Jesus Himself proclaims "Behold, I make all things new."

The selection of our Savior's name was not a chance event. Although *Jesus* a variation of *Joshua* or *Jeshua*, man did not choose it. Before the Jews built Jerusalem, before Abram left Ur, before God created Adam, before anything we can know, the Lord chose it. Luke 2:21 says:

> *On the 8th day, when it was time to circumcise him,*
> *he was named Jesus, the name the angel*
> *had given him before he had been conceived.*

We have seen the fundamental connection between [37] and the Cube. Now we will discover their close relationships to Jesus. The Cube has been our guide throughout this chapter; it represents perfect symmetry, stability, and equality in all 3 dimensions. But what is the chain that binds it and [37] to Jesus? With a sense of reverence, we take the first step in answering this question by inspecting the building blocks of our Lord's name:

$$\begin{array}{rcl}
\textbf{JESUS} & = & \textbf{888} = \textbf{[37] x 24} \\
\textbf{CHRIST} & = & \underline{\textbf{1480}} = \underline{\textbf{[37] x 40}} \\
& & \textbf{2368} = \textbf{[37] x 64}
\end{array}$$

FIGURE 12.10

The significance and symbolism of 64 will be explained. On the other hand, [37] is an old friend, one of our hexagon numbers, the 2nd terminal resurrecting quantity, and the 12th prime number. The probability of both *Jesus* and *Christ* being multiples of [37] is extremely small, but just possible. Nevertheless, the following related words and patterns — all multiples of [37] — take us beyond the realm of chaos into a world of wonders.

Let's initiate this imposing list of [37]s by considering 2 Corinthians 4:4. Its gematria is the key to the mystery of our Lord's name.

**IMAGE of GOD**
Ε ι κ ω ν      Θ ε ο υ
5 10 20 800 50   **+**   9 5 70 400 **= 1369**

**1369 is nothing less than [37] x [37],
and Εικων also means Icon.**

FIGURE 12.11

It is clear that some minute part of God's holy essence is found in the Cube's shape. However, I am not saying God *is* a Cube or any such nonsense; these are symbols. Only by images can we understand anything transcendental. How else can finite man begin to comprehend the infinite Godhead? When describing the world within the atom, scientists have a similar difficulty. From the macro-world they use images that do not quite fit the micro-world, but it is the best they, or we, can do.

Is the Cube, the Holy of Holies, directly connected to Jesus Christ? Consider. Just as God gave Moses the Cube, He also gave us His Son. Both are images of a transcendent reality. The following magnificent example of gematria reveals their relationship. It directly connects the Most Holy Place of the Jews with the most holy name of the Christians. No comment is necessary.

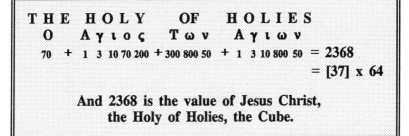

FIGURE 12.12

Romans 1:20 (KJV) refers to Jesus as the "Godhead":

> **GODHEAD**
> Θ ε ο τ η ς
> 9   5   70   300   8   200  = **592** = **[37] x 16**
>
> **The quantity of the Godhead, 592,    592**
> **plus the number of Jesus, 888,    + 888**
> **is exactly Christ, 1480.    1480**

FIGURE 12.13

Scores of Jesus' names and titles are multiples of [37]. That must have profound meaning unless you believe the Lord put all these patterns here for His idle amusement, and not for our sincere instruction. I could give a hundred illustrations of [37] in our Lord's holy names and titles. Yet, I have limited myself to a few pages at this section's end. Since these patterns undeniably exist, we should understand them.

If someone asked you to choose a single word describing the Holy Scriptures, what would it be? After reflecting, you might choose the word most often spoken by Jesus Himself. It occurs in the opening phrase He most frequently used. We, the believers, know it distinguishes the Bible from all other writings:

*I tell you the **truth** . . .*

It is not just that Jesus speaks the truth, as important as that is. It is not just that Jesus knows the truth, as profound as that is. It is that Jesus *is* the truth, as He Himself says in John 14:6:

*I am the way and the **truth** and the life.*

And what is the gematria of "truth"?

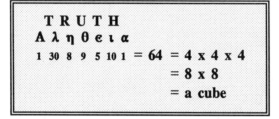

FIGURE 12.14

This quantity is the cube of 4 and the square of Jesus Resurrection Number, 8. Strikingly, it also tells us how many [37]s are in our Lord's name (see FIGURE 12.10). Assume you had a 4 x 4 x 4 cube in front of you, like the drawing at the top of the next page. Then of this larger cube/truth precisely [37] smaller cubes are visible (count them). Turn and twist as you will, but never can you see more than 3 faces at a time. This represents how much of God's truth/cube is available for man to know. Consequently, 27 parts are unseen (64 – [37] = 27) and that is the cube of The Trinity. As all Christians realize, the sacred personality has two parts: one visible and accessible to man, the other unseen and forever mysterious.

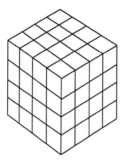

- [37] small cubes visible

- 27 small cubes unseen

- 64 cubes in total

**The Cube of Truth**

FIGURE 12.15

Further gematria wonderfully support the seen and unseen divisions of the Cube: the knowable and the unknowable parts of our Savior.

**I M A G E  OF  G O D**
Ε ι κ ω ν  Θ ε ο υ
5 10 20 800 50 **+** 9 5 70 400 = **1369** = [37] x [37]

**Representing the visible part of perfect Divinity.**

**T H E  S E C R E T  G O D**
Ο  Α π ο ρ ρ η τ ο ς
70 **+** 1 80 70 100 100 8 300 70 200 = **999** = [37] x 27

**Symbolizing the inexpressible, invisible part.**

And what is the sum ⟶ 1369 = [37] x [37]
of these two parts ⟶ **+ 999** = [37] x 27
of God's image? ⟶ 2368 = [37] x 64

**This piece of the cubical puzzle snaps exactly into place when we recall that 2368 is Jesus Christ.**

FIGURE 12.16

In the garden of God's Holy Word, the names and titles of "Jesus" blossom into a bewildering and luxuriant gematria. What follows is a brief catalogue of its contents. The full title of "the anointed" comes from Colossians 3:24:

THE    LORD    CHRIST
Τ ω    Κ υ ρ ι ω    Χ ρ ι σ τ ω
300 800 + 20 400 100 10 800 + 600 100 10 200 300 800 = [37] x 120

In Holy Scripture, references to Jesus most often take two forms. One concerns His divine nature as the image of "the Fish"; the other reflects his life on earth as the figure of "the Lamb." The first phrase is "the Son of God" (Galatians 2:20) and the second the "Son of Man" (Matthew 13:37). Jesus usually called Himself by this latter title:

THE    SON    OF    GOD
Τ η    Υ ι ο υ    Τ ο υ    Θ ε ο υ
300 8 + 400 10 70 400 + 300 70 400 + 9 5 70 400 = [37] x 66

SON    OF    MAN
Υ ι ο ς    Τ ο υ    Α ν θ ρ ω π ο υ
400 10 70 200 + 300 70 400 + 1 50 9 100 800 80 70 400 = [37] x 80

The previous title's gematria is identical to the following:

GODHEAD:  JESUS    CHRIST
Θ ε ο τ η ς    Ι η σ ο υ ς    Χ ρ ι σ τ ο ς
9 5 70 300 8 200 + 10 8 200 70 400 200 + 600 100 10 200 300 70 200 = [37] x 80

Since our Savior, as prophesied, was born of the Royal House of David, consider His earthly lineage. The following passages are from John 7:42 (KJV) and Luke 20:41 respectively. Note how The Holy Spirit has slightly changed the spelling of David ($\beta$, the middle letter, became $\upsilon$):

OF  THE  SEED  OF  DAVID
ο τ ι  ε κ  τ ο υ σ π ε ρ μ  α τ ο ς  Δ α υ ι Δ
70 300 10 + 5 20 + 300 70 400 200 80 5 100 40 + 1 300 70 200 + 4 1 400 10 4 = [37] x 70

CHRIST  IS  THE  SON  OF  DAVID
τ ο ν  Χ ρ ι σ τ ο ν  ε ι ν α ι  Δ α υ ι Δ  υ ι ο ν
300 70 50 + 600 100 10 200 300 70 50 + 5 10 50 1 10 + 4 1 400 10 4 + 400 10 70 50 = [37]x75

And [37] x 75 is a triangle number.

From start to finish, the ministry of Jesus abounds with the imagery of fish and fishermen. So, the gematria of the following title from Mark 1:17 should come as no surprise:

FISHERS     OF   MEN
α λ ι ε ι ς     α ν θ ρ ω π ω ν
1  30 10 5 10 200 $+$ 1  50 9 100 800 80 800 50 $=$ [37] x 58

Even that mysterious phrase "the sign of the Fish" has a significant value:

T H E     S I G N     OF THE     F I S H
τ ο     σ η μ ε ι ο ν     τ ο υ     ι χ θ υ ο ς
300 70 $+$ 200 8 40 5 10 70 50 $+$ 300 70 400 $+$ 10 600 9 400 70 200 $=$ [37] x 76

God created another Eden in the resplendent patterns of His Holy Word. We must not be tempted to reject this second garden and so be driven out of paradise again.

> *When man first looked down,*
> *the Devil stepped and stole his crown.*

# THE GEMATRIA OF GENESIS

The reader might ask if [37] occurs with important patterns and frequencies in the Old Testament. If so, do these harmonize with those of the New?

If this number is to be found anywhere in the Old Testament, it should be near the beginning. So let's start at Genesis 1:1, noting again that Hebrew reads right to left. Above each word is its possible literal translation, beneath each its gematria. For convenience, I have numbered these sums in parenthesis, ().

IN THE BEGINNING GOD CREATED
THE HEAVENS AND THE EARTH.

| God | created | In the beginning |
|---|---|---|
| א ל ה י ם | ב ר א | ב ר א ש י ת |
| 40 10 5 30 1 | 1 200 2 | 400 10 300 1 200 2 |
| (3) = 86 | (2) = 203 | (1) = 913 |

| .earth | and | heavens | the |
|---|---|---|---|
| ה א ר ץ | ו א ת | ה ש מ י ם | א ת |
| 90 200 1 5 | 400 1 6 | 40 10 40 300 5 | 400 1 |
| (7) = 296 | (6) = 407 | (5) = 395 | (4) = 401 |

FIGURE 12.17

This is the most powerful and momentous sentence ever written. To stamp its completeness, there are 7 immortal words; to stress its perfection, 28 triangular letters. Even the *third* word is *God*. Instantly the gematria of these words transports us into the realm of reason because their sum has transcendental significance:

**(1) + (2) + (3) + (4) + (5) + (6) + (7) = 2701**

**And 2701 is the 73th triangle number.**

FIGURE 12.18

Recall from page 32 what these quantities mean and how they are found.

```
(pre-image)
    73 --------> 1 + 2 + 3 + . . . + 73
                = 2701 (image)
                = a triangle number
```

At the beginning of this book, I wrote about this eternal first sentence. There we saw that the plural form of *God* and the singular of *created* implied *The Trinity* in the Godhead. Now we have seen that the gematria of these same words and the number of their letters are both triangular. Consequently, in the leading sentence of His Holy Word, our Lord built a triple triad structure: the meaning, the letters, the gematria. This is the topic sentence of God's Creation directing our future interpretation.

Amazingly, the triangular sum **2701** equals **[37]** x **[73]**! Again we have our hexagonal number of the Cube of Truth and this curious left-right symmetry. Of course this product also means **2701** equals **[37]** + **[37]** + . . . + **[37]**.

In God's first 7 words there are 7 relationships involving [37]. These are listed below. The parenthetical numbers represent the gematria value of each word. By using the Hebrew alphabet from page 56, the reader can verify these results:

1.  (1) + (2) + (3) + (4) + (5) = [37] x 54.

2.      (1)    +    (3) = [37] x 27.
    (In the beginning)  (God)

3.  (6) + (7) = [37] x 19 = 703 = [37]th triangle number.
    (and) (earth)

4.  (6) = [37] x 11.

5.  (7) = [37] x 8.

6.  (3)  +  (5)  +  (7) = 777 = [37] x 21.
    (God) (heavens) (earth)

7.  (1) + (2) + (4) + (6) = [37] x 52.

Return now to triangle number 2701 and its prime factors [37] and [73]. Although not emphasized previously, [37] is a star number, and, remarkably, [73] is the next one. By inspecting their diagrams (FIGURE 12.19), it is also clear these figures are constructed from two overlapping triangles: the first with 28 and the second with 55 parts.

**The third and fourth star numbers**

FIGURE 12.19

If anyone thinks there exists even the most remote possibility that all this is not God's intricate design, then they should consider the second verse of Genesis:

AND THE SPIRIT OF GOD MOVED UPON THE FACE OF THE WATERS.

| מ ר ח פ ת | א ל ה י ם | ו ר ו ח |
|---|---|---|
| 400 80 8 200 40 | 40 10 5 30 1 | 8 6 200 6 |
| (3) = 728 | (2) = 86 | (1) = 220 |

| ה מ י ם | ע ל פ נ י |
|---|---|
| 40 10 40 5 | 10 50 80 30 70 |
| (5) = 95 | (4) = 240 |

FIGURE 12.20

The gematria sum of the above is profoundly instructive:

(1) + (2) + (3) + (4) + (5) = 1369
= [37] x [37]

This total is not only a multiple of [37], but **[37]** x **[37]**. These factors bear a conspicuous resemblance to our first product, [37] x [73]. The entire passage implies a special relationship among [37], The Holy Word, and The Holy Spirit. On that special relationship rests our faith in the Bible's inerrancy. Every Christian believes God's Spirit gave divine inspiration to the Bible's authors; it was their source of knowledge, their "fountain of wisdom":

$$\text{F O U N T A I N} \quad \text{O F  W I S D O M}$$
$$\begin{array}{cccc} \pi & \eta & \gamma & \eta \end{array} \qquad \begin{array}{cccccc} \sigma & o & \phi & \iota & \alpha & \varsigma \end{array}$$
$$\underset{80\ \ 8\ \ 3\ \ 8}{} \quad + \quad \underset{200\ 70\ 500\ 10\ 1\ 200}{} = 1080$$

And, 1080 is identical to the gematria of "The Holy Spirit" itself (see page 179) — making the connection obvious.

Even before the Creation, the Bible speaks of The Word being present with God. In Genesis, The Word always comes before the world:

*And God said, "Let there be light," and there was light.*

Note the order: Word first, Creation second. The Lord sent The Word to earth to reveal His hidden designs, and it returned when the work was finished. The Word existed before Genesis. John 1:1 declares as much: "In the beginning was the Word."

*Logos* is the Greek word for *word*. Knowing how much importance the Bible places on the *logos*, it should contain wisdom and knowledge from gematria's viewpoint:

$$\text{L O G O S}$$
$$\begin{array}{ccccc} \Lambda & o & \gamma & o & \varsigma \end{array}$$
$$\underset{30\ \ 70\ \ 3\ \ 70\ 200}{} = 373$$

This symmetrical value is arrestingly similar to Genesis 1:1.

Jesus says He is the first and last, the Alpha and Omega. Beyond that, history implies He is like a fish, a being from another world:

$$\text{A L P H A} \quad \text{A N D} \quad \text{O M E G A: T H E} \quad \text{F I S H}$$
$$\begin{array}{cccc} A & \lambda & \theta & \alpha \end{array} \quad \begin{array}{ccc} \kappa & \alpha & \iota \end{array} \quad \begin{array}{ccccc} \Omega & \mu & \epsilon & \gamma & \alpha: \end{array} \quad o \quad \begin{array}{ccccc} I & \chi & \phi & \upsilon & \varsigma \end{array}$$
$$\underset{1\ \ 30\ \ 9\ \ 1}{} + \underset{20\ 1\ 10}{} + \underset{800\ 40\ 5\ 3\ 1}{} + \underset{70}{} + \underset{10\ 600\ 500\ 400\ 200}{} = 2701$$

And we know 2701 = [37] x [73].

As an appropriate end to this section, consider the last deed of
Jesus from the Cross. When Scripture says "He gave up his spirit," this
was a conscious act of His will. Christ died a victor because He had
completed His Father's purpose. Matthew 27:50 describes this last act:
Beneath each (in parenthesis) is its literal translation.

### HE GAVE UP HIS SPIRIT
(released up the spirit)

Α φ η κ ε    τ ο    π ν ε υ μ α
1 500 8 20 5 + 300 70 + 80 50 5 400 40 1 = [37] x 40

Die-hard skeptics should also consider Jesus' second last act on the
Cross: "cried out in a loud voice." Its value is [37] x 71.

Mark 15:37 uses different words to portray Jesus' final act:

### WITH A LOUD CRY, JESUS BREATHED HIS LAST
(Jesus letting out a great voice expired.)

Ι η σ ο υ ς    α φ ε ι ς    φ ω ν η ν
10 8 200 70 400 200 + 1 500 5 10 200 + 500 800 50 8 50

μ ε γ α λ η ν    ε ξ ε π ν ε υ σ ε
+ 40 5 3 1 30 8 50 + 5 60 5 80 50 5 400 200 5 = [37] x 107

The words may be different, but the message is the same.

John 19:30 phrases the Lord's last act as

### HE GAVE UP HIS SPIRIT
(delivered up the spirit)

Π α ρ ε δ ω κ ε    τ ο    π ν ε υ μ α
80 1 100 5 4 800 20 5 + 300 70 + 80 50 5 400 40 1 = 1961

You may have anticipated this final result: 1961 equals [37] x 53.

It is not just the gematria that speaks of the Cube as the image
of what man may know about God. There is a harmony between the
numerical values and the words themselves. Consider. At the instant
when Jesus died, man's sins were forgiven! Christ entered Heaven,
making it possible for us to also enter God's holy presence. Matthew
27:51 proclaims

*At that moment the curtain of the temple*
*was torn in two from top to bottom.*

The drape of the Holy of Holies was ripped away; the Cube was made visible; the knowledge was given; salvation was possible; and the symbolism was perfect.

From the Father's first recorded miracle in Genesis 1:1, to His Son's last act in John 19:30, this magnificent series of Cubes/[37]s radiates like the ascending sun, illuminating everything. The consistency electrifies. It is the force that binds the letters, words, sentences, verses, chapters, and books of the Holy Bible.

It is the image of the Cube,
the form of the Hexagon,
the pattern of the Icon,
the Cube of Truth,
the gematria of the Names,
the Holy of Holies,
the knowable part of God,
the name of the Savior.

Through them and all creation the Lord declares:

*These are My Works and My Designs,*
*what shall compare with them.*

# THE IMAGE OF THE NAMES

Before we look at our Cube of Truth in 4 dimensions, apply the Trinity Function to **Jesus Christ** and examine the results. The reader can also try this rule on other holy names; the results are consistent.

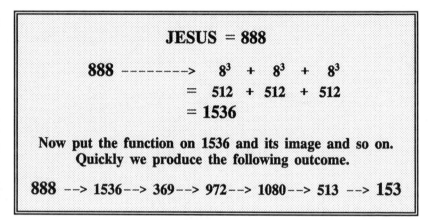

FIGURE 12.21

Therefore, Jesus, the name delivered by the angel Gabriel, is associated with the triangle number 153. Next, let's investigate the other Christian holy name, the one supposedly given by man to God.

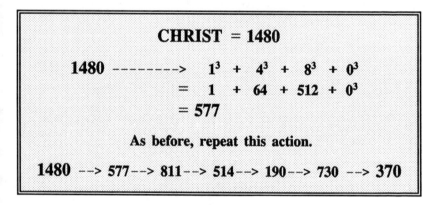

FIGURE 12.22

So 1480 transforms into the terminal number 370, which is [37] amplified. Another application of the Trinity Function leaves 370 totally unchanged. It simply resurrects itself, exactly as Jesus did, and 153 does. Truly, [37] is as mysterious and wonderful as 153.

Summary:
The two most significant names in the universe bond
with the two most meaningful numbers in the Bible.

JESUS ----------> 153
CHRIST ----------> 370

Both Jesus/888 and Christ/1480 complete their
journey through exactly 7 numbers — count them.

This line of reasoning provides a paradise of patterns and proofs on the Bible's divine origin. Use it as a means to convert unbelievers. I find they are unable to account for any of these designs except by a Designer. Their admission provides an excellent opportunity to witness for Christ and spread the "Good News" of His birth, death, and Resurrection. In this way believers can shake slumbering skeptics and scoffers into a new awakening for Jesus.

We have seen the images of our Savior's Holy Names, and we know their meanings. Now return to an earlier discussion for a deeper look into God's knowable and unknowable parts.

The Lord gave Moses the exact specifications for the Tabernacle's every feature, even down to the smallest lampstand. It, and all later temples, maintained the cubical "Sacred Sanctum" right up to the New Jerusalem as the City-Temple-Cube. The keys to understanding the Cube's purpose and imagery were the number [37] and the gematria of "truth" (64 = 4x4x4).

Jesus was and is the Holy of Holies, the Cube of Truth. Stumbling in the darkness of our sin, we cannot comprehend the fullness of the Godhead. But the three visible sides of the Cube symbolize what is shown/known to us:

VISIBLE CUBES = [37]
INVISIBLE CUBES = 27
TOTAL CUBES = 64 = TRUTH

At a deeper level, the hidden Cube $(27 = 3 \times 3 \times 3)$ of The Trinity mystery, is itself composed of two parts. At the back are three unseen sides built from 19 small cubes. In the unknowable center rests a core of 8 cubes. We may see these three hidden sides in Heaven, but the core mystery, the Resurrection Enigma, belongs to God alone.

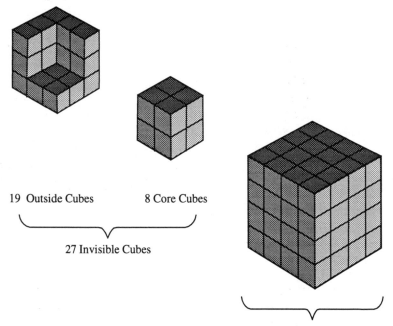

19 Outside Cubes      8 Core Cubes

27 Invisible Cubes

37 Visible Cubes

**An exploded view of
the Cube of Truth's three parts**

FIGURE 12.23

Among these numbers you will recognize our old friends the exact cubes 8, 27, and 64, and their hexagonal outlines 7, 19, and [37].

Like our Father's House, these sacred writings are a mansion with many rooms. We have merely strolled some of its wide halls and peeked into a few of its magnificent chambers. To fallen man, however, the entire structure is forever unknowable.

Fittingly, the third sentence of the Bible, the antechamber to Scripture, is concerned with the third part of The Trinity. Its gematria value, [37] x [37], emphasizes what man may know about God and the source of that knowledge. On Pentecost Day perhaps one of The Holy Spirit's gifts was this science of gematria. It is another language with a profound voice revealing hidden messages confirming our faith and deepening its meaning.

## THE HYPERCUBE

Science cannot physically find God in nature although evidence of His vast designs everywhere abounds. Consequently, we must regard the Lord as a 4-dimensional being transcending our 3-space world.

It may surprise many readers to learn that mathematicians have an excellent understanding of higher dimensions. Their difficulty, and ours, lies in the unalterable fact that no one can "see" beyond 3-space. If an object has fewer dimensions, like 0, 1, or 2, then we can easily visualize it. Higher no, lower yes. Nevertheless, it is possible to get some understanding of the 4th dimension by two uncomplicated approaches:

- Use patterns to build from lower to higher dimensions.
  (points - -> lines - -> squares - -> cubes - -> hypercube)

- Or "unfold" cubes from higher to lower dimensions.
  (hypercube - -> cubes - -> squares - -> lines - -> points)

Consider the first approach:

A line (length) is bounded at each end by 2 points.

A square (area) is bounded on each side by 4 lines.

A cube (volume) is bounded on each face by 6 squares.

By continuing the sequence 2, 4, 6, a hypercube must have 8 cubes. What 8 cubes? The 8 unknowables at the Cube of Truth's core! Notice in FIGURE 12.24 how these 8 cubes surround their central point, in effect, forming its boundary. This setup imitates, *but does not duplicate*, the situation in 4 dimensions. In higher space the 8 cubes form the boundary, not for a point, but of a hyper-volume-cube forever beyond our vision.

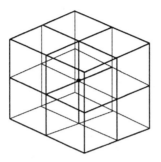

**A view of 8 cubes bounding
their central point**

FIGURE 12.24

Now try the second approach, unfolding. Pretend you are a 1-dimensional creature living in a line, like a railway car on a track. As a "line" being, how can you see a square? The best that can be done is to take the square and by cutting through a corner unfold it into your straight world. So, you would see a square as 4 line segments, like the diagram below.

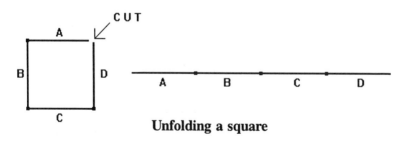

**Unfolding a square**

FIGURE 12.25

Next, imagine that you live in the more interesting world of 2 dimensions, like the surface of a table. The problem now is to visualize a cube resting on this surface. All cubes contain 19 parts: 1 volume, 6 areas, and 12 lengths. Remember, you cannot see out of the table's top; so you perceive only 5 of these pieces — the bottom area and 4 sides. By slicing 7 of its edges (see below) it unfolds into a cross of 6 squares. In the flat world, this is how you would see a cube.

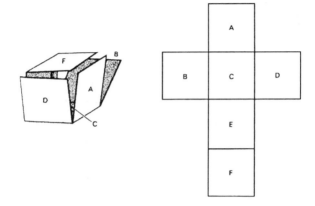

**Unfolding a cube**

FIGURE 12.26

Now we have arrived at our 3-dimensional world, needing to understand something of Jesus' 4-dimensional Cube, the Hypercube. What can we do? Clearly, exactly what was done before. Let's unfold it from 4 dimensions to 3. This is accomplished by slicing off the 8 cubes that surround its single hypervolume. Interestingly, this requires 17 cuts, and the 17th triangle is 153, the Fish Number. This produces a parallel between 17, the number of security, and the Holy Cross, the symbol of security — see the next page.

Conclusions:
- A straight-line creature sees a square as 4 line segments.
- In flatland, a cube is visualized as a cross of 6 squares.
- Similarly, in 3-space we can only perceive Jesus'
  Hypercube as 8 cubes.

Salvador Dali's *Corpus Hypercubus*,
1954, owned by Metropolitan Museum of Art

FIGURE 12.27

The Spanish artist Salvador Dali has magnificently portrayed all this symbolism involving cubes and the 4th dimension in his masterpiece *Corpus Hypercubus* (see facing page). In front of Jesus' body are 4 small cubes implying the 4th dimension. They also represent the nails driven through His hands and feet. Consider, however, the large, ominous cubes forming the Cross itself. How many can you find? Intriguingly, the dark cube at the back adds virtually nothing to the painting's composition, but for one seemingly unimportant point: it brings the total number of cubes to *exactly* 8. Dali knew his mathematics; he also knew his art, but more significantly he understood his religious symbols. The entire painting symbolizes the Resurrection Number 8 as the unfolded Hypercube of Truth.

Dali is the same artist who painted *The Sacrament of the Last Supper* (1955) with all its demonic symbolism. That painting was completed the year after *Corpus Hypercubus* (1954) with all its celestial symbolism. Obviously, sinister changes had taken place in the soul of the Spanish master.

To dramatically emphasize the 4th dimension, Dali has Jesus looking away from His mother and the viewer. The painting implies our Lord longs to leave this world of suffering and corruption to be with His Father in Heaven's higher dimensional universe.

These 8 cubes have 19 parts each: 1 volume, 6 faces, and 12 edges. So, the total number of pieces is 8 x 19 or 152. When these are added to the single hypervolume they surround, we have the complete number of parts in Jesus' Hypercube.

> This is the quantity from John 21:11
> — the 153 Fishes in the Net.

# CHAPTER — 13

# SATANIC CYCLES

*At that time if anyone says to you, "Look, here is the Christ!"*
*or, "There he is!" do not believe it. For false Christs and*
*false prophets will appear and perform great signs and*
*miracles to deceive even the elect — if that were possible.*
Jesus, Matthew 24:23-24

> *As you have heard that the antichrist is coming,*
> *even now many antichrists have come.*
> 1 John 2:18

## HISTORY AND DANIEL'S VISION

B y finding patterns and rhythms in time's passage, man strives to understand the events of the past. We long to give life meaning by discovering cycles and consistency in our lives, in the life of our country, and in the lives of previous civilizations. From Herodotus in the distant past to Arnold Toynbee in our century, all historians have known this to be their major task: find history's design.

Fortunately, this can be accomplished. One of the most striking and regular events in all the recorded past is the persecution of the Jewish People. In the earliest written records, we read of the Egyptians enslaving Jacob's Children. On the nightly TV newscasts, we have seen the former Soviet Union's and Ethiopia's oppression of the Jews and their subsequent exodus to Israel and freedom. Therefore, all attempts to explain history must, at least, account for the phenomenal constancy of Jewish persecution.

Some historians say civilizations are like flowers. They start as seeds; wiggle into small green sprouts; grow to maturity; blossom with religion, culture, and wealth; turn to seed, corrupt, and die. Yet every plant is a host for hordes of hungry parasites that gnaw at the very stalk of its being. Anti-Semitism is one such gluttonous feeder.

As a basis for their designs, secular historians could not do better than to use the Book of Daniel. Truly, this vision of man's future has been confirmed down through 2500 years. King Nebuchadnezzar had a dream, and God gave Daniel an understanding of that dream. It clearly outlined who the future oppressors of the Jews would be, from his day to ours.

In gratitude the prophet gave 15 reasons for praising God (Daniel 2:20-23). Is it just an accident that 15 is a triangle number, or did Daniel expect this number to be pleasing to the Ancient of Days? Can the Bible even have coincidences?

Our Lord has often worked through dreams to communicate with man. More than a thousand years before Daniel, God gave Pharaoh a dream of 7 fat cows and 7 lean cows. And by God's grace, Joseph correctly interpreted this as 7 years of plenty followed by 7 years of famine.

Nebuchadnezzar's dream unfolds as a statue with a golden head and silver shoulders and arms. The belly and thighs are brass, the legs and feet are iron, while the toes are a mixture of iron and clay. The golden head represented the kingdom of Nebuchadnezzar; the silver shoulders and arms, the Medo-Persian nation; and the brass belly and thighs, the empire of Alexander. The 2 legs of iron stood for the eastern and western divisions of the merciless Roman domain. Lastly, the 10 toes of iron and clay depict part of the revised Roman Empire of our day, the European Union.

Abruptly the dream ends with the statue's destruction and the establishment of Jesus' Millennial Reign. Finally, Christ will be King; justice and truth will rule forever. Daniel 2:34-35 tells us:

> *While you were watching, a rock was cut out, but not by human hands. It struck the statue on its feet of iron and clay and smashed them. . . . But the rock that struck the statue became a huge mountain and filled the whole earth.*

Uncut by human hands, this rock symbolizes the Kingdom of Heaven headed by our conquering Lord Jesus Christ. It also represents the Cube of God's holy truth that will become the immense Cube of the New Jerusalem.

The dream and the dreamer in Daniel 7 reveal more details about these empires. Here the prophet pictures the previously mentioned dictatorships as a winged lion, a two-humped bear, a four-headed leopard, and a terrifying and frightening nondescript beast. From this last creature (the Old Roman Empire) will spring the 10 horns or kings of the revised Roman Empire. And out of these will emerge the "little horn," the final Antichrist (Daniel 7:8, 24).

In chapter 8 the visions continue with the Medo-Persians as a two-horned ram and Alexander of Macedonia as a one-horned goat. The truth of these dreams lies in history's complete fulfilment of them. Thus, God granted Daniel man's greatest historical vision.

All these points are summarized in the following chart: "Taken from The NIV Study Bible. Copyright © 1985 by The Zondervan Corporation. Used by permission of Zondervan Publishing House."

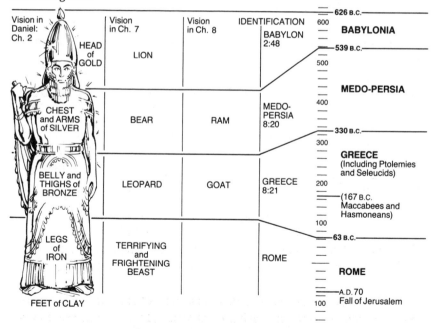

**The Kingdoms of Daniel's Vision**

FIGURE 13.1

Egypt was the first country to oppress the Jews, Assyria the second, while Nebuchadnezzar's kingdom was actually the third. Naturally Daniel did not mention the first two since by his time they were already in the past.

(It is almost necessary to read the Book of Revelation immediately after Daniel because they so strikingly complement each other. For example, John provides intriguing specifics on the empire of the Antichrist, or little horn, written about by the earlier prophet.)

The following is a complete list of the nations under Satan's influence that have — or will — maltreat, molest, and murder the Children of Israel:

1. Egypt
2. Assyria
3. Babylon
4. Medo-Persia
5. Greece
6. Roman Empire
7. The revised Roman Empire
8. The Empire of the Antichrist

My purpose is to investigate the dictators of each empire and to seek patterns in these Satanic Cycles of the past, the present, and the future.

# THE EGYPTIAN KINGDOM OF CHEOPS

Constructed at the dawn of history, the Pyramid of Cheops was more ancient to the Gospel writers than they are to us. Painstakingly cut from over 2½ million rocks weighing from 2 to 70 tons, this immense monument still excites astonishment in modern travelers to that antique land. It was the first and the oldest of the 7 Wonders of the World and the only one surviving today. Although the original cement covering vanished centuries ago, we can still calculate its vast dimensions. Covering 13 acres, it stood on a square base of 762 feet and rose an amazing 484 feet above the surrounding desert. Cheops, founder of the IV Dynasty, built this marvel.

The previous paragraph could have come from the mouth of a tour guide trying to impress and entertain foot-weary travelers. But what does this pyramid really tell us? What would the people of Cheops' day say? What would any of the 100,000 slaves, who labored 20 years in the searing Egyptian sun, say? Well it just so happens that we know the answers to these thought-provoking questions.

Around 450 B.C. the famous Greek historian Herodotus visited the pyramid and wrote about it in his *Persian Wars*. Considered the "Father of History," Herodotus is generally reliable, if too patriotic. Of Cheops he says:

> *Till the death of Rhampsinitus, the priests said,*
> *Egypt was excellently governed, and flourished greatly;*
> *but after him Cheops succeeded to the throne,*
> *and plunged into all manner of wickedness.*[1]

> *The wickedness of Cheops reached to such a pitch that,*
> *when he had spent all his treasures and wanted more,*
> *he sent his daughter to the stews [brothels],*
> *with orders to procure him a certain sum.*[2]

Egyptians so hated Cheops that for thousands of years they used his name as a curse. The great American writer Henry David Thoreau, in his classic novel *Walden*, was equally harsh on the slaves:

> *As for the pyramids, there is nothing to wonder at in them so much as the fact that so many men could be found degraded enough to spend their lives constructing a tomb for some ambitious booby, whom it would have been wiser and manlier to have drowned in the Nile, and then given his body to the dogs.*[3]

Incredibly, after the herculean task of building this stone tomb to vanity and pride, Cheops — in a diabolical twist — had himself buried elsewhere. No one knows where. For his horrific crimes against his people and his family, this Pharaoh has surely earned a high rank in Satan's legions of the damned.

There has been more occult nonsense written about the Great Pyramid then any other single object. A quick run through the New Age section in any secular book store will convince you of this. I promise not to add to this pile.

The founder of the sect called Jehovah's Witnesses, Charles Taze Russell, was deeply involved with pyramid mysticism. The third volume of his series *Studies in the Scripture* is pure pyramidology. Much of this silliness concerned various measurements of the tomb's secret chambers and hallways. It is on such measurements, especially in the Grand Gallery, that he based his fortune-telling. Again and again his dates passed with nothing happening, yet Russell continued to churn out new predictions. Contrast his pitiful prophetic results with those of Holy Scripture! On their door to door rounds, I have found that "Witnesses" are — without exception — totally unaware of their founder's occult fascinations.

The truth is we have no idea how long the basic Egyptian measuring unit was, nor are we ever likely to. Until scholars can decide this, all *ancient* measurements on the pyramid are uncertain. Ratios, however, are a different matter: they do not depend on any unit whatsoever. If one block is twice as high as a second block, you haven't said anything about the actual height of either.

The ancient Egyptian priests revealed to Herodotus that

> *the pyramid was constructed so the area of each triangular face was exactly equal to the area of a square on its height.*[4]

In other words these areas are in the ratio of 1 to 1. FIGURE 13.2 shows the precise implications of this. Interested readers should refer to the Chapter Notes for the mathematical details.

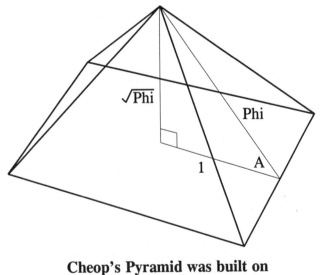

**Cheop's Pyramid was built on
Phi — Satan's signature.**

FIGURE 13.2

As a direct consequence of Herodotus' report, the ratio of the slant height to the vertical height is exactly Phi to $\sqrt{Phi}$. Only this number Phi allows the area of the pyramid's triangular face to equal its height squared. It is intriguing that, despite the actual dimensions, these distances are in this proportion. Also, the Pharaoh designed his tomb chamber and his sarcophagus in the identical ratio.

Angles, like ratios, are also independent of the length of the lines containing them. So, the slant angle A (in the previous diagram) can be found. The result (52 degrees) is in agreement with the real pyramid. From the time of the Middle Ages, these pyramid ratios and angles have been secrets of the Masonic Order.

The Prince of Darkness inspired the builder of the Great Pyramid. The evidence still exists in the ratio of the rocks. For in the pyramid, this most cruel creation, Satan has left his signature: the number of the navel, the ratio in pentagram, the sign of original sin — Phi.

# NIMROD'S ASSYRIAN KINGDOM

*Cush was the father of Nimrod,*
*who grew to be a mighty warrior on the earth.*
Genesis 10:8

*"Come, let us build ourselves a city,*
*with a tower* [of Babel] *that reaches to the heavens,*
*so that we may make a name for ourselves."*
Genesis 11:4

Cush was the offspring of Ham, the son who sinned and Noah cursed. And Cush begat the mighty hunter Nimrod, the first Assyrian conqueror and the founder of Babylon on the Euphrates and Nineveh on the Tigris Rivers.

Before Abraham left Ur of the Chaldees, Jewish literature says Nimrod tried to murder him. Apparently this was to prevent the patriarch from fathering God's Chosen People. If this is true, then the Assyrian king had a foreknowledge of events possible only from a demonic source. Because of this attempt to defy God, the Jews have always referred to the constellation of Nimrod (Orion in Greek) as

"The Fool." This title is appropriate, not only for plotting to kill Abraham, but also for building the Tower of Babel. Job 38:31 has an unusual passage describing Nimrod (Orion) being bound in chains like Satan:

*Can you loose the cords of Orion?*

To the Assyrians he was Tukulti-Ninurta; to the Greeks, Orion; to the Canaanites, Baal-Hadad; but to opponents on the battlefield he was pure terror. His queen was the beautiful Semiramis, famous for her fierce warrior skills, infamous for her incredible sexual lust. Together they produced one son, Ninyas, who inherited his parents' thirst for sacrilege, cruelty, and fornication.

Declaring herself to be the Queen of Heaven, this woman initiated the practice of temple prostitution. She even demanded blood sacrifices. Her personal sexual excesses were so legendary that after her death she became the model for sex goddesses everywhere. She was Ishtar and Astarte in Babylon, Asherah and Ashtoreth in Syria, Aphrodite in Greece, Venus in Rome, and lastly Isis in Egypt: the eternal whore-harlot. She is the true originator of the Mystery Babylon religion. Today, feminists and New Agers are campaigning to revive the worship of the mother-goddess. Following two millenniums of Christianity, she has reawakened from her long sleep like an ancient Rip van Winkle, or so they "claim."

With Nimrod and Ninyas, she formed a mocking, false trinity of father-mother-son. They taught that each was a separate deity but were united in a single godhead. After Nimrod died Semiramis lived another 42 years. Reports say that at her own death she became a dove, and her devotees worshiped her as such. This metamorphosis was one last blasphemy toward God and His Holy Spirit.

Nimrod, by his warrior ethic, established an empire throughout the Middle East. A surviving stone inscription portrays him in battle as:

*The angry and merciless one whose attack is a deluge,*
*the one who overwhelms the enemy.*

The name "Nimrod" originated from the Hebrew root word "to rebel." Furthermore, the gematria of this word supports this derivation because it is directly linked to the arch-rebel's apprentice, the Antichrist:

N I M R O D

נ מ ר ד

294 = 4 200 40 50

And 294 = 42 x 7.

The following passages directly associate 42 with the Beast:

- Daniel 7:25 says: "The saints will be handed over to him [the Antichrist] for a time [1 year], times [2 years] and a half a time [6 months]." This is 3½ years or 42 months.
- Revelation 11:2: "They will trample on the holy city for 42 months." This is ½ of the 7 years of the Great Tribulation.
- Revelation 11:3 speaks of the two witnesses during the Tribulation: "And they will prophesy for 1260 days." Biblical months in the Apocalypse as in Genesis have 30 days, implying 1260 = 42 x 30.
- Revelation 12:6 tells of the woman, a symbol of the believing Messianic community, and how the Lord will prepare a safe place for her away from the Dragon: "Where she might be taken care of for 1260 days."
- Revelation 13:5: "The beast was given . . . authority for 42 months."
- Even the parable of the 42 mocking boys and Elisha associates this number with evil (2 Kings 2:24).

If the connection with the Antichrist is still not clear enough, then consider Revelation 13:11, which speaks of "another beast":

A N O T H E R    B E A S T

α λ λ ο       θ η ρ ι ο ν

1 30 30 70    +    9 8 100 10 70 50 = 378

This equals 42 x 9 or 42 + 42 + . . . + 42.

In the entire Bible, either by itself or in combinations, this number occurs exactly 13 times. Also, 42 equals 6x6+6 — all triangle numbers. Surely Nimrod was another Beast, a False Prophet in his own time and a type of Antichrist in ours.

2 Kings 17:1-6 records the destruction of Samaria (Israel) by the Assyrian king Shalmaneser. His successor, Sargon II, deported all Samaria's leading citizens to the east, beyond the Tigris River — never to be heard of again. This forced emigration resulted in the legends of Israel's Ten Lost Tribes. Sargon's son, Sennacherib, equaled his father in military ferocity. He devastated Judah during the reign of Hezekiah, but his siege on Jerusalem failed because a plague ravaged his troops.

And so it continued! Even after 3000 years, Syria and Iraq — the core of Nimrod's ancient kingdom — still war against Israel. Undeniably, this empire has always been a major enemy of the Jewish people, both then and now. Until finally conquered by Babylon, Assyria held cruel control over vast territory, including most of modern Israel for 666 years.[5]

# BABYLON, NEBUCHADNEZZAR, AND SADDAM HUSSEIN

## BABYLON

*By the rivers of Babylon we sat and wept.*
Psalm 137

On the western banks of the southern Euphrates River lies the land of Chaldea, the area around Babylon. The people of this region dominated the city to such an extent that the words *Chaldean* and *Babylonian* became synonyms.

Chaldeans were renowned magicians, enchanters, sorcerers, and astrologers (see Daniel 2:2). Kings and commoners, presidents and prime ministers consulted them regularly — just like today. So great was their fame and influence that the adjective *Chaldean* came to mean a practitioner of the occult. During Nebuchadnezzar's reign, and with his encouragement, Babylon evolved into the world's capital for black magic, astrology, necromancy, sorcery, and fortune-telling.

Today, the New Age movement is itself enchanted by the occult. For that reason, they are reintroducing many ancient beliefs and practices directly into the 20th century. Of particular interest is a sorcery device called a magic square. Research suggests these originated in Babylon[6] but were exported everywhere. For an example, consider the well-known "Magic Square of the Sun" shown below left.

| 36 | 6 | 21 | 16 | 29 | 3 |
|----|----|----|----|----|----|
| 31 | 1 | 15 | 22 | 34 | 8 |
| 11 | 23 | 19 | 25 | 24 | 9 |
| 26 | 14 | 12 | 18 | 13 | 28 |
| 5 | 35 | 17 | 20 | 4 | 30 |
| 2 | 32 | 27 | 10 | 7 | 33 |

(a)                                    (b)

**The Magic Square of the Sun**

FIGURE 13.3

This arrangement of the numbers 1 to 36 has extraordinary properties. The reader may wish to use a calculator to confirm the following results. This list is not exhaustive:

- The total of every column is 111 or [37] + [37] + [37].
- The total of every row is 111 or [37] + [37] + [37].
- The total of every diagonal is 111 or [37] + [37] + [37].
- The sum of any symmetrically placed group of four numbers is 74 or [37] + [37] (e.g., the four corners).
- The double headed arrows in FIGURE 13.3 (b) show 18 (= 6+6+6) pairs, each with a sum of [37].
- The total of all the numbers around the outside is exactly 370/Christ.
- The sum of all the numbers in this 6 x 6 magic square is 666/Antichrist, or [37] x 18.

Why all the [37]s?

In the previous chapter, we discovered how and why the Bible built the holy names *Jesus* and *Christ* on the prime number [37].

This quantity is the main structural element in God's Holy Word. By reviving the Magic Square of the Sun, New Agers and occultists are trying to tap into God's immense power of The Holy Word. Anthropologists call this "imitative magic": a belief that like affects like, a common satanic practice. It is an attempt to gain power — despite the participants' ignorance of most of the number patterns or their biblical meanings. The last two totals listed on the previous page (i.e., 370 and 666) even try to connect *Christ* with *Antichrist*.

## NEBUCHADNEZZAR

*Nebuchadnezzar was king of the Jews. Spell*
*that in four letters and I'll give you my shoes.*
Old children's riddle-rhyme

Nebuchadnezzar, Lord of the Enemy, King of Babylon (606-562 B.C.), was perhaps the most formidable opponent ever to confront the Jewish Nation. At first he merely robbed their houses, plundered their Temple, and exiled their leading citizens. In the end he burned their homes, imprisoned their king, tore down Jerusalem's walls, and demolished her Temple.

His military career was as brilliant and brutal as his kingdoms were vast and rich. Like Cheops, he built one of the 7 Wonders of the World, the famous Hanging Gardens of Babylon. In destructive moments of anger or whimsy, he could put thousands to death by a wave of his hand. Truly, the Lord of the Enemy held everyone in his unyielding grasp. Modern Iraq's heartland is ancient Chaldea; it still wars with Israel.

How do we know this tyrant was an Antichrist — one of those whom 1 John 2:18 mentioned had already come? The evidence from Holy Scripture is clear on this point. Daniel 3:1 speaks of an image Nebuchadnezzar built to himself.

*King Nebuchadnezzar made an image of gold,*
*60 cubits high and 6 cubits wide, and set it up*
*on the plain of Dura in the province of Babylon.*

And when **6** specified musical instruments were playing, *everyone* had to worship his statue; refusal meant death. By commanding his subjects to bow to his image, Nebuchadnezzar paralleled the prophesied actions of the final Antichrist in the rebuilt Temple.

Also, judge the following. The Babylonian "golden head" toppled just twenty-four years after the death of Nebuchadnezzar. Then the Medo-Persian "silver chest and arms" took command. King Cyrus, when his victory was complete, issued a famous decree permitting the Jews to return home and rebuild God's Temple. On this dramatically high point, 2 Chronicles ends. The following book, Ezra, provides a long, detailed list of the returning exiles' family names and numbers. The 13th verse (KJV) of the second chapter is acutely striking and revealing:

> *The children of Adonikam,* [were] *666.*

The number is surprising enough, but beyond that, the name *Adonikam* in Hebrew means *Lord of the Enemy — Nebuchadnezzar.*

## SADDAM HUSSEIN

Contemporary events in the Middle East, particularly in Iraq, are simply a continuation of Daniel's ancient prophecies. Yet, Saddam Hussein is not the final Antichrist; he is just a forerunner of the future. Think how horribly different the outcome of the Gulf War might have been. Imagine if Saddam had produced a working nuclear weapon!

The media coverage of his deceitful personality, murderous behavior, and criminal past has been exhaustive. Hordes of reporters have filed thousands of stories for hundreds of radio stations, TV programs, and newspapers. What else can possibly be said about this man? Still, almost everyone has ignored one element of the entire picture — a key piece of Saddam's vision. This is why the essence of his insane plan for the future is still generally unknown in America. I don't for a moment think this is intentional on anyone's part. An architect sees only buildings; a dentist finds only teeth; the pessimist sees only the half-empty glass. Trained reporters view the world through prescribed *secular* glasses.

Briefly put, Saddam Hussein quite literally imagines himself to be the modern successor of Nebuchadnezzar, perhaps even his reincarnation. This implies his ambition is to conquer the entire Middle East, including Kuwait, Saudi Arabia, Syria, western Iran, parts of Turkey, Jordan, Lebanon, and, most important, all of Israel.

During his bloody and costly war with Iran — even at the height of the fighting — Hussein was spending millions on rebuilding ancient Babylon. Why? Because that city, when Nebuchadnezzar was king, conquered the Jews and most of the Middle East. To date, he has finished the notorious temple of Ishtar (the goddess of fertility) and the five hundred room palace of Nebuchadnezzar. *Saddam*, which means the *one who confronts* or *rebels*, pictures himself as the modern counterpart to this ancient tyrant.

An insightful (but rare) report in the *New York Times International* by John Burns made the connection. This conversation was with the chief archaeologist at the Babylonian restoration site:

> *When Mrs. Jaafar, the archaeologist, was asked if Iraqis*
> *considered Mr. Hussein to be "the new Nebuchadnezzar,"*
> *she laughed and replied, "Yes, of course!" Among Arabs,*
> *King Nebuchadnezzar is remembered as much as anything*
> *for the fact that he three times conquered Jerusalem,*
> *carrying tens of thousands of Jews back to Babylon.*[7]

Seven years to the day after his war with Iran began, which Hussein started, Iraq staged the first "Babylon International Festival." Its official theme was "From Nebuchadnezzar to Saddam Hussein, Babylon Undergoes a Renaissance." Part of the advertising for this event was the figure on the next page. The artist has stressed the dictators' facial similarities by the placement of their profiles and the drawing itself.

What does all this mean for us? Nothing, except only by knowing how a dictator views the past, and sees himself with respect to that past, can we predict his future actions. Whatever happens to this man, that area of the world is not through with his kind. Daniel 8:23 and 11:3 imply the final Antichrist may come from the Iraq-Syria region. Perhaps the next few years will reveal that Syria's president Hafez Assad is even more diabolical than Iraq's Saddam Hussein.

**The poster for the Babylon International Festival**

FIGURE 13.4

# THE MEDO-PERSIANS
## OF
# THE FOURTH KINGDOM

Like a hurricane, the Persians stormed out of the east into the land of Chaldea. From this whirlwind of war emerged Cyrus, a new conqueror sweeping away the old Babylonian Empire. Unexpectedly, a kind and generous attitude toward the Jewish people also arose out of this chaos. Not only were the Jews allowed to trek home and rebuild their Temple, but Cyrus restored its sacred articles (Ezra 1:8-11). Significantly, however, Ezra lists neither the Ark of the Covenant nor the Cherubim among the returned items.

Isaiah 44:28 describes Cyrus in glowing phrases:

*Who says of Cyrus, "He is my shepherd and will accomplish all that I please; he will say of Jerusalem, 'Let it be rebuilt,' and of the temple, 'Let its foundations be laid.' "*

The prophet's praise soars to great heights in the verse following:

*"This is what the Lord says to his anointed, to Cyrus, whose right hand I take hold of to subdue nations before him."*

This king was a midwife to the rebirth of the Jewish state and her religious life. Without Cyrus — under God's influence — the resurrection of Israel would never have occurred. Instead of being the main theme God intended, the Jews would have faded into history's mists as a mere footnote, like the Ten Lost Tribes.

There have been many Cyruses, but history calls only this one "King." The gematria of his name is composed entirely of 8s, the number of rebirth and renewal:

$$\text{K I N G} \quad \text{C Y R U S}$$
$$\text{ך ל מ} \qquad \text{ש ר ו כ}$$

$$1096 = \underset{500 \ 30 \ 40}{} + \underset{300 \ 200 \ 6 \ 20}{}$$

$$1096 = 8 \times 137$$
$$= 8 + 8 + \ldots + 8$$

Applying the Trinity Function to this name/number reveals the following:

$$1096 \dashrightarrow \quad 1^3 \; + \; 0^3 \; + \; 9^3 \; + \; 6^3$$
$$= 1\text{x}1\text{x}1 + 0\text{x}0\text{x}0 + 9\text{x}9\text{x}9 + 6\text{x}6\text{x}6$$
$$= \quad 1 \quad + \quad 0 \quad + \quad 729 \quad + \quad 216$$
$$= 946$$

By using the Trinity Rule on 946 and so on, we uncover a notable final image:

$$1096 \; \dashrightarrow 946 \dashrightarrow 1009 \dashrightarrow 730 \dashrightarrow \; 370$$

As a result, the king's number is the pre-image of 370 or [37], the building block of our Lord's Holy Word and the Cube's image. Figuratively, in this historical instance, King Cyrus/[37] is the building block of the Jewish nation and her Temple.

The Jews' 70-year Babylonian exile was God's punishment for their apostasy and sinfulness in the centuries after Solomon. When the 70 years had passed, our Lord again protected them. God did this by softening Cyrus' heart and that of later Persian kings regarding the Jews. The true successor to Cyrus was Darius the Mede. His son Xerxes, called Ahasuerus in the KJV, figures largely in the Book of Esther. And this last monarch's son, Artaxerxes, like all the Persian kings, strongly favored Israel.

Still, these kings had no such generous attitude toward their empire's other ethnic minorities. After he had captured Babylon, even Cyrus — the great liberator — impaled 5000 of its citizens on spears. Cruel, primitive religions and superstitions dominated their daily lives and activities. Herodotus in his *Persian Wars* tells how Xerxes once had a river god whipped for destroying a bridge:

> *So when Xerxes heard of it, he was full of wrath, and straight-way gave orders the Hellespont should receive 300 lashes.*[8]

Only the Lord's protection saved the Jews from the terror of these tyrants and provided for them alone a "kinder and gentler world." Yet, during the time of the Persians, by no means were Satan and his servants absent. Nor did they rest from trying to destroy the Jewish nation. Daniel 10:13 confirms this with a very unusual glimpse into the spirit world:

> *But the prince* [evil spirit] *of the Persian kingdom resisted me*
> *21 days. Then Michael, one of the chief princes* [archangels],
> *came to help me* [Gabriel] *because I was detained there with*
> *the kings of Persia.*

To mock God's design in His Word and Works, the evil spirit withstood Gabriel exactly 21 days — the 6th triangle number. This passage also clearly implies our Lord influenced the kings of Persia through His archangels: surely to the benefit of His Chosen People. Gabriel explicitly declares this support in Daniel 11:1.

The Book of Esther illustrates the preceding point. This story involves not only the heroine but also the Persian king, Xerxes; Esther's cousin and guardian, Mordecai; Haman the Agagite, and his wife, Zeresh. Let's consider Xerxes' first minister Haman, also known as "the enemy of the Jews." In the entire bible, only this phrase is applied to that man.

Mordecai would not bow to anyone but God, least of all the first minister. Because of this, Haman developed an irrational hatred for all Jews. His hatred grew into such monstrous anti-Semitism that he resolved to destroy the entire Jewish race. To gain permission for this genocide, he deceived Xerxes by telling him the Jews refused to obey the king's laws.

By using the pur (casting lots or finding horoscopes, see Esther 3:7) Haman claimed to have discovered the "most favorable day" for exterminating all the Jews. Esther 3:7, 12 tells us this was found 13 months and 13 days after they began casting the pur. Even the orders to do this genocide were written on the 13th day of the month (Esther 3:12). And the act itself was to be committed on the 13th day of the twelfth month, after the order went out to all the provinces (Esther 3:13):

> *Dispatches were sent by couriers to all the king's provinces*
> *with the order to destroy, kill and annihilate all the Jews —*
> *young and old, women and little children — on a single day*
> *the 13th day.*

This attempted holocaust is just one of many in the history books. Over two millenniums later, Adolf Hitler gave nearly identical orders.

Had Haman succeeded in his schemes, Satan would have gained his ultimate objective against God's People and forever changed the course of history. Our Lord would not allow this. The Bible records how He simply used Esther to change the mind of Xerxes. To the present time, Jews still fast on the 13th of Adar, Haman's "most favorable day." On the following day, they celebrate their deliverance by the Festival of Purim.

All the direct enemies of God, associates of Satan, and apostate rebels have biblical names that are multiples of 13 (see Chapter 9: Satanic Symbols). The gematria values of "Haman the Agagite" and his equally involved wife, "Zeresh," (5:14) harmonize perfectly with these previous results:

$$H \; A \; M \; A \; N \quad \text{the} \; A \; G \; A \; G \; I \; T \; E$$

$$ן \; מ \; ה \qquad \qquad י \; ג \; ג \; א \; ה$$

$$767 = \underset{700}{\;} \; \underset{40}{\;} \; \underset{5}{\;} \quad + \quad \underset{10}{\;} \; \underset{3}{\;} \; \underset{3}{\;} \; \underset{1}{\;} \; \underset{5}{\;}$$

$$767 = 13 \times 59$$
$$= 13 + 13 + \ldots + 13$$

$$Z \; E \; R \; E \; S \; H$$

$$ז \; ר \; שׁ$$

$$507 = \underset{300}{\;} \; \underset{200}{\;} \; \underset{7}{\;}$$

$$507 = 13 \times 39$$
$$= 13 + 13 + \ldots + 13$$

Nor are these all the 13s in this family. Consider, the names of Haman's ten sons given in Esther 9:7-9. Every original Hebrew text pointedly lists the sons' names in a vertical column, implying their gematrias are to be added. Their sum[9] is 13 x 788. Of course, this further implies the aggregate total of the entire family (father, mother, and sons) is a multiple of 13 — the Number of Rebellion.

The King James translators recognized additional pages to Esther called "The Rest of Esther." These extra chapters are normally placed in the Apocrypha, except Catholic-English versions, which put them as a supplement after Revelation.

One oddity in these extra chapters is an unusual description of Haman:

> *For Haman, a Macedonian . . .*
> *a stranger from the Persian blood.*
> Esther 16:10

Macedonia is the largest region of northern Greece and probably the homeland of Haman's mother. However that may be, it was the birthplace of Alexander the Great, the emperor of the next kingdom.

# ALEXANDER OF MACEDONIA AND THE FIFTH KINGDOM

> *Soon I* [Gabriel] *will return to fight against the prince of Persia and when I go, the prince* [fallen angel] *of Greece will come;*
> Daniel 10:20

> *The two-horned ram that you saw represents the kings of Media and Persia. The shaggy goat is the king of Greece, and the large horn between his eyes is the first king* [Alexander].
> Daniel 8:20-21

What Alexander of Macedonia could not accomplish with brute force and terror, Jesus of Nazareth will do with love and kindness: conquer the world.

In matters concerning only the Jews, Satan had no final influence over the minds and hearts of the Persian kings. So, in what must have been frustrated rage, the Devil resolved to destroy Israel from without. Satan acts through men, and this time he chose well.

No conqueror ever subdued so much territory, so quickly, so brilliantly, or so thoroughly as Alexander. Always outnumbered, sometimes 20 to 1, yet he never lost a single battle. His entire force consisted of 5000 cavalry and 30,000 infantry. Darius III, his Persian opponent, could probably have mustered ten times as many horsemen and a hundred times as many troops. At the battle of Issus (333 B.C.), the Persians had somewhere between 300,000 and 600,000 soldiers.

Nevertheless, in one of history's most incredible encounters, the vastly outnumbered Macedonians ravaged the entire Persian army. They even captured the king's family: mother, wife, sons, and daughters.

Secular historians cannot truly account for Alexander's unequaled success, but from a Christian perspective his career is easily explained. For a deep understanding of his triumphs, the opening quotation from Daniel 10:20 delivers the key. When the Bible talks about the "princes of this world," it means Lucifer and his legions of fallen angels. This passage clearly implies that Greece, and therefore Alexander, had the help of a fallen angel, perhaps even Satan himself.

Between the life of Alexander and the final Antichrist, the parallels are astonishing: two men of infamy, one that was and one that will be. The following list of comparisons clearly establishes that parallel.

- The number 13 swirls around Alexander's life and his every activity. His conquests took place in the short span of precisely 13 years. Even his magnificent stallion Bucephalas, which no one else could ride, cost 13 gold talents (coins). Astride this great beast Alexander won all his major battles:

$$\begin{array}{ccccccccc}
B & U & C & E & P & H & A & L & A & S \\
B & o & \upsilon & \kappa & \epsilon & \phi & \alpha & \lambda & \alpha & \nu \\
2 & 70 & 400 & 20 & 5 & 500 & 1 & 30 & 1 & 50 & = 1079
\end{array}$$

$$1079 = 13 \times 83$$
$$= 13 + 13 + \ldots + 13$$

Perhaps one could argue that the 13s in the famous horse's name, like his price, are coincidences. Although, I doubt that the price of any other horse from the ancient world is known. This is a very curious event.

- The preceding could be accidental since it was the work of man; in any case, the following is not. You may recall the detailed list (pages 130-134) of associations between the Devil's many names and the False Trinity Number, 13. Remarkably, the gematria of "Antichrists" again confirms that the Bible uses this quantity, but this time it's for the Beasts in Satan's service:

### A N T I C H R I S T S

Α ν τ ι χ ρ ι σ τ ο ι

1  50 300 10 600 100  10 200 300 70 10  = 1651

$$1651 = 13 \times 127$$
$$= 13 + 13 + \ldots + 13$$

So strong is the relationship between the numbers 13 and 1651 that even the digital root of 1651 (=1+6+5+1) is 13.

- Olympias, Alexander's wild and beautiful mother, was fond of sex orgies, revengeful murder, and snake handling. In her bed she kept a large pet serpent, which undoubtedly must have kept her bewildered husband Philip out. In Book 12 of his *Philippic Histories*, the historian Pompeius Trogus (5th century A.D.) records the intriguing story of Alexander's conception. By Trogus' account, it occurred when Olympias had sexual intercourse with the god Ammon-Ra (Satan) in the form of a great snake.

- In what seems a mockery of Jesus' love for His mother, Mary, Alexander worshiped his mother, Olympias. He even elevated her to the level of a goddess. On one occasion, mother and son endured exile together to protest Philip's (his father's) marriage to a younger woman. When the king's passion and interest in his young bride faded, Olympias had her and her child murdered. Note:

### O L Y M P I A S

Ο λ υ μ π ι α ς

70 30 400 40 80 10 1  6  = 637

$$637 = 13 \times 49$$
$$= 13 + 13 + \ldots + 13$$

Interestingly, "Philip" (Φιλιππος) equals 786, and this *is not* a multiple of 13.

- Alexander's sexual perversions were legendary, his drunkenness longstanding, and his homosexuality concealed behind three political marriages. For his male lover Hephaestion, who died in a drunken stupor, he built an enormous shrine in Babylon.

- The Macedonia's cruelty was outstanding even for that time. Try to imagine the intense terror of the inhabitants in his captured cities. He slaughtered all the males of Tyre (northwest of Jerusalem) and sold their wives, daughters, and children into slavery — 30,000 souls. Earlier he had done the same for Thebes in Greece, and later he would do even worse for Gaza in Judea. When Alexander dedicated Hephaestion's shrine in Babylon, his butchers sacrificed an incredible 10,000 victims[10].

- During his lifetime, Alexander consciously tried to imitate the deeds of the previous Antichrists: Cheops, Nimrod-Semiramis, and Nebuchadnezzar. He even had plans to build a colossal pyramid[11] in Greece of identical size, ratio, and design as Cheops' in Egypt. Also, in a totally unnecessary act of competition with the Semiramis' feats, he disastrously drove his troops across the Gedrosian desert of southern Pakistan. By this one act of vanity, he lost more men than in any single battle. In Babylon, he enlarged the temple of Marduk and rebuilt the ziggurat in the city's center (Nimrod's Tower of Babel). And Like Saddam Hussein, he repaired Nebuchadnezzar's palace — it was to be his empire's capital.

- According to his ancient Greek biographer Arrian, Alexander had a nonrational longing for the unknown and mysterious. Clearly he was an avid lover of the occult in all its forms. To forecast events he kept dozens of soothsayers and seers in his court and camp and was forever sacrificing to pagan gods.

- In parody of our Lord's Resurrection, Satan will cause the last Antichrist (Revelation 13:3) to suffer a deadly wound but still recover. Similarly Alexander, in the Indian city of Malli, had an arrow pierce right through his lung[12]. Nonetheless, he miraculously avoided death from bleeding, infection, or vital organ collapse. The very fact he even lived, not to mention his speedy recovery, brought wonderment to his troops and terror to his enemies.

- In the last 3½ years of the Great Tribulation, the final Beast will declare himself to be a god and set up his image in Jerusalem's rebuilt Temple (2 Thessalonians 2:4).

Analogously, at the oracle and temple in Siwah[13] Egypt Alexander declared himself to be the son of Ammon-Ra (Satan). To the Greeks he actually issued an edict[14] demanding they place his statue in their temples and worship him as a god. In addition, he instituted the practice whereby everyone in his "divine" presence had to fall on their face until acknowledged.

(Very recent archaeological evidence indicates Alexander was buried at Siwah. Considering the great importance he attached to his role as the son of Ammon-Ra, this is not totally unexpected.)

- Consider Alexander's image on Greek coinage circulating at that time.

Coin with Alexander's head showing the horn of Ammon-Ra (Satan) from the ancient mint at Pergamum. The totem of this Egyptian god was a goat — the image in Daniel's dream.

Alexander reversed the Persian policy of hoarding gold in the imperial treasuries. Instead, he had it minted and spent on grandiose projects and megalomaniac schemes. Of course his image graced the front of the coin. Often the back was stamped with Satan's pentagram and by implication Phi, the second member of the unholy number trinity. By doing this, everyone would bear *in* — but not yet *on* — their hand the mark of the Beast.

Because the Macedonian's birth was occasioned by three victories for his father Philip[15], Greek prophets said the newborn child would be invincible. In battle he was; in life he was not. At the same age as Jesus conquered death, death conquered Alexander with a strange suddenness. He died in the Babylonian palace of the former Antichrist, Nebuchadnezzar; some say even in the same room.

This is the multi-chambered edifice Saddam Hussein has recently reconstructed. Archaeologists believe the building itself was the site of the Hanging Gardens of Babylon.

The abruptness of Alexander's death at age 33 ended all his fabulous plans for capturing Arabia, Spain, Italy, France, and North Africa. Had he lived and subdued these countries, the Roman Empire could not have existed. If that had happened, many biblical prophecies would have been lies. This, our Lord would not allow.

During his 13-year rampage across the known world, Alexander did not have the least doubt concerning his own abilities or destiny. Flavius Josephus, the eminent Jewish historian, writes knowingly about the Macedonian in his *Antiquities of the Jews*:

*And when the book of Daniel was shewed him* [Alexander], *wherein Daniel declared that one of the Greeks should destroy the empire of the Persians, he supposed that himself was the person intended.*[16]

Once, someone asked Alexander to whom he would leave his empire; he replied "to the strongest." Again Daniel (7:6) — centuries earlier — knew the correct answer:

*After that, I looked, and there before me was another beast, one that looked like a leopard. And on its back it had four wings like those of a bird. This beast had four heads, and it was given authority to rule.*

The swift, merciless leopard stands for Alexander; the four heads symbolize his successors.

Daniel 8:8 has a similar vision:

*The goat* [Alexander with the horn] *became very great, but at the height of his power his large horn was broken off* [his sudden death], *and in its place four prominent horns grew up toward the four winds of heaven.*

After Alexander's death his generals quarreled and fought like starving wolves over his kingdom's carcass. Antipater took Greece to the west; Lysimachus captured Turkey and Thrace in the north. Alexander's boyhood friend Ptolemy subdued Egypt to the south, but Seleucus grabbed the largest share to the east. Just as Daniel had prophesied, they divided the Macedonian's empire toward the four winds of heaven.

It only remains for us "to count the number of the beast" by the wonderfully revealing method of gematria. When we analyze the full and proper name of this dictator, his lineage is clear:

---

**A L E X A N D E R      O F      M A C E D O N I A**
Αλεξανδρος    των    Μακεδονια
1 30 5 60 1 50 4 100 70 200 **+** 300 800 50 **+** 40 1 20 5 4 70 50 10 1 $= 1872$

Strikingly, $1872 = 13 \times 144$
$= 13 + 13 + \ldots + 13.$

Besides 13, the number of rebellion, 144 equals 12 x 12, the number of the chosen and governmental authority.

---

FIGURE 13.5

The associations of 12 with governmental power and authority are the very stamp of Alexander's reign, as 13 is of his character. Undeniably, Satan and his minions chose and assisted the Macedonian into a unique place in history as the Master of the Fifth Kingdom.

For us the importance of Alexander lies not in his deeds, but as another dress rehearsal for the ultimate Antichrist. Such are the close parallels between these two that even the birthplace of the final Beast will be one of the Grecian Empire's four divisions (Daniel 8:8-9). Still, Alexander's acts of terror will be like a stroll in the gentle light of dawn compared to the black midnight ramble of the final Antichrist.

The modern Spanish-American philosopher George Santayana once said:

*Those who don't know history are bound to repeat it.*

Daniel would have said:

*Those who understand history know it is bound to repeat.*

# THE CAESARS OF
# THE SIXTH KINGDOM

*After that, in my vision at night I looked, and there before me*
*was a fourth beast* [since Daniel] — *terrifying and frightening*
*and very powerful. It had large iron teeth; it crushed and*
*devoured its victims and trampled underfoot whatever was left.*
Daniel 7:7

## NERO CAESAR

In 37 A.D., out of the dank cellars and sewers of mankind crawled one of history's most loathsome creatures, Nero Caesar. Born to privilege and power, he ascended to the full emperor's throne at just eighteen. From then to his early thirties, he left an unequaled trail of lust and brutality. To his stepbrother Britannicus he was treacherous; to his wife Octavia, unfaithful; with his mother Agrippina, incestuous. Afterward, he had all three poisoned or butchered. Poppaea, his second wife, died while pregnant from a kick to her womb, most probably delivered by Nero. After this he married — in a full formal ceremony — a young boy named Sporus whom he castrated. He obeyed neither the laws of man nor God. Finally, with everyone sickened by his cruelty and debauchery, the army forced him to commit suicide.

Ancient historians unanimously declared Nero responsible for the great fire that ravaged Rome for 9 days in July 64: fire is Satan's destructive element. But the legends of Nero "fiddling while Rome burned" are clearly false since the violin hadn't been invented yet. Curiously though, in modern folklore, the fiddle is the Devil's own instrument. Nero dreamed of rebuilding Rome, of being its second founder, even of renaming it Neropolis. His conceit was limitless.

However, Satan's real purpose with his servant Nero Caesar lay in Rome's slums with a small obscure religion. The authorities tortured the poor wretches of this group to take complete responsibility for starting the many fires that consumed the great city. So, they provided the emperor with very convenient scapegoats. The Devil's designs and Nero's schemes meshed perfectly.

Throughout these tragic times lived Rome's most celebrated historian, Tacitus. In his *Annals of Imperial Rome* he diligently recorded the scapegoats' fate. His writings, although generally reliable, give a very distorted view of early Christians:

> *To suppress this rumour* [that he started the fire], *Nero fabricated scapegoats — and punished with every refinement the notoriously depraved Christians (as they were popularly called). Their originator, Christ, had been executed in Tiberius' reign by the governor of Judaea, Pontius Pilatus. But in spite of this temporary setback the deadly superstition had broken out afresh, not only in Judaea (where the mischief had started) but even in Rome. All degraded and shameful practices collect and flourish in the capital.*

(Yet, happily, these "notoriously depraved Christians" are still growing in number, and shortly they may reach every home on the entire globe.)

Tacitus continues:

> *First Nero had self-acknowledged Christians arrested. Then on their information, large numbers of others were condemned — not so much for incendiarism as for their antisocial tendencies. Their deaths were made farcical. Dressed in wild animals' skins, they were torn to pieces by dogs, or crucified, or made into torches to be ignited after dark as substitutes for daylight Nero provided his Gardens for the spectacle, and exhibited displays in the Circus, at which he mingled with the crowd — or stood in a chariot, dressed as a charioteer. Despite their guilt as Christians, and the ruthless punishment it deserved, the victims were pitied. For it was felt that they were being sacrificed to one man's brutality not the national interest.*[17]

Tradition says, and we have no reason to doubt it, that Saint Paul and Saint Peter both died during these horrific events.

Up to this point we have looked at the compelling historical evidence for Nero Caesar as an Antichrist. Recall that his gematria in both biblical languages decisively confirms this. First, reconsider his common name in Hebrew:

FIGURE 13.6

Secondly, the effect in Greek is equally strong:

NERO        CAESAR
Ν ε ρ ω ν        Κ α ε σ α ρ
50 5 100 800 50   +   20 1 5 200 1 100   =   1332

Earlier we saw that 1332 = 666 x 2
                           = 666 + 666.

FIGURE 13.7

As a result, in either biblical language, "Nero Caesar" was an Antichrist. By his deeds or by his gematria, he was possibly the most abominable Beast in human history.

The False Trinity Number, 13, is also intimately interwoven with the life and death of Nero. Tacitus unknowingly wrote about this when he described the Roman court intrigues after the poisoning of Claudius, Nero's predecessor:

*Moreover, the appropriate steps were being taken to secure Nero's accession. . . . Agrippina [Nero's mother] issued frequent encouraging announcements about the emperor's health [Claudius was already dead; she was stalling for time], to maintain the army's morale and await the propitious moment forecast by the astrologers.*

*At last on midday on October 13, the palace gates were suddenly thrown open. . . . he was hailed as emperor.*[18]

Coincidentally, the birth-*day* of this Beast was the 15th, just two days away. Why not wait for this perfect time? Obviously, for Nero, there was something irresistible and compelling about the 13th. As was his reign's beginning, so was its end decided by the False Trinity Number. According to Josephus, a contemporary of these events, Nero Caesar ruled for 13 years[19], the same period as Alexander.

By demanding worship as a god, Nero matched the careers of the preceding Antichrists. At the entrance to his temple, he had the finest Greek sculptors chisel a colossal 120 foot statue of beautiful features and form — of himself. Actually, at twenty-five he was a degenerate with a swollen stomach, weak and slender limbs, fat face, blotched skin, curly yellow hair, and dull gray eyes. Even the officially minted coins of the day could not hide his true features:

Note his puffy face and the undeserved title "Augustus" on the coin's right side. Observe also that every "U" was written as a "V."

As a youth, Nero gave no hint of his later character; rather, much the opposite was shown. The Roman philosopher Seneca tutored him in the milder aspects of Roman life and culture. Everyone expected a second Augustus (the stepfather of the Caesar to whom Jesus referred); instead they got a new Beast. Significantly, Nero's original name, Lucius Domitius, has no numerical importance whatsoever, whether in Hebrew, Greek, or Latin. But, when he as emperor adopted his new name — whose number is 666 — Satan entered into him and ruled the world for 13 years.

## CAESAR AND CHRIST

*Finally, there will be a fourth kingdom* [since Daniel], *strong as iron — for iron breaks and smashes everything — and as iron breaks things to pieces, so it will crush and break all the others.*
Daniel 2:40

If we identify Nero as the *only* Antichrist John meant in Revelation 13:18, then we have a serious problem with the time involved. Nero was forced to suicide in 68 A.D., but John wrote the last book of the Bible in 96 A.D. — 28 years later. So, it is not possible the author was implying only this emperor: he was writing for all times in human history. This is abundantly clear from Revelation 17:8:

> *The inhabitants of the earth . . . will be astonished when they see the beast, because he once was, now is not, and yet will come.*

Plainly, many Beasts have occurred in the past, and at least one more will crawl to the surface in the future.

Various ancient peoples used the notorious "number of the beast" centuries before Saint John. In his age and before, it was the secret symbol of the ancient pagan mystery religions connected with Devil worship. Today it's the hidden link between those ancient rites and the New Age movement. New Agers believe 666 is a holy number and a commanding symbol of man's ascendance to godhood.

The secret symbol of the old religious mysteries consisted of the three letters "SSS" ("ςςς" in Greek). Since the Greeks used their peculiar form of the letter "S" for 6, the symbol was really three 6s or 666. Recall (page 49) that $\alpha = 1$, $\beta = 2$, $\gamma = 3$, $\delta = 4$, $\epsilon = 5$. However, when it came to 6, this alphabetical numbering was broken by introducing a different letter. They should have picked the 6th, zeta (ζ), not their odd "ς" called stigma. Beyond this, there are further complications. This character "ς" was normally used for 200 when it appeared last in a word, and then the Greeks call it sigma.

A "stigma" was also a mark, especially one made by a brand. Often owners burned it on their cattle or slaves, and generals stamped it on their soldiers. Some religious zealots would brand themselves to symbolize they belonged to their gods. The Greeks came to use it for scars, and the Apostle Paul used it for his. These, Paul regarded as medals of his sufferings: the marks he carried on his body as Christ's witness, the One to whom he belonged (Galatians 6:17).

Earlier than any other society, the Egyptians adopted SSS as their religious symbol for the mother-goddess, Isis. Throughout the Roman empire she was the sovereign of sexuality, under names like Ishtar, Aphrodite, and Venus. By having sexual intercourse with priestess-prostitutes, followers imagined they were communicating directly with Isis. Devotees praised and revered her as the triple harlot, a reference to SSS and the body's three openings for sexual practices: oral, anal, vaginal.

The images of Egyptian gods were composites of humans and animals. Artists generally depicted Isis' son, Ammon-Ra, with a human torso and a goat's head. Millions worshiped him as such and as the Great Serpent of the Underworld. Alexander of Macedonia proclaimed himself to be the son of Ammon-Ra. By this one act, he declared his submission to Satan and his close connection with the family symbol SSS (666).

Goddess worship also surrounded ancient Israel and, on occasion, infected Jerusalem. Despite all his renowned wisdom, Solomon in old age was a tragic figure of apostasy. The declining monarch disobeyed God by taking 700 women and girls as brides, mostly from foreign nationalities. Because of their origins, these wives worshiped the mother-goddess, and they turned Solomon away from the one true God (see 1 Kings 11:5). So widely did he stray that the perversions of goddess worship were introduced even into the Temple itself.

As part of this sexual "worship," the Temple's wicked priests gave Solomon 666 gold talents per year (1 Kings 10:14) — the number is hardly an accident. This was probably payment for allowing them to charge clients for the profane services of the Temple prostitutes.

*The weight of gold that Solomon received yearly was 666 talents.*

Since the adoration of Isis flourished for centuries throughout the empire, why did her addicts never receive any persecution? Conversely, why were the Christians and Jews under such continuous oppression? The reader can readily deduce the answers to these questions from Matthew 22:21. When the Pharisees asked Jesus whether it was right to pay taxes or not, He replied:

*Give to Caesar what is Caesar's, and to God what is God's.*

What exactly was Caesar's? According to Jesus, just the coins bearing the hated image (see next page). Surely it was neither the worship the emperors demanded, nor what the coins' sacrilegious inscriptions implied. The devotees of the mother-goddess, however, had no difficulty adding another pagan deity to their already crowded pantheon. On the other hand, Christians and Jews totally refused to bow or bend to the emperor as a god. *This* was the reason for their persecution.

Shown to the right is the "tribute penny" Jesus referred to in the previous quotation. Minted in the reign of Tiberius (A.D. 14-37), the Latin inscription reads "Tiberius Caesar, son of the divine Augustus."

The Roman Beast, as Daniel said, "was different from all the others." In his timeless vision, this was the only unrecognizable creature and the only one not associated with a specific king. Differences lay also in the enormity of its cruelty and the many centuries of its existence. All these points imply that the whole Roman Empire should be considered as the Antichrist.

The numerical evidence for identifying the Beast as the Roman Empire is compelling. Numbers captivated the Romans; they often numbered/named their children Primus, Secondus, Tertius, etc. Paul's secretary, mentioned in Romans 16:22, was Tertius (the third), and two verses later we hear of a man named Quartus (the fourth). The Roman counting system itself was just a thinly veiled symbol for the number of the Beast. It is remarkable that they did not use all the letters of their alphabet for counting as the Greeks and Hebrews did. Instead, they chose just six: I, V, X, L, C, and D. And it is even more remarkable that the sum of these is exactly 666. As the Bible says, "count the number of the beast."

1. I = 1
2. V = 5   } 6
3. X = 10
4. L = 50  } 60
5. C = 100
6. D = 500 } 600   } 666

**The Numbers of the Beast**

There is an arresting parallelism in the Roman *titles* of Christ and Antichrist. The Roman state charged Jesus with claiming to be the "King of the Jews." For this reason, they placed the words Iesus Nazarenus, Rex Iudaeorum (I.N.R.I.) above His head on the Cross. These letters were to identify the supposed criminal and His crime. If I.N.R.I. identifies Christ, then surely I.V.X.L.C.D. identifies Antichrist.

The Jews called Latin "Romiith," the Roman language. Its prominent gematria again implies the Empire was the Antichrist:

R O M I I Th

ת י מ ו ר

666 = 200 6 40 10 10 400

As unlikely as the previous value is by chance alone, consider what the Greeks called the Latin language and people:

L A T E I N O S

Λ α τ ε ι ν ο ς

30 1 300 5 10 50 70 200 = 666

Since these results are so startling, the reader is encouraged to check them. Conclusively, Latin, Hebrew, and Greek all labeled the ancient Romans with "the number of the beast."

The Roman emperors form a special group in world history, forcibly illustrating that power corrupts, and absolute power corrupts absolutely. The emperor Caligula (37-41 A.D.) set up his own image in Jerusalem's Temple for the Jews to worship; he even declared his horse divine. To glorify the mother-goddess Isis, Caligula made her adoration an official Roman religion. In John's time, the emperor Domitian (81-96 A.D.) proclaimed his own divinity! He demanded all citizens address him as "Dominus et Deus Noster," that is, "Our Lord and God."

A decade before Domitian's reign, the entire Jewish nation rose up aflame in hopeless rebellion. This was after repeated abominations in their Temple and suppression of their religion. The revolt lasted only five months. Yet, during this period they cleansed the Temple, reinstated ancient religious practices, and minted new coins without the hated images. For all that, these were utterly futile gestures with the Roman Dragon at the gate.

Josephus, an eye witness to the revolt (from the Roman side), tells how during the battle the corpses clogged the streets of Jerusalem. Those still living tossed more than 100,000 dead bodies over the defence walls. When the Roman general Titus had captured half the city, he offered what he considered lenient terms to the defenders, but they rejected them. No one surrendered, neither man, women, nor child. More than 1 million[20] died by sword, suicide, or crucifixion. The Romans "crushed and devoured victims and trampled underfoot whatever was left." As Jesus had predicted in Matthew 24:1-2, they also destroyed the Temple:

> *I tell you the truth, not one stone here will be*
> *left on another; every one will be thrown down.*

No people in human history has fought harder, longer, or more bravely for freedom, country, and religion. Their dreams of liberty would have to wait nearly 19 centuries until Zionists established the modern state of Israel on 14 May 1948.

During and after the reign of emperor Hadrian (117-138 A.D.), the Romans prohibited all Jews from entering Jerusalem. The Roman Senate even renamed the great city, Aelia Capitolina, and they built pagan temples to Jupiter and Venus on holy Temple ground. Jesus says in Matthew 23:37-39:

> *O Jerusalem, Jerusalem, . . . how often have I longed to*
> *gather your children together, . . . but you were not willing.*

> *Look, your house is left desolate. For I tell you,*
> *you will not see me again until you say,*
> *"Blessed is he who comes in the name of the Lord."*

For the second time, a conqueror had demolished the Temple and dispersed her people. The victors sold almost a 100,000 of the living into slavery and scattered them throughout the empire. Without family or friend, without mother or daughter, without father or son — like dust in the whirlwind — they vanished from the Promised Land. What Alexander was not permitted to destroy, Titus was destined to.

The name "Titus" derives from the word "Titan." In Greek religious mythology, the Titans were the 12 children of Uranus and Gaea: 6 boys and 6 girls. When they grew up, they usurped the power and position of their parents. In turn, they were deposed by the 12 Olympian gods. Undoubtedly, literate/numerate Greeks knew the unusual gematria of "Titan":

$$\text{T I T A N}$$
$$\text{T ε ι τ α ν}$$
$$\text{300 5 10 300 1 50} = 666$$

Intriguingly, our calendar system has *no year zero*. Therefore, from 1 B.C. to 1 A.D. is only one year, not two. Had it been otherwise, Titus would have destroyed Jerusalem in 69, not 70 A.D. As we have seen, however, the Jerusalem Number, 70, has always been associated with the completion of judgment.

Consider a second, but only apparent, consequence of the missing year zero. In 31 B.C. Augustus Caesar defeated Marc Anthony at the battle of Actium, and Jerusalem became part of the Roman Empire. It remained trodden down by the emperors, these Sons of Darkness, until the Saracen conquest of 636 A.D. It is a curious fact that the entire time of the Roman Beasts' authority and dominion over the Jews — just like the Assyrians' — was exactly 666 years.

# HITLER AND NAPOLEON

*The Bible is a revelation of what was, what is, and what will be.*

We have seen the Antichrists of the ancient world: Cheops, Nimrod-Semiramis, Nebuchadnezzar, Alexander, Nero, and the Roman Empire. Now we will investigate two Beasts of modern times: Hitler and Napoleon.

The old Roman Empire's western leg fell to the barbarians in 476 A.D., but the eastern leg, with its capital at Constantinople (Istanbul), continued until 1453. This was the fourth kingdom of Nebuchadnezzar's dream, but the sixth to oppress the Children of Abraham. The head became the chest and arms, and these turned into the belly and thighs. The thighs diverged into the legs that will eventually grow into the 10 toes or kingdoms of the revised Roman Empire. John (Revelation 12:3) visualizes these kingdoms as 10 horns. Whether horns or toes, the number is always 10.

In great wrath, because he knows his time is growing short, Satan strives with ever increasing fury to subvert God's plans and timetable. As horrible as Napoleon's reign was, Hitler's surpassed it and all others by the sheer extent of its butchery. But, obviously, neither Napoleon nor Hitler was the ultimate Antichrist. Just as obviously, they were under satanic control and direction. At least four events, however, must precede the appearance of the final Beast:

- The state of Israel must be reborn.
- Jews in large numbers are to return to Israel.
- The 10 kingdoms will be established in the area of the old Roman Empire.
- The Temple in Jerusalem must be rebuilt on the original foundation stones.

The first two have already happened; the third (the European Union) is taking place as I write, and the last is being planned.

Although the times of Napoleon and Hitler did not fit God's design, Satan influenced both to try to revive the Roman Empire. From the broad general outlines to the small particulars, their careers were eerily similar. After we have studied them, we will better appreciate history's recurrent nature and the depth of Daniel's vision.

Napoleon created a nightmare from which Europe longed to awake. What began in the French Revolution as Liberty, Equality, and Fraternity ended in the crushing cold of a Russian winter as disease, starvation, and death. Hitler's terrifying vision of empire cost the lives of 60 million people, including the near genocide of the Jewish race. From Pharaoh the Pursuer to Titus the Destroyer, the cry has always been the same: *exterminate the Jews! Listen! You can hear it today!*

# THE ANTICHRIST ARCHETYPE

The lives of all the Antichrists contain striking parallels. This must imply Satan has a set pattern of behavior for his tethered Beasts, a certain pasture they may devour and no more.

Since Napoleon and Hitler are much closer to our time, we have more information on their campaigns and characters. A careful comparison of this rich storehouse will produce additional pieces of the pattern for the last Beast. Everyone — not just Christians — should know the Antichrist's designs. Understand them and you will more easily identify the Beast. Remember though, the Bible provides the ultimate description of the final Antichrist, and all we learn must harmonize with Daniel, Revelation, and the Gospels.

It's impossible to give here a detailed account of both brutes. So I have limited myself to comparing the same event in each life: their invasions of Russia. The main source on Napoleon is the famous historical novel *War and Peace* by Leo Tolstoy (1828-1910). For Hitler I have used *The Rise and Fall of the Third Reich* by William L. Shirer.

Tolstoy was a follower of Jesus and perhaps the most influential Christian in Russian history. In old age, he gave away large portions of his estate and all the money earned from his final book, *Resurrection*. Most of it went to Russian Christians, particularly to help the persecuted Dukhobor sect emigrate to Canada and a new life.

This great Christian writer's insights into the human soul are legendary. Only by comparison to Holy Scripture do his books pale to insignificance. Less well known is his deep interest in the field of numbers. He regarded 28 as his special quantity. Born on 28 August 1828 (old style), he purposely left his home for the last time on 28 October 1910. His eldest son Sergei was born on June 28. When asked to select poems by French poets for his article "What is Art?", Tolstoy deliberately picked them from page 28 of different poetry books. In his last novel, *Resurrection*, the hero, Prince Nekhlyudov, experiences his spiritual revival on April 28. Beyond this, some unpublished notes from Tolstoy's short story "The Kreuzer Sonata" contain these words:

> *I was then young and in love.*
> *I was 28, and was going to visit my future*
> *wife's family to propose to her.*

What is so special about 28? The reader may recall that not only is 28 triangular, but it's also the second "perfect" number. Tolstoy chose well. As we shall learn, this knowledge of numbers was useful to him.

His panoramic novel *War and Peace* paints a spectacular picture of the French Emperor's entire Russian campaign. On the first page, in the very first paragraph, the main theme is set out: Napoleon as the Antichrist. The Czarina's maid is speaking to a friend; she says:

> *But I warn you, if you don't tell me that this means war, if you still try to defend the infamies and horrors perpetuated by that Antichrist [Napoleon] — I really believe he is the Antichrist — I will have nothing more to do with you and you are no longer my friend, no longer my 'faithful slave,' as you call yourself.*

The Russian people knew then, as they did in World War II, the true nature of their enemy. For that reason they fought both Beasts with great determination and surprised the world with their unexpected victories.

The Western Allies were also aware of the similarities between Napoleon and Hitler. In 1941 the *London Sunday Graphic* newspaper printed a cartoon showing Adolf Hitler and Air Marshal Hermann Goering saluting an army of men. Overhead a swarm of planes moves eastward to Russia. Hitler is saying, "Do you ever get the feeling all this has happened before, Hermann?" Behind the pair rises the ghost of Napoleon. It's a cliché, but many a true word has been spoken, written, or drawn in jest.

- The parallels between these two sons of Satan began at birth. Napoleon wasn't French; he was born on the island of Corsica and always spoke French with an Italian accent. Hitler wasn't German; he was Austrian; he spoke High German with an Austrian accent. For that matter, Alexander wasn't completely Greek; he was Macedonian, and he always spoke in a Greek dialect.
- By 1812 Napoleon was the master of Europe, and in 1942 Hitler was dictator of Europe. The former tried to impose his Continental Monetary System; the latter forced his New Order Economics for buying and selling on a defeated continent. Sound familiar? Aren't we hearing identical phrases today? In each case Russia and England refused to fit into these controlling webs of economic domination.

- Before attacking Russia, both tyrants attempted an invasion of England. To protect their island from Napoleon, the English built circular towers all along their coast. They even refurbished them during Hitler's reign. The Führer had, of course, not only waterships but airships, and London felt the full force of these. Yet, there was no true invasion in either case.
- To prevent an attack on their eastern flank, each dictator signed a short-lived nonaggression pact with Russia: Napoleon with Czar Alexander, Hitler with Stalin.
- The French Emperor tried to persuade the Russian Czar to join him in an alliance against England. And deputy Führer Rudolf Hess parachuted into Scotland to ask the English people and Parliament to join Hitler in an alliance against Russia. In both cases — despite radically different political systems — England and Russia allied themselves against their common enemy.
- Napoleon had Prussia and Austria as puppets; Hitler had Finland, Rumania, and Italy. Sadly, both England and Russia had their appeasement groups, the peace-at-any-price people.
- Each Beast's decision to invade Russia took place on the summer solstice — a satanic high Black Sabbat. Napoleon's was on 22 June 1812; Hitler's, on 21 June 1941.
- The Corsican felt he was destroying Asiatic barbarism. The Austrian intended to obliterate all major Russian cities and enslave the remaining population as agricultural serfs.
- Initially, both enjoyed huge military successes — they were given dominion. Even the roads traveled and the cities captured were the same.
- Each met his downfall in a single battle: Napoleon at Borodino, Hitler at Stalingrad. These titanic struggles, however, did not totally destroy either Antichrist. Nevertheless, their wounds were mortal and they began to stagger toward a fall.
- The French Emperor was deeply involved with the occult. During the Russian campaign, he consulted his astrologers daily. These horoscopes inevitably flattered his ego with predictions of great victories and cheering crowds.

Like Alexander, he was convinced of his high place in history. On one occasion he gave his empress Josephine a ring engraved "to destiny."

- The extent of Hitler's entanglement with the black arts is startling. Almost as arresting is how little the war scholars have mentioned this. It's nearly a conspiracy of silence. In Washington, DC, the National Archives contain privileged material on the Ahnenerbe, the occult wing of the Nazi SS. Lewis Sumberg, the American translator of Jean-Michel Angebert's *The Occult and the Third Reich*, hints at secret records. Apparently both the Nazis and the Allies spirited away files and withheld them from historians.

The Nazi party grew out of the old German Thule Society, long known for practicing every supernatural art imaginable. At one meeting Hitler actually claimed he was the dictator named "Hister" predicted by the notorious sixteenth century seer Nostradamus. Hitler's reaction to Nostradamus' predictions sounds like Alexander's response to Daniel's prophecies.

The swastika, also called the hooked cross or anti-cross, is the perfect symbol for the occult. Yet, contrary to general knowledge, Hitler *did not create* the swastika. This very ancient pagan figure flourished throughout a world unfamiliar with Christ and the true Cross. The Hindus still employ it as a major symbol in their religion, as did the Aztecs of Mexico, and the Druids of England. Satan is eternally busy!

In *The Life and Death of Adolf Hitler*, the Führer's major biographer Robert Payne gives some interesting details on Hitler's design variations of the swastika:

*Most of these designs came from Hitler's drawing board. . . .*
*It was a masterly design, and he evidently experimented*
*at considerable length to find the exact proportions.*
*All together, more than 300 flags were designed.*[21]

Many hooked crosses were purposely drawn to contain Phi (1.618...), the number of the pentagram, original sin, and Satan. See FIGURE 13.8 for one common design; compare it to the one on Hitler's left arm.

**The Swastika and Phi**          **Adolf Hitler**

FIGURE 13.8

To mock Christ's Millennial Reign, Hitler proclaimed the Third Reich would last a 1000 years. The propaganda for this attempt at reviving the Holy Roman Empire (the First Reich) was under the masterful control of a Second Beast, Joseph Goebbels. This False Prophet organized all Hitler's propaganda triumphs, including the hugely successful Nuremberg Nazi rallies. From a strange sense of duty, the Second Beast remained with the First in the Berlin Bunker until the very end. After Hitler's suicide, Goebbels poisoned his own six children and then had an SS officer shoot him in the back of the head. Both Beasts gave strict orders to have their bodies burned beyond recognition. Revelation 19:20 describes the death of the Antichrist and the False Prophet in terms hauntingly similar to what really happened in the Berlin Bunker.

> *But the beast was captured* [in the Bunker] *and with him the false prophet who performed the miraculous signs* [propaganda] *on his behalf. With these signs he had deluded those* [Nazi members] *who had received the mark of the beast* [swastika] *and worshiped his image. The two of them were thrown alive into the fiery lake of burning sulphur* [gasoline soaked pit].

Returning to Tolstoy and his account of Napoleon's Russian campaign, we find an astonishing demonstration of gematria in the first part of the third volume, chapter 19, of *War and Peace*. He writes:

*If the French alphabet is treated like the Hebrew system of enumeration, by which the first ten letters represent the units, and the next the tens, and so on, the letters have the following value:* [22]

## FRENCH ALPHABET

| | | |
|---|---|---|
| A = 1 | K = 10 | T = 100 |
| B = 2 | L = 20 | U = 110 |
| C = 3 | M = 30 | V = 120 |
| D = 4 | N = 40 | W = 130 |
| E = 5 | O = 50 | X = 140 |
| F = 6 | P = 60 | Y = 150 |
| G = 7 | Q = 70 | Z = 160 |
| H = 8 | R = 80 | |
| I = 9 | S = 90 | |

FIGURE 13.9

Now use the full title of the French dictator, "Le Empereur Napoleon," and sum the value of his letters:

L E   E M P E R E U R   N A P O L E O N
20 5 + 5 30 60 5 80 5 110 80 + 40 1 60 50 20 5 50 40 = 666

Interestingly, as Tolstoy also shows, you get the identical result when you add up "quarante-deux," 42. This is the number of months God permits the Antichrist to reign:

Q U A R A N T E - D E U X
70 110 1 80 1 40 100 5 + 4 5 110 140 = 666

There exists a little known and anonymous gematria of "Hitler." During World War II, it made the rounds of Christian circles and was even published. Because the letters of our alphabet have no numerical value, we must give them one in some justifiable manner. If you use a familiar code in which A is 100, B is 101, and C is 102, and so on, then "Hitler" very neatly sums to 666:

# ENGLISH ALPHABET

| A = 100 | J = 109 | S = 118 |
|---------|---------|---------|
| B = 101 | K = 110 | T = 119 |
| C = 102 | L = 111 | U = 120 |
| D = 103 | M = 112 | V = 121 |
| E = 104 | N = 113 | W = 122 |
| F = 105 | O = 114 | X = 123 |
| G = 106 | P = 115 | Y = 124 |
| H = 107 | Q = 116 | Z = 125 |
| I  = 108 | R = 117 |         |

FIGURE 13.10

H I T L E R
107 108 119 111 104 117 = **666**

What are we to think of these "beastings" of Napoleon and Hitler? Standing alone, without the other supporting evidence, they should convince no one. After all, neither the letters of the old French alphabet nor our own have numerical values. Any we give them may be incorrect. Only Hebrew, Greek, and six Latin characters truly did double service. For that reason, this modern gematria is not a means to discover the Antichrist — although it may afterward confirm it.

Military advisers cautioned both dictators against invading Russia and by that opening a second fighting front. But pride, Satan's sin, had deeply imprinted Hitler and Napoleon. Outrageous egotism and self-confidence marked each life. They shared the same strange outbursts of anger, the same savage threats, the same fury, the same ability to hypnotize an audience. Ultimately they shared the same character. Century after century we see these features in one type of man: the Antichrist.

Hitler was acutely aware of the similarities between himself and the French Emperor; he stressed them on many occasions. Immediately after conquering Paris, he went directly to the Tomb of Napoleon where he stayed for a considerable time. While viewing the sarcophagus, he murmured to his faithful photographer Heinrich Hoffmann, "This is the greatest and finest moment of my life." [23] It was a unique event for the Führer to pay respect to any man, living or dead.

*We have met the Beasts of the past.*
*We are waiting for the final Antichrist.*

# CHAPTER — 14

## APOCALYPSE 2000

*So when you see standing in the holy place "the abomination
that causes desolation," spoken of through the prophet Daniel
— let the reader understand —*
Jesus, Matthew 24:15

A n outstanding feature of the Bible is its emphasis on numbers
and exactness. In the Book of Numbers this almost becomes a
fixation with its census lists, roles of personal names, columns
of instructions, travel itineraries, and so on. Accordingly, attention to
detail is a conspicuous characteristic of the Holy Scriptures. The
following example comes from Exodus 12:41 (KJV):

> *And it came to pass at the end of 430 years,*
> *even the selfsame day it came to pass, that all*
> *the hosts of the Lord went out from the land of Egypt.*

The Bible is a magnificent landscape of vivid symbols and
precise numbers. We are going to travel through this landscape in
search of the mathematics of the *end times*. Our guides on this pilgrimage will again be the three levels of mathematical interpretation
outlined in Chapter 4. These are restated below:

Level 1. References to quantities, times, measurements,
and the number of occurrences of important
words, phrases, or events.
Level 2. The gematria of the words.
Level 3. The triangular form of God's Word as revealed
by the Triad Rules.

This journey will be unlike any other because the final destination is history's omega point. As we ascend and descend from level to

level, the domain of the Lord's numbers will become strikingly clear. I propose to prove that biblical numbers, at all levels, point directly to an apocalyptic event *around* the year 2000.

# DANIEL'S DREAM OF THE END

In the previous chapter we learned about Daniel's majestic vision concerning the kingdoms that would persecute the Jews. So far we have examined six of these; now we will investigate the last two: the revised Roman Empire and the final Kingdom of the Antichrist. Some say history is the only true philosophy. If that is so, then Daniel is history's only true philosopher.

In the present chapter's opening quotation, Jesus refers to the heart of Daniel's vision: the *last days*. The exactness of this revelation is affirmed by its mathematics; its divinity, by the source; and its truthfulness, by history:

*Seventy "sevens"* [70 x 7 or 490] *are decreed for your people and your holy city* [Jerusalem] *to finish transgression, to put an end to sin, to atone for wickedness, to bring in everlasting righteousness, to seal up the vision and prophecy and to anoint the most holy.*

*Know and understand this: From the issuing of the decree* [by Artaxerxes in 445 B.C.] *to restore and rebuild Jerusalem until the Anointed One, the ruler* [Jesus Christ], *comes, there will be seven "sevens," and sixty-two "sevens"* [483 years]. *It will be rebuilt with streets and a trench, but in times of trouble.*

*After the sixty-two "sevens" the Anointed One will be cut off* [rejected and crucified] *and will have nothing. The people of the ruler who will come* [the Romans under Titus] *will destroy the city and the sanctuary* [70 A.D.]. *The end will come like a flood: War will continue until the end, and desolations have been decreed.*
Daniel 9:24-26

With the next verse (Daniel 9:27) the focus of the vision changes to the final "week" and the ultimate Antichrist. When a prophecy shifts in this manner, scholars call it a double reference:

*He* [the Antichrist] *will confirm a covenant with many* [the Jews] *for one "seven"* [obviously 7 years]. *In the middle of the "seven"* [3½ years, 42 months, or 1260 days] *he will put an end to sacrifice and offering. And on a wing of the temple* [to be rebuilt] *he will set up an abomination* [a statue of himself] *that causes desolation, until the end that is decreed is poured out on him.*

To rebuild the Temple destroyed by Nebuchadnezzar's armies in 586 B.C., the Jews needed seven "sevens" (49 years). An additional sixty-two "sevens" (434 years) passed before the Messiah was "cut off" (rejected). Their sum is sixty-nine "sevens" (483 years). To this, add the last seven years of the Tribulation Week, producing a grand total of 490 years.

Since the Jews rejected Jesus at His First Coming, God has stopped the cosmic clock for over 19 centuries. It is due to start again. While the clock is (was?) on hold, the Age of the Church or Gentiles continues (continued?). This age began after the sixty-nine "sevens" (483 years) and ends before the final seventieth "seven."

Sir Robert Anderson, a brilliant biblical scholar and a former head of Scotland Yard, wrote a masterful book called *The Coming Prince*[1]. In it he gives the complete details and astronomical evidence that this period was exactly 483 *biblical years*, even to the "selfsame day." This was from the decree to rebuild the Temple on 14 March 445 B.C., to the rejection of Jesus on Palm Sunday, 6 April 32 A.D.

On that day, Jesus rode into Jerusalem on a foal, and his disciples identified Him as the Messiah, proclaiming, "Blessed is the King who comes in the name of the Lord" (Luke 19:38). But the Pharisees and most of the people refused to recognize Him as such. They called out to Jesus, "Teacher, rebuke thy disciples" (verse 39).

Significantly, Anderson's date for this historic rejection is Palm Sunday, 6 April 32 A.D., which is the 10th of Nisan in the Jewish calendar. Therefore, the day of the Resurrection fell on the 17th of Nisan, one week later. As mentioned previously (pages 167-168), 17 is the number of security.

A *biblical year* has 360 days. Genesis tells us the Flood lasted for 150 days — from the 17th day of the 2nd month to the 17th day of the 7th. This is a total of 5 months, implying each had 30 days (see Genesis 7:11-24 and 8:3-4). So, 12 months would have 360 days (12 x 30 = 360). Furthermore, Revelation 13:5-7 speaks of the

Antichrist's reign of terror lasting 3½ years or 42 months. Elsewhere in the same book, John uses 1260 days as equivalent to 42 months. Again this implies each month has 30 days (42 x 30 = 1260). From beginning to end, the Bible is marvelously consistent, even down to its time units.

God the Father granted Daniel this immortal vision hundreds of years before the actual events occurred. Or, as with the final week, have yet to occur. All the above dates and calculations may have been confusing, so I have summarized everything in the following chart.

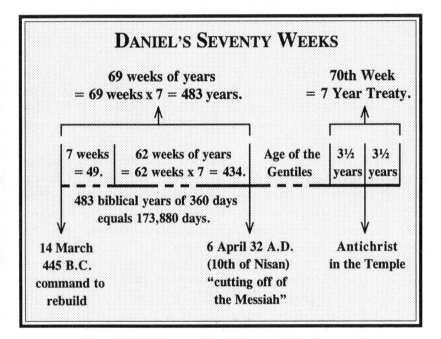

FIGURE 14.1

# WHY 490 YEARS?

What is the purpose of these time periods? Why does God use them? In answer to these questions, we must understand these are testing times for the Jews — testing them with God's covenants. An American Bible scholar from the turn of the century C. I. Scofield called each period a "dispensation." In his *Reference Bible* he defined these as

*a period of time during which man is tested in respect*
*of obedience to some specific revelation of the will of God.*[2]

Furthermore,

*These periods are marked off in Scripture by some change*
*in God's method of dealing with mankind, in respect to two*
*questions: of sin, and man's responsibility. Each dispensation may*
*be regarded as a new test of the natural man, and each ends in*
*judgement — marking his utter failure in every dispensation.*[3]

The mathematical reasons for the length of a dispensation are intriguing. Earlier chapters stressed how 7 symbolizes the completeness of a list, usually only once. On the other hand, 10 stands for the completeness of a cycle, usually more than once. So 70, Jerusalem's Number, represents a complete cycle of lists. Similarly, 70 x 7, or 490, signifies in some sense the major completion of a large and important time period.

Let's change our point of view, and consider 490 in terms of triangle numbers. By doing this, we get another look into the Bible's triad structure. In the notes to Chapter 4, there is a proof that every "perfect" number is also a triangle number. In those same notes you will find a table of all presently known perfects. The first is 6, the third is 496. Of course, 490 is just the difference between them:

$$490 = 496 - 6$$

| 490 | 496 | 6 |
|:---:|:---:|:---:|
| dispensation period | 3rd perfect number | 1st perfect number |

This number, 490, has recurred *at least* four times in Jewish history. These intervals have always been about the Jews' covenant relationship to God. For that reason I call 490 the *Covenant Number*. Again these periods remind us of our Lord's judgment and His repeated forgiveness.

In Matthew 18:21-22 (KJV), Peter asked Jesus how many times he should forgive his brother. It is singularly remarkable that Christ answered 70 x 7 or 490:

*Then came Peter to him, and said, Lord, how oft shall my*
*brother sin against me, and I forgive him? till seven times?*
*Jesus saith unto him, I say not unto thee,*
*Until seven times: but, Until seventy times seven.*

Now that we have seen Daniel's magnificent 490 year cycle; let's
learn about the others.

## THE COVENANT WITH ABRAHAM

The first dispensation began when Abraham was born. It continued
until God, by His promise, called Abraham out of Ur (in modern
Iraq). This period was 75 years (Genesis 12:4). To this, add 430 years
(Galatians 3:17), the time until the Ten Commandments when a new
covenant began. However, this gives a sum of 505 years (75 + 430)
— an apparent error in our totals.

The reader must understand that years count only when the
Hebrews are in a covenant relationship with the Lord. By analogy,
consider the following. A football game is an hour long, although the
actual game may last several hours because of timeouts, penalties, half
time, and so on. Similarly the cosmic clock runs only when the Jews
are in a strict covenant relationship with the Father. The Bible says as
much in Numbers 6:12:

*The previous days do not count because*
*he became defiled during his separation.*

Since Abraham doubted God's promise (Genesis 12:1-3)
concerning Sarah's ability to have children, he broke the covenant.
Because of this abandonment of faith — motivated by concern over
producing descendants — Abraham had sexual intercourse with his
wife's Egyptian maid, Hagar. From this coupling came Ishmael, the
Arabic people, and eventually the Islamic religion. They could have
been Abraham's true seed. Nevertheless, just as the Lord pledged,
Sarah did give her husband a son. From the time Abraham first slept
with Hagar until the birth of Isaac, 15 years lapsed (Genesis 16:3 and
21:5). When 15 is subtracted from 505, the result is exactly 490, the
Covenant Number.

## The Covenant With Moses

When Moses received the Law, a new dispensation began. God fully acknowledged this by His presence in the Tabernacle at the Ark of the Covenant. During intervals, this Divine Presence, the Shekinah Glory, continued until Solomon built the Temple, and then the Lord entered into the Most Holy Place. From the Law to the Temple is 601 years:

      40 years in the wilderness (Acts 13:18)
      20 years under Joshua (scholars disagree on these years)
    450 years under the Judges and Samuel (Acts 13:20)
      40 years under Saul (Acts 13:21)
      40 years under David (1 Kings 2:11)
      11 years under Solomon until the dedication of
 +__ the Temple (1 Kings 6:1, 6:38, and 8:1-11)
   601 years in total.

The years, when the Hebrews fell from obedience to God's Holy Word, must be subtracted from this total. Judges records all these Jewish apostasies — mostly the worship of Baal (Satan) and the goddess Ishtar. Invariably, they resulted in foreign captivity. Here is a summary:

      8 years captive in Mesopotamia (3:8)
    18 years captive in Moab (3:14)
    20 years captive under the Canaanites (4:3)
      7 years under the Midianites (6:11)
    18 years under the Ammonites and Philistines (10:8)
 + 40 years again under the Philistines (13:1)
  111 years of captivities.

By subtracting 111 from 601, we have the Covenant Number, 490.

Some biblical scholars are unsure about the exact length of time the Jews were under Joshua's leadership. For that reason, there may be uncertainty in the previous reckoning. The subject is very involved and technical. Fortunately, we can easily calculate this cycle by a different method. From the total of 601 subtract the length of time the Ark was absent from the Tabernacle until Solomon installed it in the Temple. This includes:

    20 years under Samuel (1 Samuel 4:22 and 7:2)
    40 years under Saul
    40 years under David
+ _11_ years under Solomon
    111 years in all.

Thus, by this second method, we get the same 490 years. Since both methods arrive at the identical answer, this implies the 20 years under Joshua's leadership is probably correct.

## THE COVENANT WITH DAVID

From Solomon's dedication of the Temple in 1005 B.C. to Artaxerxes' commandment to rebuild it in 445 B.C. is 560 years. Secular historians confirm both dates. For worshiping pagan gods and goddesses, the Jews spent 70 of these years in Babylonian captivity. When we take 70 from 560, this intriguing 490 reappears.

## THE FOURTH DISPENSATION: DANIEL'S VISION

This is the celebrated seventy "sevens" of Daniel's dream discussed earlier. With this, the Covenant Age and God's direct dealings with the Jews ends, except for the last 7 years of the Great Tribulation.

# THE AGE OF THE GENTILES

*I do not want you to be ignorant of this mystery, brothers, so that you may not be conceited: Israel has experienced a hardening in part until the full number of the Gentiles has come in.*
Paul, Romans 11:25

It seems unusual that from the "cutting off" of Christ to the present time is exactly 4 more periods, each of 490 years. Could God have decreed 4 cycles for the Jews and 4 cycles for the Gentiles? This would produce a grand total of 8 cycles, each of 490 years duration.

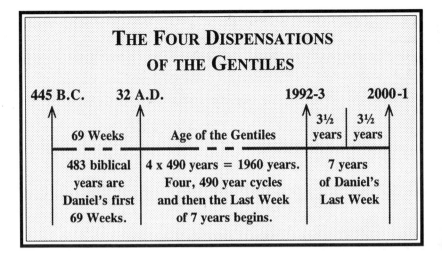

FIGURE 14.2

# THE GREAT SABBATH WEEK

*For a thousand years in your sight are like a day that has gone by.*
Psalm 90:4

> *With the Lord a day is like a thousand years,*
> *and a thousand years are like a day.*
> 2 Peter 3:8

The Trinity is beyond space and time! For God, time is purely relative; modern physics has shown the truth of relativity. When viewed in the light of all eternity, a thousand years are truly just a day.

But how long is eternity? An Eskimo legend says that in Canada's far northern wastes in the midst of ice and snow stands an immense rock. This rock is a cube a mile long, a mile wide, and a mile high. Once every 1000 years, a small white bird flutters to the top of the rock and gently cleans its tiny bill. When the cube has been worn away, one day of eternity will have passed.

The 6 Creation Days and the 1 Sabbath Day are the model for man's duration on earth. If the Lord created Adam in approximately 4000 B.C., and the Apocalypse comes around 2000 A.D., then these dates span 6000 years. This 6000-year period matches the 6 Days of Creation, and the final day of rest corresponds exactly to the 1000-year Millennial Reign. The previous quotations from Psalm 90 and 2 Peter confirm this is how God views time. Shouldn't we?

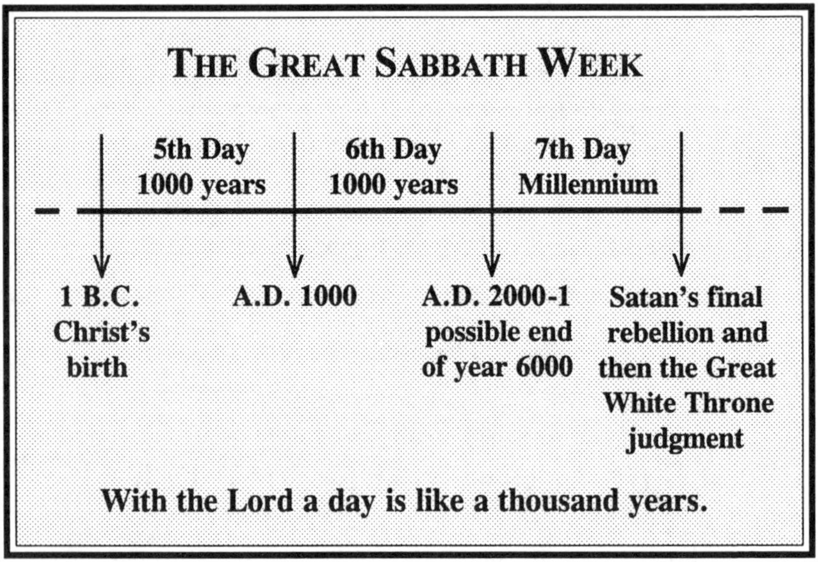

FIGURE 14.3

I am not saying anything here about the age of the earth or the universe. Both may be many millions, or even billions, of years old. Genesis 1:1 proclaims:

*In the beginning God created the heaven and the earth.*

These immortal lines do not reveal when God created man. It could have been eons later. Evidence from astronomy, specifically the red shift in the light spectrum and background radiation in the universe, implies a "Big Bang" in the very, very distant past. Also, the recently discovered large-scale hexagonal structure of the universe (Chapter 7) points to a Grand Designer, our Lord of the Cosmos. What the Bible has always known, modern science now affirms: the universe had a beginning; therefore, we may reasonably expect it to have an end.

Many early church leaders noted the similarities between the Creation Week and the Great Sabbath Week. Writing about Genesis in his book *Against Heresies*, Irenaeus (150 A.D.) said:

> *This is an account of the things formerly created, as also it is a prophecy of what is to come. For the day of the Lord is as a thousand years; and in 6 days created things were completed; it is evident, therefore they will come to an end at 6000 years.*[4]

History attributes one of the first pseudepigrapha (writings wrongly ascribed) to Barnabas, companion to Mark and the Apostle Paul. The Epistle of Barnabas, whether written by him or not, provides valuable information on the early church teachings. Here Barnabas writes about the Creation:

> *And God made in 6 days the works of His hands; and He finished them on the 7th day, and He rested on the 7th day and sanctified it. Consider, what that signifies, He finished them in 6 days. The meaning of it is this: that in 6000 years the Lord God will bring all things to an end. For with Him, one day is a thousand years; as Himself testifieth, saying, behold this day shall be as a 1000 years. Therefore children, in 6 days, that is, 6000 years, shall all things be accomplished.*[5]

After 6000 years of human history and the 1000-year Millennial Reign, the Lord will have completely finished with His triangular Creation. Following this — *on the 8th day* — John joyously tells us:

> *Then I saw a new heaven and a new earth,*
> *for the first heaven and the first earth passed away.*
> Revelation 21:1

# THE GEMATRIA OF THE END TIMES

So far we have investigated only Level 1 of the mathematical structure of the *end times*. Now consider Level 2, the gematria. By a diligent hunt through Greek and Hebrew words, it might be possible to find a few whose gematrias are *around 2000*. Yet, what would that prove except the single-mindedness of the researcher? The gematria of these times must describe the terrible Tribulation and the actions of the people. In addition, the words must agree with the numbers, and all the passages must harmonize with each other. I believe such words and numbers are abundant in God's Holy Word. You be the judge.

On the "day of the Lord" many will call on the "name of the Lord":

NAME    OF THE    LORD (1 Corinthians 1:2)
Ο ν ο μ α      τ ο υ      Κ υ ρ ι ο υ
70 50 70 40 1  +  300 70 400  +  20 400 100 10 70 400 = 2001

Of course, they may call on the "Name of Jesus" to be saved:

NAME          OF      JESUS      (Acts 5:40)
Ο ν ο μ α τ ι      τ ο υ      Ι η σ ο υ
70 50 70 40 1 300 10 + 300 70 400 + 10 8 200 70 400 = 1999

When Jesus comes again, it will not be as the Suffering Messiah but with the "power of God":

POWER          OF      GOD      (Romans 13:2)
Ε ξ ο υ σ ι α      τ ο υ      Θ ε ο υ
5 60 70 400 200 10 1 + 300 70 400 + 9 5 70 400 = 2000

The New Testament contains 16 (8 + 8) references to the *coming* Son of Man, Jesus' favorite title for Himself. After 6000 years of human sinfulness, He is coming again, this time as the Conquering Messiah, to right wrongs and punish wickedness.

If we had learned to add our letters, as the Greeks, Jews, and Romans did, how differently we should regard our alphabet! By habitual practice, we would have forged an absolute bond between letter and number. The letters of a word would appear as a number, and the digits of a number would suggest a word. Gematria would be as natural as talking. Perhaps this explains why the early church leaders Irenaeus and Barnabas wrote so convincingly on the *end times* and the year 6000.

# TRINITY, TRIANGLE, AND 2000

In our explorations of Levels 1 and 2, we have seen some of the wonder in God's Word. Level 3, the final and deepest, will confirm and expand our previous results. Yet where and how can triangle quantities point to a design involving the number 2000 and the *end times*? To explain this, we will take a short detour.

All the biblical authors from Moses to John used certain poetic forms. Poetry in English is a matter of meter and rhyme, but poetry in Hebrew and Greek was a matter of parallelism and repetition. The author said it; then in different words, he said it again. The structure could be as short as a sentence or as long as an entire book (e.g., Isaiah and Daniel). Even some prophecies are parallel and repetitive. It is important to know this; otherwise, you could entirely misinterpret them.

What are these passages? Where are they found in the Bible? Consider the following examples. The first is from Genesis 1:27:

> A — So God created man
> B — in his own image,
> B — in the image of God
> A — he created him.

The pattern is A B = B A, expressing just two ideas: God created man, and man is in God's image. For a second illustration, consider this famous verse from Isaiah 55:8:

> A — For my thoughts
> B — are not your thoughts
> B — neither are your ways
> A — my ways , declares the Lord.

Again the structure is A B = B A, like a stepladder, first up then down. It contains four phrases but expresses only two ideas: God's thoughts and ways, our thoughts and ways.

Mark 5:3-5 has a longer example of this structure. These verses describe the well-known scene of the Gadarene swine and the demon-possessed man whom Jesus healed.

A — This man lived in tombs,
   B — and no one could bind him any more,
      C — not even with a chain.
      C — For he had often been chained hand and foot.
   B — No one was strong enough to subdue him.
A — Night and day among the tombs.

The poetic form is A B C = C B A, expressing three ideas, not six. English teachers call this device a *chiasmus* and illustrate it with examples like "she went to Los Angeles; to New York went he."

Occasionally a chiasmus can be a noble structure ranging over several books and uniting them all in a profound vision. One such[6] is found in the Prologue to Revelation. Here John refers to the Old Testament and Jesus exactly 8 times, the Resurrection Number. These references are set out in a chiasmus of great beauty and illumination. The first is from the same book as the eighth, and the second corresponds to the seventh. The third matches the sixth, and the fourth goes with the fifth. (Note, the first number after each capital letter gives the verse from the Prologue.)

   A — 5. Isaiah 55:4
     B — 7. Daniel 7:13
       C — 7. Zechariah 12:10
         D — 8. Isaiah 41:4, 44:6, 48:12
         D — 11. Isaiah 41:4. 44:6, 48:12
       C — 12. Zechariah 4:2
     B — 13-15. Daniel 7:9, 13, 22; 10:5-6
   A — 16. Isaiah 49:2

Other examples are possible, but the point is clear: Holy Scripture uses these arrangements. By their very nature, you can read any chiasmus *forward or backward*.

Most biblical numbers, including triangular ones, also have this reversible property. Briefly recall:

**Jesus = 888    Cross = 777    Antichrist = 666**

Obviously, these may be read both ways. Many others exist, however, without identical digits (see the notes for Chapter 8) that may also be read both ways. In the next chapter we will investigate 3003, another meaningful number of this type. Still, some extremely important triangles are not reversible, for instance Jesus' Celestial Number, 153. Although in this case, the reverse itself is triangular, and together they do form the required pattern: 153—351. The second quantity is the spiritual inverse of the first since it is an exact multiple of 13, the False Trinity Number of Rebellion. Plainly, 153 is not.

Remarkably, the situation goes much deeper than these self-evident cases. Consider the transcendently powerful first sentence of Genesis. It really says it all; how else should the Lord's Holy Word begin? On pages 229-230, I verified that the gematria value of those 7 words and 28 letters is the triangle number 2701.

---

**This is God's chiasmus in the Bible's first sentence:**

**2701 = [37] x [73]**

---

Also, the same chapter explained how John 1:1, "In the beginning was the Word," implies a similar but more compact chiasmus. He speaks of the word *logos* as God, and its gematria is **373**.

Therefore, much of the Bible's mathematics has the same structure as its words, sentences, paragraphs, and books. Everything inspired by the Lord is a harmony and a unity; it never contains chaos, the domain of Satan.

How is all this related to The Trinity, triangle numbers, and the year 2000? Return to the Triangle of Creation/Pascal (page 21) and inspect the *3rd digit* of its *3rd column*. Remember, this column contains every triangle quantity.

```
Δ
000     To the left are the triangle numbers (i.e., the
001     3rd column). Their 3rd digit (i.e., the hundreds)
003     is marked by a "Δ". This vertical line of numbers
006     forms a magnificent chiasmus (palindrome), 2000
010     digits long. Here it is in part:
015
021     -------------------------------->
028     0 0 0 0 0 0 0 0 0 0 0 0 0 0 0 1 1 1 1 1 1 2 2 2
036     2 3 3 3 3 4 4 4 4 5 5 5 6 6 7 7 7 8 8 9 . . . .
045     . . . . 5 5 5 (centered on 28 fives) 5 5 5 . . . . .
055     . . . 9 8 8 7 7 7 6 6 5 5 5 4 4 4 4 3 3 3 3 2
066     2 2 2 1 1 1 1 1 1 0 0 0 0 0 0 0 0 0 0 0 0 0 0 0
078         < --------------------------------
091
105     As shown above, the center of this grand structure
120     contains 28 fives, our seventh triangle and the
136     second perfect number.
153
. . .
. . .
. . .
```

What follows is the full, majestic 2000-digit chiasmus from the *trinity digit* of the *triangle numbers*. (The Chapter Notes have a complete proof.) Make no mistake concerning the initial and final zeros: they are part of the pattern. The second group of 2000 digits is identical to the ones listed below, and so on. *Know the first 2000, and you know them all.*

It's a useful exercise to check some numbers at both ends. You might also inspect the symmetry of the two middle (highlighted) lines. Each of the 80 rows contains 25 digits, and 80 x 25 = 2000.

```
0 0 0 0 0 0 0 0 0 0 0 0 0 0 0 1 1 1 1 1 1 2 2 2 3
3 3 3 4 4 4 4 5 5 5 6 6 7 7 7 8 8 9 9 9 0 0 1 1 2
2 3 3 4 4 5 5 6 7 7 8 8 9 0 0 1 2 2 3 4 4 5 6 7 7
8 9 0 0 1 2 3 4 4 5 6 7 8 9 0 0 1 2 3 4 5 6 7 8 9
0 1 2 3 4 5 6 7 8 9 1 2 3 4 5 6 7 9 0 1 2 3 5 6 7
8 0 1 2 3 5 6 7 9 0 1 3 4 5 7 8 0 1 2 4 5 7 8 0 1
```

```
3 4 6 7 9 0 2 4 5 7 8 0 2 3 5 6 8 0 1 3 5 7 8 0 2
4 5 7 9 1 2 4 6 8 0 2 3 5 7 9 1 3 5 7 9 1 3 5 7 9
1 3 5 7 9 1 3 5 7 9 1 3 5 7 0 2 4 6 8 0 3 5 7 9 2
4 6 8 1 3 5 7 0 2 4 7 9 2 4 6 9 1 4 6 8 1 3 6 8 8
1 3 6 1 3 6 8 1 4 6 9 1 4 7 9 2 5 7 0 3 5 8 1 4 6
9 2 5 7 0 3 6 9 1 4 7 0 3 6 9 1 4 7 0 3 6 9 2 5 8
1 4 7 0 3 6 9 2 5 8 2 5 8 1 4 7 0 4 7 0 3 6 0 3 6
9 3 6 9 2 6 9 2 6 9 2 6 9 2 6 9 3 6 9 3 6 0 3 7 0
4 7 1 4 8 1 5 9 2 6 9 3 7 0 4 7 1 5 8 2 6 0 3 7 1
5 8 2 6 0 3 7 1 5 9 3 6 0 4 8 2 6 0 4 8 2 6 0 4 8
2 6 0 4 8 2 6 0 4 8 2 6 0 4 9 3 7 1 5 9 4 8 2 6 1
5 9 3 8 2 6 0 5 9 3 8 2 7 1 5 0 4 9 3 7 2 6 1 5 0
4 9 3 8 2 7 1 6 1 5 0 4 9 4 8 3 8 2 7 2 6 1 6 1 5
0 5 0 4 9 4 9 4 8 3 8 3 8 3 8 2 7 2 7 2 7 2 7 2 7
2 7 2 7 2 7 2 7 2 7 3 8 3 8 3 8 3 9 4 9 4 9 5 0 5
0 6 1 6 1 7 2 7 3 8 3 9 4 9 5 0 6 1 6 2 7 3 8 4 9
5 0 6 1 7 2 8 4 9 5 0 6 2 7 3 8 4 0 5 1 7 3 8 4 0
6 1 7 3 9 4 0 6 2 8 4 9 5 1 7 3 9 5 1 7 3 9 5 1 7
3 9 5 1 7 3 9 5 1 7 3 9 5 1 8 4 0 6 2 8 5 1 7 3 0
6 2 8 5 1 7 3 0 6 2 9 5 2 8 4 1 7 4 0 6 3 9 6 2 9
5 2 8 5 1 8 4 1 8 4 1 7 4 1 7 4 1 7 4 1 7 4 1 8 4
1 8 5 1 8 5 2 9 5 2 9 6 3 0 7 3 0 7 4 1 8 5 2 9 6
3 0 7 4 1 8 5 2 9 6 4 1 8 5 2 9 6 4 1 8 5 2 0 7 4
1 9 6 3 0 8 5 2 0 7 4 2 9 6 4 1 9 6 3 1 8 6 3 1 8
6 3 1 8 6 3 1 9 6 4 1 9 7 4 2 9 7 5 2 0 8 6 3 1 9
7 4 2 0 8 5 3 1 9 7 5 2 0 8 6 4 2 0 8 6 4 2 0 8 6
4 2 0 8 6 4 2 0 8 6 4 2 0 8 7 5 3 1 9 7 6 4 2 0 9
7 5 3 2 0 8 6 5 3 1 0 8 7 5 3 2 0 9 7 5 4 2 1 9 8
6 5 3 2 0 9 7 6 5 3 2 0 9 8 6 5 4 2 1 0 8 7 6 5 3
2 1 0 8 7 6 5 4 2 1 0 9 8 7 6 4 3 2 1 0 9 8 7 6 5
4 3 2 1 0 9 8 7 6 5 5 4 3 2 1 0 9 9 8 7 6 5 5 4 3
2 2 1 0 9 9 8 7 7 6 5 5 4 3 3 2 2 1 0 0 9 9 8 8 7
7 6 6 5 5 4 4 4 3 3 2 2 2 1 1 0 0 0 9 9 9 9 8 8 8
8 7 7 7 7 6 6 6 6 6 6 5 5 5 5 5 5 5 5 5 5 5 5 5 5
5 5 5 5 5 5 5 5 5 5 5 5 5 5 6 6 6 6 6 6 7 7 7 7 8
8 8 8 9 9 9 9 0 0 0 1 1 2 2 2 3 3 4 4 4 5 5 6 6 7
7 8 8 9 9 0 0 1 2 2 3 3 4 5 5 6 7 7 8 9 9 0 1 2 2
3 4 5 5 6 7 8 9 9 0 1 2 3 4 5 5 6 7 8 9 0 1 2 3 4
5 6 7 8 9 0 1 2 3 4 6 7 8 9 0 1 2 4 5 6 7 8 0 1 2
```

```
3 5 6 7 8 0 1 2 4 5 6 8 9 0 2 3 5 6 7 9 0 2 3 5 6
8 9 1 2 4 5 7 9 0 2 3 5 7 8 0 1 3 5 6 8 0 2 3 5 7
9 0 2 4 6 7 9 0 3 5 7 8 0 2 4 6 8 0 2 4 6 8 0 2 4
6 8 0 2 4 6 8 0 2 4 6 8 0 2 5 7 9 1 3 5 8 0 2 4 7
9 1 3 6 8 0 2 5 7 9 2 4 7 9 1 4 6 9 1 3 6 8 1 3 6
8 1 3 6 8 1 3 6 9 1 4 6 9 2 4 7 0 2 5 8 0 3 6 9 1
4 7 0 2 5 8 1 4 6 9 2 5 8 1 4 6 9 2 5 8 1 4 7 0 3
6 9 2 5 8 1 4 7 0 3 7 0 3 6 9 2 5 9 2 5 8 1 5 8 1
4 8 1 4 7 1 4 7 1 4 7 1 4 7 1 4 8 1 4 8 1 5 8 2 5
9 2 6 9 3 6 0 4 7 1 4 8 2 5 9 2 6 0 3 7 1 5 8 2 6
0 3 7 1 5 8 2 6 0 4 8 1 5 9 3 7 1 5 9 3 7 1 5 9 3
7 1 5 9 3 7 1 5 9 3 7 1 5 9 4 8 2 6 0 4 9 3 7 1 6
0 4 8 3 7 1 5 0 4 8 3 7 2 6 0 5 9 4 8 2 7 1 6 0 5
9 4 8 3 7 2 6 1 6 0 5 9 4 9 3 8 3 7 2 7 1 6 1 6 0
5 0 5 9 4 9 4 9 3 8 3 8 3 8 3 7 2 7 2 7 2 7 2 7 2
7 2 7 2 7 2 7 2 8 3 8 3 8 3 8 4 9 4 9 4 0 5 0
5 1 6 1 6 2 7 2 8 3 8 4 9 4 0 5 1 6 1 7 2 8 3 9 4
0 5 1 6 2 7 3 9 4 0 5 1 7 2 8 3 9 5 0 6 2 8 3 9 5
1 6 2 8 4 9 5 1 7 3 9 4 0 6 2 8 4 0 6 2 8 4 6 0 2
8 4 0 6 2 8 4 0 6 2 8 4 0 6 3 9 5 1 7 3 0 6 2 8 5
1 7 3 0 6 2 8 5 1 7 4 0 7 3 9 6 2 9 5 1 8 4 1 7 4
0 7 3 0 6 3 9 6 3 9 6 2 9 6 2 9 6 2 9 6 2 9 6 3 9
6 3 0 6 3 0 7 4 0 7 4 1 8 5 2 8 5 2 9 6 3 0 7 4 1
8 5 2 9 6 3 0 7 4 1 9 6 3 0 7 4 1 9 6 3 0 7 5 2 9
6 4 1 8 5 3 0 7 5 2 9 7 4 1 9 6 4 1 8 6 3 1 8 6 3
1 8 6 3 1 8 6 4 1 9 6 4 2 9 7 4 2 0 7 5 3 1 8 6 4
2 9 7 5 3 0 8 6 4 2 0 7 5 3 1 9 7 5 3 1 9 7 5 3 1
9 7 5 3 1 9 7 5 3 1 9 7 5 3 2 0 8 6 4 2 1 9 7 5 4
2 0 8 7 5 3 1 0 8 6 5 3 2 0 8 7 5 4 2 0 9 7 6 4 3
1 0 8 7 5 4 2 1 0 8 7 5 4 3 1 0 9 7 6 5 3 2 1 0 8
7 6 5 3 2 1 0 9 7 6 5 4 3 2 1 9 8 7 6 5 4 3 2 1 0
9 8 7 6 5 4 3 2 1 0 0 9 8 7 6 5 4 4 3 2 1 0 0 9 8
7 7 6 5 4 4 3 2 2 1 0 0 9 8 8 7 7 6 5 5 4 4 3 3 2
2 1 1 0 0 9 9 9 8 8 7 7 7 6 6 5 5 5 4 4 4 3 3 3
3 2 2 2 2 1 1 1 1 1 0 0 0 0 0 0 0 0 0 0 0 0 0
```

The Lord is telling us something marvelously profound through His chosen numbers from His Trinity Creation. After 2000, this structure is exhausted, nothing new is forthcoming. As Jesus said, "It is finished."

# TRIANGLE NUMBERS
# AND THE END TIMES

While attempting to uncover the mathematical designs in the Bible, I have been strongly impressed by how many triangle numbers *focus around 2000*. The following examples illustrate this:

- The 2000th triangle number is 2001 emphasized.
  Remember how we find such quantities:

$$2000 \text{ --------->} 1 + 2 + 3 + \ldots + 2000$$
$$= 2001,000$$
$$= 2001 \times 10^3$$
$$= \text{a triangle number}$$

- When the Trinity Function is repeatedly used on 2001, or 2001,000, the image is John 21:11, the 153 fishes. By continuing to apply the rule to each new image, we find:

$$2001 \text{ ---> } 9 \text{ ---> } 729 \text{ ---> } 1080 \text{ ---> } 513 \text{ ---> } 153$$

  As we know, when you use the Trinity Rule on 153, it resurrects itself. Like life, this mathematics ends and then begins again with Jesus!
- The quantity 2000 is the sum of exactly three significant triangle numbers. Before we show this, however, recall David's star, the Flag of Israel Number (pages 186-187), and David's gematria. Intriguingly, "David" is the first and last human name mentioned in the New Testament.

$$\begin{array}{ccccc} D & A & V & I & D \\ \Delta & A & B & I & \Delta \\ 4 & 1 & 2 & 10 & 4 \end{array} = 21$$

This value, 21, is the sixth triangle number. In the chapter dealing with the 144,000, we saw that star numbers are composites of triangles. What could be more natural than to use David's number to construct David's Star? In point of fact, the sixth star is built from the sixth triangle. Take 12 triangles/tribes of 21 points each; center them on one point, God the Father. From this you get the sixth star, 253:

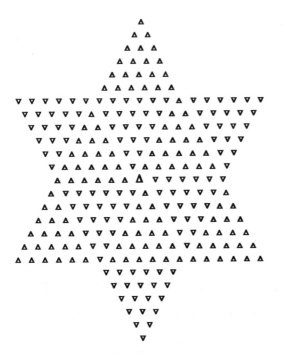

- 21 is David's number.

- 12 is the number of tribes of the "chosen."

- The central 1 is for God as a unity and a unifier.

- The 253 points form both a star and a triangle.

**The Flag of Israel Number or David's Star**

FIGURE 14.4

Since 12 represents both governmental power and the tribes of the "chosen," it is appropriate. The 1 is also correct because the Jews have always looked on God as a unity, never as a trinity. They rejected Jesus at His first coming; they reject Him now. Moreover, and as unlikely as it may seem, David's Star is also a triangle. It's the 22nd, the same as the number of Hebrew letters. Here is the distinctive triple triangle structure of 2000:

**2000 = 253 + 666 + 1081**
David's Star   Antichrist   God's Holy Spirit

Figuratively this implies the Antichrist is separating or standing between Israel and God's Holy Spirit trying to prevent the conversion of the 144,000 Jews of the *end times*.

- If the preceding equation was meaningful, then the following seems ominous. In the *last days*, Satan, the Antichrist, and the False Prophet will unite in a mocking anti-trinity of rebellion, wickedness, and deception. What better symbol could they choose then a triad of 666s? The date/sum of these three triangles is swiftly approaching, like the hoof-beats of the horsemen of the Apocalypse.

$$1998 = 666 + 666 + 666 =$$

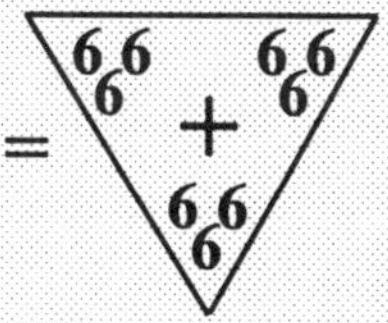

**Never again will this arrangement occur.**

FIGURE 14.5

Perhaps during the Tribulation Week, 1998 will be the high point in the horror of the Antichrist — "the abomination that causes desolation." This number conceals many things. We will meet it again in the final chapter and learn of its connection to the Bible's last verse.

- Pointing directly at 2000, the following property is deeper than the others. It uncovers a profound relationship between the Trinity Function and 2000. When applying this rule to any quantity greater than 2000, *a lower number always results*. If reapplied, it keeps lowering the number until it reaches a quantity less than 2000. The starting number could have a zillion digits, and still the image *always* grows smaller until it passes the watershed of 2000. This is not so for all quantities under 2000. Consider:

Above 2000 the images always go down.

```
9999 ---> 2916 ---> 954
          down       down
79,895 ---> 2438 ---> 611
          down       down
9,999,999 ---> 5103 ---> 153
          down       down
```

Below 2000 the images may go up or down.

```
 2 --->    8  ---> 512
      up         up
21 --->    9  ---> 729
      down       up
99 ---> 1458  ---> 702
      up        down
```

Mathematically-minded readers will not find this property difficult to prove. For the rest, these examples, and any others you may wish to try, should be enough. But the question remains: Why is 2000 such a dividing point, such a watershed, unless something momentous is going to occur around that time?

# NOT THE DAY NOR THE HOUR

*No one knows about that day or hour, not even*
*the angels in heaven, nor the Son, but only the Father.*
Jesus, Matthew 24:36

In the lines immediately following the above quotation, Jesus unmistakably says He is speaking of His second coming. This passage squarely confronts all would-be date-setters. Many books, pamphlets, and sermons have vainly tried to wiggle and squirm around this famous verse. More to the point, when Jesus spoke of not knowing "that day or hour," He obviously meant the week, the month, and the year as well. In the same discourse our Lord tells of the many signs of the end: wars and rumors of wars, earthquakes, famines, and so on. By reading these signs you *can know* the season, but you *cannot know* the exact day, hour, or even year of deliverance.

In 1 Thessalonians 5:1-5 Paul speaks on the same topic; he uses two comparisons:

*Now, brothers, about times and dates we do not need to write to you, for you know very well that the day of the Lord will come like a thief in the night. While people are saying, "peace and safety," destruction will come on them suddenly, as labour pains on a pregnant woman, and they will not escape.*

The Apostle continues with a crucial point:

*But you, Brothers, are not in darkness so that this day should surprise you like a thief. You are the sons of the light and the sons of the day. We do not belong to the night or to the darkness.*

Conclusively, we cannot know the exact time, not even the year. Yet we, the believers, can know the season — that the times are pregnant. How do we do this? As Jesus and Paul said, by reading the signs. Just as it was in the days of Noah, the disbelievers and skeptics were not ready. However, the patriarch and his family knew the season. They spent years building the Ark and boarded it precisely 7 days before the rains began.

At this point, some readers may be thinking the author has deeply contradicted himself. Haven't I been giving the year 2000 as the date of Christ's return? No I haven't; no I won't! All my dates have been *around or about 2000*. It could be anywhere from 1998 to 2002, approximately. This is sin's season. The reader is encouraged to quickly go over my gematria and mathematics to confirm this.

One source of confusion was touched on earlier: our calendar has no year zero. For that reason, from 1 B.C. to 1 A.D. is only a single year, not two. The first decade of the Christian era began in 1 A.D. and ran to the *end* of 10 A.D. The second century began in 101 and continued until the *end* of year 200. The 20th century started in 1901 and will continue until the *end of 2000* (i.e., midnight, 31 December 2000). As a result, the 21st century begins on 1 January 2001. So, do my calculations refer to the year 2000 as a date, or to the passage of 2000 years? They are not the same, and I do not know which to choose! It's almost as if the Father has built-in this point of confusion to keep the exact time of His Son's return a mystery. On all dates concerning Jesus' second coming, which I may use, the reader is forewarned. Be alert for such small words as *around* and *about*: They keep us honest.

# THE REVISED ROMAN EMPIRE

*This calls for a mind with wisdom. The seven heads are seven hills* [Rome] *on which the woman sits.*

*They are also seven kings. Five have fallen,* [Egypt, Assyria, Babylon, Medo-Persia, and Greece] *one is,* [Rome — in John's time] *the other* [the revised Roman Empire] *has not yet come; but when he does come, he must remain for a little while.*

*The beast who once was, and now is not, is an eighth king* [the Antichrist]. *He belongs to the seven and is going to his destruction. The ten horns you saw are ten kings who have not yet received a kingdom, but who for an hour* [a short time] *will receive authority as kings along with the beast.*
Revelation 17:9-12

Plainly, biblical prophecy is declaring there will be a 7th kingdom, a revised Roman Empire, and an 8th, the empire of the Antichrist. Although written in symbolic language, John's implication is clear. Also, with that wonderful consistency we have come to expect from the Bible, Daniel 7:24 made the same point, but six centuries earlier:

*The ten horns are ten kings who will come from this kingdom. After them another king* [the Antichrist] *will arise, different from the earlier ones; he will subdue three kings. He will speak against the Most High and oppress his saints and try to change the set times and the laws. The saints will be handed over to him for a time* [1 year], *times* [2 years], *and half a time* [6 months].

History records many futile attempts to revive the ancient empire of the Romans. For Europeans it has always been the ultimate symbol of unity and power. In 800 A.D. the illiterate Charlemagne, king of the Franks, united several countries in a short-lived, mini-Roman kingdom. Napoleon tried to imitate Charlemagne, and for 13 years he succeeded. In the time between these two rulers, the Holy Roman Empire existed as an uneasy sharing of power between many kings and a succession of popes. Of course our century has witnessed Hitler's demonic attempt to cement Europe under his swastika into one enormous concentration camp.

None of these previous Beasts were totally successful. Yet Europe — as I write — is uniting from a groundswell of popular opinion from businessmen, trade unions, and politicians. What arms and the man could not accomplish, history and time are. What single political guru foresaw the events in Europe: the collapse of the Berlin Wall, the merging of the two Germanies, the overthrow of communism, and the disintegration of the Soviet Union? The straight, honest answer is no one, although the Holy Scriptures have for 25 centuries predicted a revised Roman Empire. Score another brilliant point for biblical prophecy!

With headquarters at Brussels, Belgium, the European Union (EU) correctly targeted 1992-3 as the date for economic union. Presently the EU consists of more than 10 countries, but already England has said *no* to any full monetary alliance. Besides, several smaller members are also uneasy concerning fiscal union. Isn't it quite conceivable that by the late 1990s there will be exactly 10 members as Daniel and John predicted?

Since the Age of the Gentiles probably ended in 1992-3, these are particularly portentous times:

$$32 + 490 + 490 + 490 + 490 = 1992\text{-}3$$

| Crucifixion of Jesus | Age of the Gentiles | European Union |
|---|---|---|

After the Age of the Gentiles comes the *time of the end.*

The expectation of a united Europe with a common monetary policy on buying and selling is not universally welcomed. Japanese and U.S. businessmen are already voicing alarm over the prospect of a new mega-economic power some call Fortress Europe.

EU trade and promotional symbols strike this author as openly prophetic. Prominent among these is a large poster copied from *The Building of the Tower of Babel*, a 1563 painting by the Flemish artist Pieter Brueghel. The modern caption on it says "Europe, many tongues, one voice." Even its pentagrams are all arranged "horns up," in the manner of Satan. A second logo, used as a trademark by some Italian manufacturers, consists of an oval split by a horizontal line. Above the line is a drawing of a lamb with two horns (Revelation 13:11) and beneath it the number 666.

(a)                                        (b)

**European Union promotional symbols**

FIGURE 14.6

First, Europe will have an economic union under 10 kings, horns, or presidents, then political union under the Antichrist. This 7th kingdom will be short-lived. It's just an appetizer for the coming ravenous Beast. So the stage is set, the season is soon to arrive, the players are ready: enter Antichrist.

# THE FINAL ANTICHRIST

*While I was thinking about the horns, there before me was
another horn, a little one, which came up among them; and three
of the first horns were uprooted before it. This horn had eyes like
the eyes of a man and a mouth that spoke boastfully.*
Daniel 7:8

*And I saw a beast coming out of the sea* [of mankind].
*He had 10 horns and 7 heads, with 10 crowns on his horns,
and on each head a blasphemous name.*
Revelation 13:1

With the advent of signs of the *end times*, naming someone as the
Antichrist has become almost a pastime. One American writer has
pointed to Mikhail Gorbachev as the Beast, mainly because of the
birthmark on his forehead. Other favorite targets have been Henry
Kissinger, Saddam Hussein, computers, the entire Islamic world, and
so forth. By incorrectly labeling some politician, religious leader, or
group as the Antichrist, these authors have inflicted some injustice.
The identification of the Beast may not be apparent in the first half of
the Tribulation. Without question, however, you will know him when
he sets up a statue of himself in Jerusalem's rebuilt Temple.

# THE GEMATRIA OF THE ANTICHRIST

*I have come in my Father's name, and you do not accept me;
but if someone else comes in his own name, you will accept him.*
Jesus, John 5:43

*And what rough beast, its hour come round at last,
Slouches towards Bethlehem.*
William Butler Yeats, *The Second Coming*

Everyone knows the sum of the letter values in his name will be 666.
But what about the False Trinity Number, 13, used in the Bible as the
Number of Rebellion? Is it found in the gematria of the Beast's names?
The answer is yes, and this is another powerful affirmation of the

extraordinary mathematical form in the Holy Scriptures. Remarkably, *every name and title* of "the Antichrist" is a multiple of 13! Judge this:

T H E     A N T I C H R I S T       (John 2:22)

O     Α ν τ ι χ ρ ι σ τ ο ς

70   +   1   50   300   10   600   100   10   200   300   70   200   = 1911

$$\text{And } 1911 = 13 \times 147$$
$$= 13 + 13 + \ldots + 13.$$

A N T I C H R I S T S       (1 John 2:18)

Α ν τ ι χ ρ ι σ τ ο ι

1   50   300   10   600   100   10   200   300   70   10   = 1651

$$\text{Similarly, } 1651 = 13 \times 127$$
$$= 13 + 13 + \ldots + 13.$$

B E A S T       (Revelation 13:1)

Θ η ρ ι ο ν

9   8   100   10   70   50   = 247

$$\text{Again, } 247 = 13 \times 19$$
$$= 13 + 13 + \ldots + 13.$$

The final Beast will be equal to Satan in rebellious intentions. Authors of the Talmud have long recognized this. They frequently referred to the "Little Beast" whose number is 666:

L I T T L E     B E A S T

נ ו י ר ת

666 =   400   200   10   6   50

The False Prophet, called "another beast" in Revelation 13:11, has another but connected number, i.e., 42:

A N O T H E R     B E A S T

α λ λ ο       θ η ρ ι ο ν

1   30   30   70   +   9   8   100   10   70   50   = 378

This gematria relates to the second Beast and Nimrod (a former Antichrist type) because 378 = 42 + 42 + . . . + 42.

John's Apocalypse (16:2), speaks about "the mark of the beast":

THE    MARK   OF THE   BEAST

τ ο    χ α ρ α γ μ α   τ ο υ   Θ η ρ ι ο υ

300 70 + 600 1 100 1 3 40 1 + 300 70 400 + 9 8 100 10 70 400 = 2483

$$\text{And } 2483 = 13 \times 191$$
$$= 13 + 13 + \ldots + 13.$$

When referring to the Antichrist and the False Prophet, the Apocalypse uses the word "beast" on exactly 36 occasions, and the 36th triangle number is 666. The notorious reference "the number of the beast" (Revelation 13:18) has a double meaning, 666 and 13:

THE   NUMBER   OF THE   BEAST

τ ο ν    α ρ ι θ μ ο ν   τ ο υ   Θ η ρ ι ο υ

300 70 50 + 1 100 10 9 40 70 50 + 300 70 400 + 9 8 100 10 70 400 = 2067

$$\text{Similarly, } 2067 = 13 \times 159$$
$$= 13 + 13 + \ldots + 13.$$

Even the name "Gog" is nothing but 13s.

GOG

Γ ω γ

3 800 3 = 806

This sum is 13 x 62 or sixty-two 13s.

The NIV calls the apostasy engineered by Satan in the *last days* "the rebellion." The KJV calls it "a falling away." Whatever the translation, Paul, in the original Greek, uses the definite article "the" to distinguish it from all other apostasies (2 Thessalonians 2:3):

THE   REBELLION

η    α π ο σ τ α σ ι α

8 + 1 80 70 200 300 1 200 10 1 = 871

This number, like the word, is composed entirely of 13s.

$$\text{Once again, } 871 = 13 \times 67$$
$$= 13 + 13 + \ldots + 13.$$

The Book of Revelation calls Satan the "dragon":

**D R A G O N**
Δ ρ α κ ω ν
4 100 1 20 800 50 = 975

Which is 13 x 75 or 13 + 13 + . . . + 13.

Significantly, this book uses the word *dragon* precisely 13 times. Nowhere else is it found in the entire New Testament.

As we have seen, the most common name for the Antichrist's master is "Satan"; it is also a multiple of 13. (See pages 132-134 for a detailed list of his many names.)

**S A T A N**
Σ α τ α ν ς
200 1 300 1 50 1 6 = 559

This is 13 x 43 or 13 + 13 + . . . + 13.

The word *Satan* in Hebrew — which has a value of 13 x 28 — means *adversary*. E. W. Bullinger in his book *Number in Scripture* gives a longer list[7] of the 13s in the Antichrist's and the Devil's many names.

And lastly, between Jesus' Celestial Number and Satan's False Trinity Number there exists a unique polar relationship. By multiplying them, we find the following:

153 x 13 = [Celestial Number] x [False Trinity Number]
= 13 + 13 + . . . + 13 (153 times)
= 153 + 153 + . . . + 153 (13 times)
= [153 + 153] + [351] + [666 + 666]
Christ        reverse        Antichrist
= all triangle numbers.

As Bullinger says:
*Numbers must occur. The only question is, shall they be used by design or by chance? In order, or disorder? According to law, or without law? In the works of God they are used always in perfect order. Surely then we ought to look for the same order in His Word.*[8]

# THE FORTY-TWO MONTHS

*Antichrist is coming.*
1 John 2:18

The French call the Antichrist the "Antechrist," meaning the false Christ prophesied to come first. The Bible says he will precede our Lord by 7 years, Daniel's 70th week. In particular, the last 3½ years, often called the time of Jacob's Trouble, will be the most horrible in man's history. Consider this biblical time period:

$$3½ \text{ years} = 42 \text{ months of } 30 \text{ days each}$$
$$= 1260 \text{ days}$$
$$= 630 + 630 \text{ triangle days.}$$

At first, it seemed reasonable that the Antichrist's reign of terror would endure for 1332 or 666 + 666 days. (Despite this, God has more majestic patterns than any man can ever dream of. We see only a few threads in His immense garment.) On further reflection I realized the nearest triangle number to 666 is 630, and 1260 equals 630 + 630. The final days will center on Jerusalem, and even the last battle will be nearby. Notably, these 1260 days are a multiple of 70, Zion's Number?

$$1260 = 70 \text{ x } (6 + 6 + 6)$$
$$= 70 + 70 + \ldots + 70.$$

The Bible mentions these last 1260 days exactly 7 times:

1. Daniel 7:25 (KJV) in the Chaldee language as "a time and times and the dividing of time."
2. Daniel 12:7 in Hebrew as "a time, times and an half."
3. Revelation 12:14 in Greek as "a time, and times, and half a time."
4. Revelation 11:2 in Greek as "42 months."
5. Revelation 13:5, the same as 4.
6. Revelation 11:3 in Greek as "1260 days."
7. Revelation 12:6, the same as 6.

These verses give the time period in three languages, in two Testaments, and in three forms (years, months, and days). Nevertheless, the complete number of occurrences is still 7.

# ARMAGEDDON

*Then they gathered the kings together to a place that in Hebrew is called Armageddon.*
Revelation 16:16

*I saw heaven standing open and there before me was a white horse, whose rider is called Faithful and True. With justice he judges and makes war.*
Revelation 19:11

At the *time of the end* the mass of men will lead lives of open desperation. There will be no more wise counselors speaking the truth and standing by their word. Old people destitute of wisdom try to behave like the young, and the young affect the manner of their elders. Desire for material success has risen to supreme heights; love has vanished; self interest is the law of life.

> *Property is the only asset that confers rank!*
> *Wealth, the only source of virtue!*
> *Falsehood, the only wellspring to success!*
> *Lust, the only bond between man and woman!*
> *Sex, the only means of enjoyment!*
> *Life has slipped back into the chaos*
> *out of which God had originally created it!*

This is how it will end, not with a bang or a whimper, but with a cry of anguish. The Archangel who would be God has arrayed his brutes, the Antichrist and the False Prophet. Their armies of millions blanket an ancient plane northwest of Jerusalem in a place the Hebrews call Megiddo. Like Haman, Nero, and Hitler, these last Beasts have a final solution for the Jews. God has other plans.

When all seems lost and the Sons of Darkness appear in command and the green fields are awash in blood, then the sky will open and the Son of Light will descend. Jesus as almighty God will smite and defeat this demonic army *without hand*. Just as in Nebuchadnezzar's dream, the statue was demolished at its 10 toes by the Cube of God's truth — *cut without hand*.

Revelation 19:19-20 announces the outcome:

*Then I saw the beast and the kings of the earth and their armies gathered together to make war against the rider on the horse and his army. But the beast was captured, and with him the false prophet who had performed the miraculous signs on his behalf. With these signs he had deluded those who had received the mark of the beast [666] and worshiped his image. The two were thrown alive into the fiery lake of burning sulphur.*

Revelation 20:1-4 pronounces Satan's fate:

*And I saw an angel coming down out of heaven, having the key to the Abyss and holding in his hand a great chain. He seized the dragon, that ancient serpent, who is the devil and Satan, and bound him for a thousand years.*

After 6000 years of futile human attempts to find love and security by rebellion, it descends from Heaven. Now Jesus will rule the earth in true "peace and safety" for 1000 years.

I cannot leave this chapter without stating two final pieces of outstanding gematria. Both concern salvation: one particular, the other general. Each tacitly speaks of Jesus. Specifically, the Bible mentions "the salvation of Israel" just 3 times:

THE    SALVATION    OF  ISRAEL

η  Σ ω τ η ρ ι α  Ι σ ρ α η λ

8 + 200 800 300 8 100 10 1 + 10 200 100 1 8 30 = 1776

**This memorable number/date is 888 + 888.**

The general statement applies to the reader, the writer, and all mankind. In Isaiah 52:10 the mighty prophet declares:

*In the sight of all nations, and the ends*
*of the earth will see the salvation of our God.*

THE SALVATION OF OUR GOD

י שׁ ו ע ת    א ל ה י נ ו

888 = 6 50 10 5 30 1  +  400 70 6 300 10

The numbers, like the words, are for all eternity. By their very presence they imply design and divinity. They are not mute! They shout of man's redemption from his first disobedience which brought sin and death into the world and all our suffering. They sing of our Lord's birth, death, and resurrection. They redeem us!

# CHAPTER — 15

# THE MILLENNIUM

*When the thousand years are over, Satan will be released from*
*his prison and will go out to deceive the nations in the four corners*
*of the earth — Gog and Magog — to gather them for battle.*
Revelation 20:7-8

The word *millennium* cannot be found in the Bible. Yet the phrase "a thousand years" does appear in the Apocalypse (20:1-7) exactly 6 perfect triangle times. Two other versions of *millennium* frequently referred to are "Thy kingdom come" and "the age to come." To live in this Golden Age will be a blessing and a reward for the faithful, the dream of all the ages.

## THE NUMBER OF FINALITY
## AND JUDGMENT

Up to this point, I have not mentioned the biblical significance of the number 9. This final chapter seems the appropriate place for its introduction. It represents the end of all things concerning man and God's judgment or wrath upon them.

The gematria and the context of Hebrews 3:11 (KJV), "my wrath," imply that 9 pertains directly to God's just anger against sin:

$$\begin{array}{ccc} \text{M Y} & \text{W R A T H} \\ \tau\ \eta & o\ \rho\ \gamma & \mu\ o\ \upsilon \\ 300\ 8 + 70\,100\ 3 & 8 + 40\ 70\ 400 = 999 \end{array}$$

And 999 builds on the block of [37]: the Image of the Cube, the Holy of Holies, and the knowable part of God:

$$999 = [37] \times (9 + 9 + 9)$$
$$= [37] + [37] + \ldots + [37]$$

Consider the following examples involving 9, both sacred and profane. All relate to *final or last things*.

- God's last creation was Adam/45, the 9th triangle.
- Abraham was finally circumcised in his 99th year, but Ishmael was in his 13th (Genesis 17:24).
- Jesus died at the 9th hour (in all the Synoptic Gospels).
- During the 40 days before the Ascension, our Lord appeared 3 times to His Apostles. The last was the 9th and final "great sign" in John's Gospel.
- The digits are 0, 1, 2, 3, 4, 5, 6, 7, 8, and 9. Therefore, of all these, 9 is the final one. More important, it is the sum of a trinity of 3s.

$$9 = 3 + 3 + 3 =$$

- The final total of all the Hebrew (and Greek) letters is 4995 or 999 + 999 + 999 + 999 + 999.
- In old Greek manuscripts the number 99 was often written at the end of a benediction or a prayer. For centuries the meaning of this was a tiny mystery, until the 1900s. But consider:

A M E N

α μ η ν

1  40  8  50  = 99

What could be more natural? Significantly the last word in the entire Bible is *Amen* or *99*.

- The Millennial Reign will be a literal earthly kingdom with Jesus at its Head and His saints assisting. It will also be the 9th and final kingdom before the judgment of the Great White Throne. After the 8 empires of Hell ruled by a succession of Antichrists (Revelation 17:11), this is the promised earthly paradise.

# HISTORY'S FINAL TIME-LINE

While doing research for this book, the triangle structure underlying the Holy Scriptures repeatedly emerged. For instance, 3003 is the 77th triangle number, implying perhaps a special completeness:

$$77 \; \text{---------->} \; 1 + 2 + 3 + \ldots + 77$$
$$= 3003$$
$$= \text{a triangle number}$$

Interestingly, 3003 is a chiasmus like 888, [37] x [73], 373, and so many other biblical numbers, verses, and books.

In his time James Ussher (1581-1656), Archbishop of Armagh, was an eminent biblical scholar. By counting back through the generations, dates, and ages of the Pentateuch, he fixed the year of the Creation at 4004 B.C. For centuries afterward this date was always a marginal note in Genesis. It is uncertain if Reverend Ussher took into account the missing year zero between 1 B.C. and 1 A.D. Nevertheless, it seems more than a coincidence that 4005 is the 89th triangle number and almost the Archbishop's exact date (see Chapter Notes):

$$89 \; \text{---------->} \; 1 + 2 + 3 + \ldots + 89$$
$$= 4005$$
$$= \text{a triangle number}$$

The apparent time between 4005 B.C. and 3003 A.D. is 7008 years. By subtracting 1 for the missing year zero, we get 7007 years. On the surface this 7007 seems at odds with the Great Sabbath Week's 7000. But the extra 7 refers to the Creation Week of 7 seconds, days, months, years, millenniums, or whatever time unit God wanted. The previous count was from the end of the Week; this one is from its beginning.

FIGURE 15.1 shows a time-line from 1998, the middle (?) of the Tribulation, to 3003, the date of Satan's last battle. Following immediately after this is the Great White Throne Judgment and then the *first day of forever*. Remarkably, the triangle year of this revolt is a multiple of both the numbers of rebellion and completeness:

$$3003 = 13 + 13 + \ldots + 13 \; \text{(rebellion)}$$
$$= 7 + 7 + \ldots + 7 \; \text{(completeness)}$$

## TIME-LINE TO ETERNITY

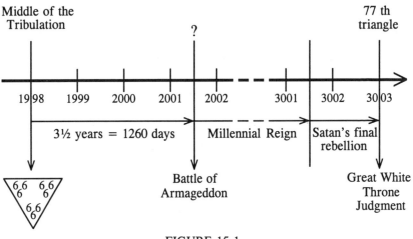

FIGURE 15.1

Scripture does not tell us the duration of Lucifer's last revolt. We are told it will extend over the whole earth, and that must take some months or perhaps even years. For one last time, Satan will tempt mankind: specifically, all those malcontent and mutinous souls born during the Millennium. Still, God — in His own time — will extinguish this final rebellion. Ultimately the evil will end when the Lord's angels hurl Satan into the Lake of Fire where the Antichrist and the False Prophet sank 1000 years earlier. With this, the Dark Angel is dead.

# FIRST AND LAST THINGS

The last book of the Bible, the 66th, is a triangle number. The last verse is the 21st, another triangle number. Of course Genesis 1:1, the first book and the first verse, are also triangles. And since this first verse contains so many wonders, it's natural to expect Revelation 22:21, the last verse, to as well. So let's consider its gematria. (Further details are in the Chapter Notes.)

---

**THE GRACE OF THE LORD JESUS CHRIST**
**BE WITH ALL OF YOU. AMEN.**

H  χ α ρ ι ς    τ ο υ    Κ υ ρ ι ο υ
8 + 600 1 100 10 200 + 300 90 400 + 20 400 100 10 70 400

η μ ω ν   Ι η σ ο υ    Χ ρ ι σ τ ο υ
+ 8  40 800 50 + 10 8 200 70 400 + 600 100 10 200 300 70 400

μ ε τ α   π α ν τ ω ν   υ μ ω ν.  Α μ η ν.
+ 40 5 300 1 + 80 1 50 300 800 50 + 400 40 800 50 + 1 40 8 50 = **8991**

---

FIGURE 15.2

In the Lord's Holy Word, this number 8991 has truly wondrous associations. By itself it may be expressed as two triangles in only one way:

$$8991 = 990 + 8001$$

The interested reader can check 990 and 8001 for triangularity by referring to the last page of the Chapter Notes. All three numbers in the above equation are multiples of 9, emphasizing the end of the Bible. Yet, 8991 can be written in another way, making its connection with finality perfectly clear:

$$8991 = 9 \times 999$$
$$= 999 + 999 + \ldots + 999 \text{ (9 times)}$$

This last verse consists of 10 words and 45 letters: both triangle numbers. With the final four from "Amen," the total rises to 49 or 7 x 7. Compare this to Genesis' initial sentence of 7 words and 28 perfect triangle letters. As we shall soon see, however, the similarities between the first and last verses penetrate far, far, far deeper.

At this point, let's summarize the most notable gematria results we have uncovered. These are 2701, the Bible's first verse; 8991, its last verse; [37], the building block number; and 888/Jesus, the quantity that suffuses the whole.

```
┌─────────────────────────────────────────────┐
│  ┌─────────────────────────────────────────┐ │
│  │                                         │ │
│  │        THE BIBLE'S GEMATRIA             │ │
│  │                                         │ │
│  │   2701 is the value of Genesis 1:1.     │ │
│  │   [37] is the building block.           │ │
│  │   888 is Jesus.                         │ │
│  │   8991 is Revelation 22:21.             │ │
│  │                                         │ │
│  └─────────────────────────────────────────┘ │
└─────────────────────────────────────────────┘
```

FIGURE 15.3

Incredibly, 8991, as well as being a multiple of 9, is also a multiple of [37] and the Trinity Number, 3.

$$8991 = [37] + [37] + \ldots + [37]$$
$$= 3 + 3 + \ldots + 3$$

Consequently, 2701, 888, and 8991 are all composed of [37]: the biblical building block. Even the word "savior" occurs exactly [37] times in Holy Scripture.

Revelation 22:21 completes the perfect Word of God — with finality. In one way, it is the direct opposite of Satan's wickedness in 1998 (= 666 + 666 + 666). This will likely be the middle of the Great Tribulation when the Antichrist sets up his image in Jerusalem's rebuilt Temple. The reader may have already noticed that 1998 and 8991 form a chiasmus of numerical as well as spiritual opposites.

1998 <----------> 8991

# THE THREE LAWS
# OF BIBLICAL MATHEMATICS

We have seen many marvels in the Lord's Holy Word, but the best is yet to come. The following three equations exhibit a trinity of transcendentally profound relationships connecting the gematria of the Bible's most prominent numbers: 2701, [37], 888, and 8991.

The First Law proves how the number/name of Jesus is found in Genesis 1:1. By summing a trinity of 888s cemented together by the building block number, [37], we get the exact gematria value of the Bible's initial triangle verse: 2701. Clearly Jesus is the binding energy in these eternal words.

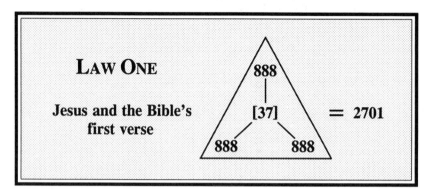

FIGURE 15.4

The Second Law displays how the number/name of Jesus is found in Revelation 22:21. By adding the amplified number of Jesus to a trinity of [37]s, we get the exact gematria of the Bible's last verse. These two laws are symmetrical. That is, by interchanging the [37]s and the 888s, Law One becomes Law Two and vice versa. Conclusively, Jesus is the essence in the final verse.

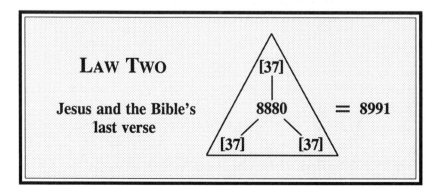

FIGURE 15.5

The Third Law reveals how our Savior joins the first and last verses together. This connection is at once both simple and profound. Look for yourself!

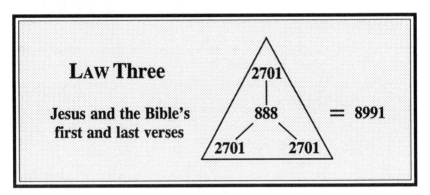

FIGURE 15.6

Decisively, Jesus is the energy that binds the Bible's initial and final verses. He is the *truth* woven through the fabric of the Holy Garment. This stamp of Divinity, this mark of the Godhead, is what makes the Bible different from every other book.

> *With immovable bonds Jesus unites the Bible.*
> *He is The Trinity in the first verse.*
> *He is the Essence in the last.*
> *He is the Universal Life Force joining*
> *the first and last, the Alpha and Omega.*

In our special time, as we approach the millennium, these new insights provide striking confirmation of the Bible's eternal verities and divine origin. They also reveal startling new truths that look back to the past and forward to a very different future.

# WHAT THEN MUST WE DO?

Prophecy is always for a future age; we cannot completely comprehend it. However, as its time draws near, The Holy Spirit makes future events clearer to us. Remember Daniel's inability to fully understand his own *end-time* prophecies; the great visionary was aware of his limitations. Yet, Gabriel told him (12:4):

> *But you, Daniel, close up and seal the words*
> *of the scroll until the time of the end. Many will*
> *go here and there to increase knowledge.*

Ecclesiastes 3:1 implies a similar idea:

> *To every thing there is a season,*
> *and a time to every purpose under the heaven.*

That time is about to arrive! What then must we do? Clearly, every possible means and effort must be taken to convert skeptics, atheists, and followers of false faiths. I believe the mathematical evidence set out in this book will gain any evangelist — however humble — a hearing in the homes of the godless and the halls of the damned. Prove, then proselytize.

> But, it is not enough to use mathematics!
> It is not enough to go to church on Sunday!
> It is not enough to be baptized!
> It is not enough to do good works!
> It is not enough to be born again!

We must call upon the name/number of Jesus, and do what He says to be saved! His Great Commission from the last verse of Matthew's Gospel commands us:

> *Therefore go and make disciples of all nations, baptizing them*
> *in the name of the Father and of the Son and of The Holy Spirit,*
> *and teaching them to obey everything I have commanded you.*
> *And surely I am with you always, to the very end of the age.*

**99**

Δ
Δ  Δ

# CHAPTER NOTES

All notes are referenced in the main text by the words *Chapter Notes* or by a numerical superscript.

## CHAPTER — 2

1 Bertrand Russell, *Why I Am Not a Christian* (London: George Allen & Unwin Ltd., 1958), p. 14.

## CHAPTER — 3

[P. 19] Calculating Probabilities:

To calculate the probability that 7 randomly chosen numbers from the first 1081 (inclusive) are all triangular, use the "choose" notation. The "n" in this formula represents the total number of objects, and the "r" is the number of these you choose.

$$C(n,r) = \frac{n!}{(n - r)! \; r!}$$

For example, imagine a jar containing 6 different varieties of candies, and a child who wishes to choose 2 of them. In how many different ways could he do this?

$$C(6,2) = \frac{6!}{(6 - 2)! \; 2!}$$

$$= \frac{720}{(24) \times (2)}$$

$$= 15$$

Therefore, the lucky youngster has 15 different choices.

So, the probability we are seeking is the number of ways of choosing 7 triangles from 46 divided by the total number of ways of choosing any 7 numbers from 1081. In symbols,

$$\frac{C(46,7)}{C(1081,7)} = \frac{46!}{(46 - 7)! \ 7!}$$

$$= 0.000000000159462482957$$

$$= \frac{1}{6,271,067,535} .$$

Or, the odds are 1 to 6,271,067,534.

[P. 22] The Next Row of Pascal's Triangle:

1  11  55  165  330  462  462  330  165  55  11  1

# CHAPTER — 4

[P. 26] Perfect Numbers:

I wish to prove that *every* even perfect number is also a triangle number. Before this can be done, it is necessary to develop a general test for triangularity. Fortunately, this isn't difficult.

PROVE: X is a triangle number
       if and only if $8X + 1$ is a square.

PROOF:          Let X = a triangle number
    $<=>$      $X = (n^2 + n)/2$   (n, a natural number)
    $<=>$     $8X = 8[(n^2 + n)/2]$
    $<=>$     $8X = 4n^2 + 4n$
    $<=> 8X + 1 = 4n^2 + 4n + 1$
    $<=> 8X + 1 = (2n + 1)^2$
    $<=> 8X + 1 =$ a square number

The symbol " $<=>$ " means "implies both ways" or "if and only if." This shows the argument can be worked from the top down or the bottom up. Now that we have a test for triangle numbers, let's try it on 10 and 13.

$$8 \times 10 + 1 = 80 + 1$$
$$= 81$$
$$= 9^2$$
$$= \text{square (Therefore, 10 is a triangle.)}$$

$$8 \times 13 + 1 = 104 + 1$$
$$= 105$$
$$\neq \text{square (So, 13 is not a triangle number.)}$$

For 2000 years, the world's best selling book has been the Holy Bible. Everybody knows this, but what is the second best? You might be surprised to learn it is a book on mathematics, written around 300 B.C., called Euclid's *Elements*.

In his celebrated text, Euclid proved that the formula $2^{n-1}(2^n-1)$ produces "even" perfect numbers if the bracketed expression is a prime number. For $(2^n-1)$ to be prime, it is necessary but not sufficient that the exponent, n, also be prime. Two thousand years later, Leonhard Euler (1707-1783) showed that this formula gives *all* the even perfects. No human knows of an "odd" perfect or whether one can exist. With the use of Eucild's formula and the previous theorem, we are ready to prove our main idea.

PROVE: If X is an even perfect number,
  then X is a triangle number.

PROOF:  Let X = an even perfect number
$$\Rightarrow \quad X = 2^{n-1}(2^n - 1)$$
$$\Rightarrow \quad 8X = 8[2^{n-1}(2^n - 1)]$$
$$\Rightarrow \quad 8X = 2^3[2^{2n-1} - 2^{n-1}]$$
$$\Rightarrow \quad 8X = 2^{2n+2} - 2^{n+2}$$
$$\Rightarrow 8X + 1 = 2^{2n+2} - 2^{n+2} + 1$$
$$\Rightarrow 8X + 1 = (2^{n+1} - 1)^2$$
$$\Rightarrow 8X + 1 = \text{a square number}$$

Therefore, by our previous theorem, X is a triangle number.

What follows is a list of all presently known perfects:

## PERFECT NUMBERS

| | FORMULA | NUMBER | NUMBER OF DIGITS |
|---|---|---|---|
| 1. | $2^1(2^2-1)$ | 6 | 1 |
| 2. | $2^2(2^3-1)$ | 28 | 2 |
| 3. | $2^4(2^5-1)$ | 496 | 3 |
| 4. | $2^6(2^7-1)$ | 8128 | 4 |
| 5. | $2^{12}(2^{13}-1)$ | 33,550,336 | 8 |
| 6. | $2^{16}(2^{17}-1)$ | 8,589,869,056 | 10 |
| 7. | $2^{18}(2^{19}-1)$ | 137,438,691,328 | 12 |
| 8. | $2^{30}(2^{31}-1)$ | | 19 |
| 9. | $2^{60}(2^{61}-1)$ | | 37 |
| 10. | $2^{88}(2^{89}-1)$ | | 54 |
| 11. | $2^{106}(2^{107}-1)$ | | 65 |
| 12. | $2^{126}(2^{127}-1)$ | | 77 |
| 13. | $2^{520}(2^{521}-1)$ | | 314 |
| 14. | $2^{606}(2^{607}-1)$ | | 366 |
| 15. | $2^{1,278}(2^{1,279}-1)$ | | 770 |
| 16. | $2^{2,202}(2^{2,203}-1)$ | | 1,327 |
| 17. | $2^{2,280}(2^{2,281}-1)$ | | 1,373 |
| 18. | $2^{3,216}(2^{3,217}-1)$ | | 1,937 |
| 19. | $2^{4,252}(2^{4,253}-1)$ | | 2,561 |
| 20. | $2^{4,422}(2^{4,423}-1)$ | | 2,663 |
| 21. | $2^{9,688}(2^{9,689}-1)$ | | 5,834 |
| 22. | $2^{9,940}(2^{9,941}-1)$ | | 5,985 |
| 23. | $2^{11,212}(2^{11,213}-1)$ | | 6,751 |
| 24. | $2^{19,936}(2^{19,937}-1)$ | | 12,003 |
| 25. | $2^{21,700}(2^{21,701}-1)$ | | 13,066 |
| 26. | $2^{23,208}(2^{23,209}-1)$ | | 13,973 |
| 27. | $2^{44,496}(2^{44,497}-1)$ | | 26,790 |
| 28. | $2^{86,242}(2^{86,243}-1)$ | | 51,924 |
| 29. | $2^{110,502}(2^{110,503}-1)$ | | 66,530 |
| 30. | $2^{132,048}(2^{132,049}-1)$ | | 79,502 |
| 31. | $2^{216,090}(2^{216,091}-1)$ | | 130,100 |
| 32. | $2^{756,838}(2^{756,839}-1)$ | | 455,663 |

[P. 28] Friendly Numbers:

Friendly numbers have other interesting properties I have neglected to mention. Presently, mathematicians know over 1000 pairs. Here are the first 7:

## FRIENDLY NUMBERS

| | |
|---|---|
| 220 | 284 |
| 1,184 | 1,210 |
| 2,620 | 2,924 |
| 5,020 | 5,564 |
| 6,232 | 6,368 |
| 10,744 | 10,856 |
| 12,285 | 14,595 |

Jacob's flocks weren't infinite. Judging from the size of the above quantities, it seems reasonable that the angels should direct him to the smallest pair of friendly numbers. Of these he chose the smaller half. All known couples have a common divisor and are either both even or both odd.

These pairs are just a generalization of perfect numbers. Let me explain. Pick any quantity and add all its divisors to obtain a second number. Then add all the divisors of this second number and continue the chain, hoping to return to the original quantity. If the first step immediately produces the original number, then the chain has a single link, and we call the number perfect. Two links, and the quantities are termed friendly. It is possible to have more than two links.

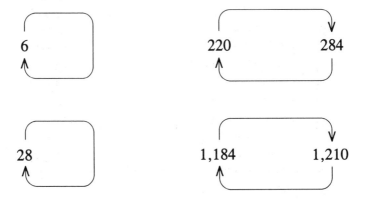

[P. 32] The Triangle Function:

Good diagrams can be effective aids to understanding certain formulas. Their truth can often be seen at a glance, rather than wading through a dull page of algebraic manipulation. Consider the sum of the first "n" numbers:

$$1 + 2 + 3 + \ldots + n = (n^2 + n)/2$$
$$= n(n + 1)/2 \text{ (factored form)}$$

The left side of the above equation is the definition for triangle numbers, while the right side is its very compact equivalent. At least that is what we wish to prove. The first n consecutive numbers are shown as specks in a triangular formation (see left illustration below). Two such triangles fit together to form a rectangle containing $n(n + 1)$ dots. Now divide by 2, and we have our equation:

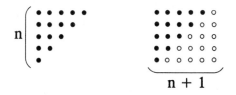

This formula dates from the ancient Greeks.

[P. 36] Three Rules in One:

Our present task is to show how Rules 1 and 2 can be considered as special cases of Rule 3, the Trinity Function. Initially, we will use only numbers with consecutive digits starting with 1, or scrambled versions of these, for example,

123, 321, 312, 132, 231, 213.

Note that the Digital Root Function becomes the Triangle Function when operating on these quantities. The digital root of 123 is $1 + 2 + 3$ or 6, a triangle number. Again, the digital root of 12345 (or any of its 120 permutations) is $1 + 2 + 3 + 4 + 5$ or 15, another triangle number. So, under these conditions, Rules 1 and 2 are identical.

Now we will prove that Rule 2 derives from Rule 3, with the type of numbers shown on the previous page. Consider the following remarkable formula:

$$(1 + 2 + 3 + \ldots + n)^2 = 1^3 + 2^3 + 3^3 + \ldots + n^3$$

On the left is the square of the nth triangle number while the right side is the Trinity Function applied to the same numbers. Before seeing the general proof, here is an example:

$$
\begin{aligned}
(1 + 2 + 3 + 4)^2 &= (10)^2 \\
&= 100 \\
&= 1 + 8 + 27 + 64 \\
&= 1^3 + 2^3 + 3^3 + 4^3
\end{aligned}
$$

So, $(1 + 2 + 3 + 4)^2 = 1^3 + 2^3 + 3^3 + 4^3$.

Therefore, the statement is true for n = 4. On the other hand, showing a formula is true for a few cases is not good enough to be considered a "mathematical proof," so let's continue.

The number arrangement on the following page, which extends infinitely down and to the right, is simply the multiplication table you learned in public school. Every entry is the product of the quantity to the far left of its row and the quantity at the top of its column. The table has been divided into *bent* strips, and the sum of all the numbers in the nth strip is $n^3$. In a square of five bent strips we have $1^3 + 2^3 + 3^3 + 4^3 + 5^3$. Since this figure is the multiplication table up to 5 times 5, it must be the product of all the following numbers:

$(1 + 2 + 3 + 4 + 5)(1 + 2 + 3 + 4 + 5)$ or $(1 + 2 + 3 + 4 + 5)^2$
And therefore, $(1 + 2 + 3 + 4 + 5)^2 = 1^3 + 2^3 + 3^3 + 4^3 + 5^3$.

Because our table goes to infinity in two directions, this result clearly generalizes to n terms.

So, $(1 + 2 + 3 + \ldots + n)^2 = 1^3 + 2^3 + 3^3 + \ldots + n^3$.

This is a very old formula, and due to the French mathematician Joseph Liouville (1809-1882), a generalization exists to numbers other than those containing consecutive digits.

## THE MULTIPLICATION TABLE

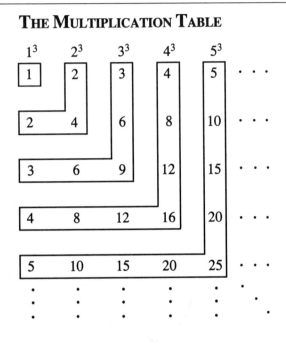

## CHAPTER — 5

[p. 43] The Trinity and the Triangles:

Here is an exhaustive list of all possible types of triangles:

1. Equilateral or perfect – – – – (all sides equal)
2. Right–angled scalene – – – – – (no sides equal)
3. Right–angled isosceles – – – – (two sides equal)
4. Acute scalene – – – – – – – – – (no sides equal)
5. Acute isosceles – – – – – – – – (two sides equal)
6. Obtuse scalene – – – – – – – – (no sides equal)
7. Obtuse isosceles – – – – – – – (two sides equal)

It's intriguing that the visual form of The Trinity comes in only 7 different varieties. The compact design on the next page shows one way these figures and the numbers 3 and 7 are related.

# THE SEVEN POSSIBLE TRIANGLES

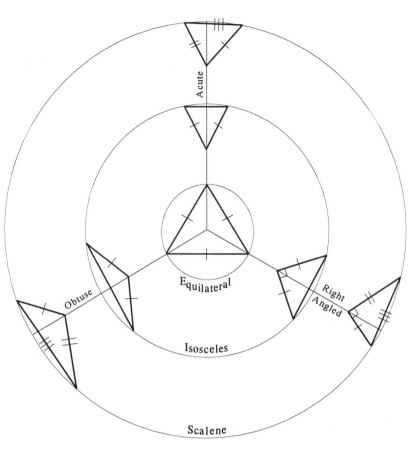

Emerging from the center of the equilateral triangle are 3 straight lines that cut 3 concentric circles. Each of these three lines slices through triangles with similar angles. Simultaneously, each of the 3 circles passes through triangles with a like number of sides. So, angles are on the lines; sides are on the circles; triangles are at the intersections.

1 Bryant Wood, "Score One for the Bible," *Time* magazine, 5 March 1990, p. 61.

# CHAPTER — 7

[P. 68] Computer Program:

Readers with a home computer can generate the Triangle of Creation with the surprisingly simple program listed below, written in Microsoft QBASIC. If you are using a different programming language, check your handbook for any slight variations, especially in the plot (my circle) command.

```
REM: This program prints the Triangle of Creation.
SCREEN 12
REM: Plot any three small circles to represent The Trinity.
CIRCLE (320, 4), 3
CIRCLE (106, 366), 3
CIRCLE (534, 366), 3
REM: The following line determines the number of points plotted.
FOR n& = 1 TO 1000000
    RANDOMIZE (n&)
    R = INT(RND * 3) + 1
  IF R = 1 THEN
    REM: The next two program lines divide the distance in half
    from any particle to point 1. To produce the hexagonal pattern
    of our present universe, divide by 3 or any larger number.
    X = INT((X + 320)/2)
    Y = INT((Y + 4)/2)
    REM: This line plots a circle of zero radius, i.e., a point.
    CIRCLE (X, Y), 0
  ELSEIF R = 2 THEN
    X = INT((X + 106)/2)
    Y = INT((Y + 366)/2)
    CIRCLE (X, Y), 0
  ELSE
    X = INT((X + 534)/2)
    Y = INT((Y + 366)/2)
    CIRCLE (X, Y), 0
  ENDIF
NEXT n&
```

[P. 70] Some Properties of the Triangle of Creation:

- Each nonempty triangle is similar to the whole figure (mathematicians say it is self-similar).
- The pattern is infinite in depth.
- The figure itself is just a speck in a continuous design.
- Combining the previous two points implies the pattern goes to infinity in both directions.
- Let the area of FIGURE 7.1 be 1 square unit. Then the area of the largest empty triangle is ¼, and the area of the three second largest empty triangles is (¼) x (¾). Continuing, we find the area of the nine next smaller triangles is (¼)(¾)², and so on. This process may be taken to infinity; in fact, the total sum of all the empty triangles can be found:

$$\text{SUM} = (\tfrac{1}{4}) + (\tfrac{1}{4})(\tfrac{3}{4})^1 + (\tfrac{1}{4})(\tfrac{3}{4})^2 + \dots$$
$$= \frac{\tfrac{1}{4}}{1-\tfrac{3}{4}} \text{ (sum of an infinite geometric series)}$$
$$= 1$$

Consequently, the sum of the empty spaces is identical to the total area — a very surprising result. This amazing outcome implies that our Lord can create something out of nothing. Something whose very form is as important as its filling.

[P. 81] Properties of Pascal's Triangle:

Running down the center are triangles of increasing size marked by empty circles; each made up entirely of even numbers. (See the diagram on the next page.) Near the top is the "triangle" of 1 circle, then the series continues with triangles of 6, 28, and 120 circles, etc. Two of those shown (i.e., 6 and 28) are perfect numbers. By definition, each is equal to the sum of all its divisors, except itself (for example, $6 = 1+2+3$ and 1, 2, and 3 all divide into 6).

Every even perfect number will be found among the "o" triangles. See page 338 for a complete list of all those presently known. Of course by the geometry of this setup, all these numbers are triangular whether perfect or not. For different values of n, these quantities can be found from Euclid's formula $2^{n-1}(2^n-1)$. For example:

$$n = 1 \text{ implies } 2^{1-1}(2^1-1) = 2^0(1) = 1$$
$$n = 2 \text{ implies } 2^{2-1}(2^2-1) = 2^1(3) = 6 \text{ (perfect)}$$
$$n = 3 \text{ implies } 2^{3-1}(2^3-1) = 2^2(7) = 28 \text{ (perfect)}$$
$$n = 4 \text{ implies } 2^{4-1}(2^4-1) = 2^3(15) = 120$$

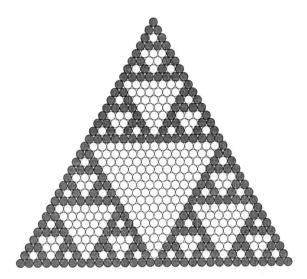

This is Pascal's Triangle with the even numbers as empty circles and the odds as shaded circles. Note the clear triangles.

[P. 81] Pascal's Pyramid:

Some readers may be asking themselves, "Can a flat 2-dimensional triangle provide a true and complete image of God's material creation, the Cosmos, and His spiritual creation, the Bible?" True, yes. Complete, no.

Remarkably, everything we have shown about the Triangle of Creation and its alter ego, Pascal's Triangle, can be done in 3 dimensions, all properties are then generalized. Consider for a moment Pascal's Pyramid, shown on the following page. Every entry is the sum of the 3 numbers *above*. Imagine you are at the third level in the pyramid, standing on the number 6. When you look directly above, you see three 2s forming a triangle. The entry you are standing on is the sum of these 2s. Each of the pyramid's faces is a Pascal Triangle, but the interior has additional structure.

As a second example of how these properties generalize, assume we replaced every odd number by a shaded dot and every even by an empty dot. The entire structure would now be partitioned into pyramids of even dots increasing in size — analogous to our triangles on the previous page. But the faces do not form part of any pyramid; they are as before.

## PASCAL'S TRIANGLE OR THE PYRAMID OF CREATION

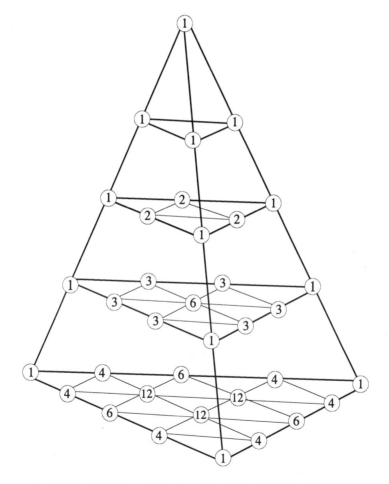

1. Each of the 3 upright faces is a Pascal Triangle.
2. The whole structure is infinitely large.
3. All properties from 2 dimensions generalize to 3 dimensions.

1 Heinz R. Pagels, *Perfect Symmetry* (New York: Bantam Books, 1986), pp. 211-220.

# CHAPTER — 8

[P. 90] Reverse Triangle Numbers:

| | |
|---|---|
| 55 | 55 |
| 66 | 66 |
| **[153]** | **[351]** |
| 171 | 171 |
| 595 | 595 |
| 666 | 666 |
| 3003 | 3003 |
| 5995 | 5995 |
| 8778 | 8778 |
| 15051 | 15051 |
| [17578] | [87571] |
| 66066 | 66066 |
| [185745] | [547581] |
| 617716 | 617716 |
| 828828 | 828828 |
| 1269621 | 1269621 |
| [1461195] | [5911641] |
| 1680861 | 1680861 |
| 3544453 | 3544453 |
| 5073705 | 5073705 |
| 5676765 | 5676765 |
| 6295926 | 6295926 |

Reversible triangle numbers can be divided into three groups:

1. Those with identical repeated digits (e.g., 55).
2. Symmetrical ones with different repeated digits (e.g., 3003).
3. Those rare ones with nonsymmetrical digits [bracketed above, e.g., 153].

[P. 91] Truncated Triangle Numbers:

Readers with a home computer and some knowledge of programming can quickly prove that only 6 truncated triangle numbers exist. After you have written and run your program, the print-out will be a short list of a half dozen numbers. But how do we know this inventory is complete for the infinity of possibilities? Let's reason as follows. To have a truncated triangle number with five digits implies you had one with four digits. But, if your program is correct, then there are none with four digits. Accordingly, there cannot be any with five. And reasoning in a similar fashion, there can be none with six digits or seven or eight, and so on.

[P. 92] Hexagonal Numbers:

Two types of hexagonal numbers exist: vertex-centered and centered. Here, we are dealing with the former. The proof that these quantities are embedded in the triangle numbers follows:

Let's call the rth n-gonal number $P(r,n)$. There is a little known formula[2] that easily allows you to find such quantities. It says,

$$P(r,n) = r/2[r(n-2) - n + 4]^{\diamond}.$$ For example:
$$P(153,6) = 153/2[153(6-2) - 6 + 4]$$
$$= 46665.$$

Now we will test in general for triangularity by multiplying both sides of $\diamond$ by 8 and adding 1:

$$8P(r,n) + 1 = 4r[r(n-2) - n + 4] + 1$$
$$= 4r[nr - 2r - n + 4] + 1$$
$$= 4nr^2 - 8r^2 - 4nr + 16r + 1$$
$$= (4n-8)r^2 + (16-4n)r + 1.$$

All this gives us a quadratic expression in r.
For triangularity, $8P(r,n) + 1$ must equal a perfect square.
That is, $b^2 - 4ac$ must equal 0 ($a = 4n - 8$, $b = 16 - 4n$, $c = 1$).

Which means $(16 - 4n)^2 - 4(4n - 8)(1) = 0$.
Therefore, $256 - 128n + 16n^2 - 16n + 32 = 0$,
or $n^2 - 9n + 18 = 0$, where $(n - 3)(n - 6) = 0$.

So, n = 3 or n = 6. Unexpectedly, this last equation has only two solutions. One of which implies all hexagonal numbers (i.e., n = 6) are also triangular. This means that out of an infinity of choices only the 6-gonal numbers are wholly contained within the 3-gonal. In fact, every second triangle is also a hexagon. Compare FIGURES 3.2 and 8.3.

By substituting n = 6 in ✩ (from the previous page), we get $2r^2 - r$: a general formula for the rth hexagonal number. For example, the 9th such quantity is $2x9^2 - 9 = 2x81 - 9 = 153$.

[P. 93] The Roots:

To uncover more of the structure in Holy Scripture use the Digital Root Rule on 153 and 666:

$$153 \; ---> \; 1 + 5 + 3 = 9$$
$$666 \; ---> \; 6 + 6 + 6 = 18$$
$$\text{and again } 18 \; ---> \; 1 + 8 = 9$$

The digital roots are identical, although 666 missed it on the first application.

[P. 95] The Proof that 153 is the Center of the Net:

Perhaps the easiest method of proof is to write a short computer program to sum the cubes of all the digits of every multiple of 3 less than 2000. By inspecting the print-out, you can quickly confirm that all such numbers end at exactly 153. Quantities larger than 2000 need not be tested since the Trinity Function automatically reduces them to a number below it. Barring the above approach, you will find a proof in the *New Scientist*, 21 December 1961, p. 753.

1 David Ulansey, "The Mithraic Mysteries," *Scientific American*, Dec. 1989, p. 133.
2 Ross Honsberger, *Ingenuity in Mathematics* (New York: Random House, 1970), pp. 118-119.

# CHAPTER — 9

[P. 107] Phi and the Pentagram:

PROVE: In the Satanic Pentagram the ratio of each
length to the next larger length is 1 to $\phi$.

PROOF:

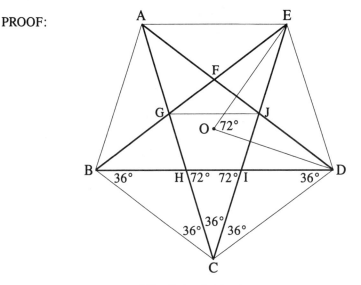

**The Satanic Pentagram**

AB = BC = CD = DE = EA (a regular pentagon).
Therefore, AC = AD = BD = BE = CE (equal diagonals).

Let "O" be the center of the figure.
∠ EOD = 360°/5 = 72° (angle at the center).
So, ∠ OED = ∠ ODE = 54° (base angles in isosceles triangles).

Therefore, ∠ A = ∠ B = ∠ C = ∠ D = ∠ E = 108°.
So ∠ CBD = ∠ CDB = 36°, and therefore ∠ HCB = ∠ ICD = 36° also
(base angles in isosceles triangles). Therefore, ∠ HCI = 36°.

Let CH = CI = a, and HI = 1 unit. Now consider ∆HIC:

$$\frac{\sin(72°)}{a} = \frac{\sin(36°)}{1} \quad \text{(by the Sine Law).}$$

So, $a = \dfrac{\sin(72°)}{\sin(36°)} = \dfrac{2\sin(36°)\cos(36°)}{\sin(36°)} = 2\cos(36°).$

Also, $1^2 = a^2 + a^2 - 2(a)(a)\cos(36°)$ (by the Cosine Law).
Therefore, $1 = 2a^2 - 2a^2\cos(36°) = 2a^2 - a^2[2\cos(36°)]$.
So, $1 = 2a^2 - a^3$ (by substituting "a" for $2\cos(36°)$).
To find "a" we have only to find the correct root of
$a^3 - 2a^2 + 1 = 0$, or $(a - 1)(a^2 - a - 1) = 0$.

From the first factor, $R_1 = 1$, which is not "a" since it would make $\triangle HIC$ equilateral. From the second factor, and by using the quadratic formula, we can find two more roots. $R_2 = (1 - \sqrt{5})/2 = -0.618 \ldots$, which is also impossible since "a" is a distance and hence positive.

$$\begin{aligned} \text{Therefore, } R_3 &= (1 + \sqrt{5})/2 \\ &= 1.618\ldots \\ &= \phi \text{ (Phi)} \\ &= a \ (= CH = CI). \end{aligned}$$

So, $CH{:}HI = \phi{:}1 = \phi$.

Therefore, isosceles triangles with angles 72°, 72°, and 36° have a ratio of short base to long side of 1 to $\phi$. Just as 666 is the 36th triangle number, so $\phi$ is the number in the triangle whose angles are all multiples of 36. Consider triangles $\triangle HIC$, $\triangle GJC$, and $\triangle AEC$ which are isosceles and share $\angle ACE = 36°$:

$$\begin{aligned} \text{Therefore, } &\triangle HIC \\ &\sim \triangle GJC \\ &\sim \triangle AEC \text{ (similar triangles).} \end{aligned}$$

This implies a large number of equal ratios among the sides; in particular

$$GH{:}CH{:}CG{:}CA = 1{:}\phi{:}\phi^2{:}\phi^3.$$

For this reason, the ratio of every length to the next larger length is 1 to Phi. The Satanic Pentagram is, in reality, a geometrical illustration of the number of original sin.

[P. 110] Phi and the Navel:

PROVE: The navel divides the human body in
the ratio of $\phi$ to 1 (i.e., KM:AK = $\phi$).

PROOF:

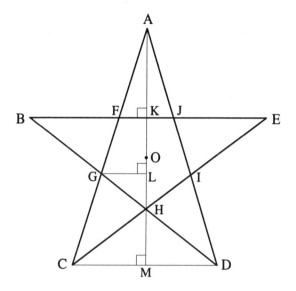

**The Man in the Pentagram**

Draw a perpendicular line from A to CD, cutting BE at K and
touching CD at M. From G draw a perpendicular to AM at L.

Therefore, $\triangle$AFK (similar right–angled
$\sim \triangle$AGL    triangles and they
$\sim \triangle$ACM    all share $\angle$CAM).

So, AF:AG = AK:AL = AG:AC = AL:AM.
Therefore, $1:\phi$ = AK:AL = $1:\phi$ = AL:AM (see previous proof).
So, (AK)(AM) = (AL)$^2$, and (AK)($\phi$) = AL.
And (AK)(AM) = (AK)$^2$($\phi$)$^2$ (by substitution).
So, AM:AK = $\phi^2$.

Hence, AM:AK $-$ 1 = $\phi^2$ $-$ 1, ($\phi^2$ $-$ 1 = $\phi$, see next proof).
And so, (AM–AK):AK = $\phi$. Finally, KM:AK = $\phi$.

> Therefore, the navel exactly divides
> the ordinary human body in the ratio of $\phi$ to 1.

[P. 109] The Three Forms of Phi:

Show that the decimal (irrational) part of Phi is unchanged by taking its reciprocal or by squaring.

RECIPROCAL:

$$\text{Since Phi} = \frac{(1 + \sqrt{5})}{2} = \phi,$$

$$\text{therefore } \frac{1}{\text{Phi}} = \frac{2}{(1 + \sqrt{5})}$$

$$= \frac{2}{(1 + \sqrt{5})} \frac{(1 - \sqrt{5})}{(1 - \sqrt{5})}$$

$$= \frac{2(1 - \sqrt{5})}{-4}$$

$$= \frac{\sqrt{5} + 1 - 2}{2}$$

$$= \frac{\sqrt{5} + 1}{2} - 1.$$

$$\text{Therefore, } \frac{1}{\phi} = \phi - 1,$$

$$\text{or } \frac{1}{1.618\ldots} = 1.618\ldots - 1.$$

SQUARING:

$$\phi^2 = \frac{(1 + \sqrt{5})^2}{2^2}$$

$$= \frac{1 + 2\sqrt{5} + 5}{4}$$

$$= \frac{3 + \sqrt{5}}{2}$$

$$= \frac{1 + \sqrt{5}}{2} + \frac{2}{2}$$

$$\text{Therefore, } \phi^2 = \phi + 1,$$

$$\text{or } (1.618\ldots)^2 = 1.618\ldots + 1.$$

SUMMARY:

$$\text{Phi} = \phi = 1.618\ldots = \phi \pm 0$$

$$\frac{1}{\text{Phi}} = \frac{1}{\phi} = 0.618\ldots = \phi - 1$$

$$(\text{Phi})^2 = \phi^2 = 2.618\ldots = \phi + 1$$

These results may be checked by using a hand-held calculator. The preservation of the irrational part of Satan's sin number after flipping and squaring is unique in all of mathematics.

[P. 113] Satan's Sequence and Phi:

$$1, 1, 2, 3, 5, 8, 13, 21, 34, 55, 89, 144, \ldots$$

The entries in the sequence are named "Fibonacci" after their 13th century discoverer, but I call the entire series and the process of formation satanic. In 1843 the French mathematician J.P.M. Binet discovered the peculiar formula given below. It will generate the nth term of this sequence without knowing the previous two terms.

$$F_n = \frac{\left(\dfrac{1 + \sqrt{5}}{2}\right)^n - \left(\dfrac{1 - \sqrt{5}}{2}\right)^n}{\sqrt{5}}$$

Surprisingly, this formula is exact. That is, if you substitute 10 for n, you will get precisely 55, the 10th Fibonacci number. It is totally unexpected that the irrationals on the right should produce the whole numbers on the left. The generating agents are two forms of the Devil's number: 1.618... and 0.618....

Since $\phi = \dfrac{1 + \sqrt{5}}{2}$, therefore $-\phi^{-1} = \dfrac{1 - \sqrt{5}}{2}$.

Now substitute these into Binet's formula.

Therefore, $F_n = \dfrac{\phi^n - (-\phi)^{-n}}{\sqrt{5}}$.

By using this formula, we can now prove that Phi is cleverly hidden in Satan's sequence.

PROVE: Limit as n $\longrightarrow \infty$ of $\dfrac{F_{n+1}}{F_n}$ is $\phi$.

PROOF: $\underset{n \longrightarrow \infty}{\text{Lim}} \dfrac{F_{n+1}}{F_n} = \underset{n \longrightarrow \infty}{\text{Lim}} \dfrac{\phi^{n+1} - (-\phi)^{-n-1}}{\sqrt{5}} \times \dfrac{\sqrt{5}}{\phi^n - (-\phi)^{-n}}$

$\qquad = \underset{n \longrightarrow \infty}{\text{Lim}} \dfrac{\phi^{n+1} - (-\phi)^{-n-1}}{\phi^n - (-\phi)^{-n}}$

$\qquad = \underset{n \longrightarrow \infty}{\text{Lim}} \dfrac{\phi - (-1)^{-n-1} \phi^{-2n-1}}{1 - (-1)^{-n} \phi^{-2n}}$

$\qquad = \dfrac{\phi - (-1)^{-n-1} \times 0}{1 - (-1)^{-n} \times 0}$

$\qquad = \phi$

Therefore, $\underset{n \longrightarrow \infty}{\text{Lim}} \dfrac{F_{n+1}}{F_n} = \phi$.

So the exact limit is Phi.

1 Manley P. Hall, *The Secret Teaching of All Ages*, p. CIV.
2 Rudolf Koch, *The Book of Signs* (New York: Dover Publications Inc., 1955), p. 6.
3 Peter S. Stevens, *Patterns in Nature* (Boston: Atlantic-Little, Brown Books, 1974), p. 127.
4 David Bergamini, *Mathematics* (New York: Time-Life Books, 1963), p. 94.
5 O. A. W. Dilke, *Reading the Past: Mathematics and Measurement* (London: British Museum Publications, 1987), p. 34.
6 Ladislao Reti, *The Unknown Leonardo* (New York: McGraw-Hill Book Co., 1974), p. 7.
7 Kenneth Clark, *Leonardo da Vinci* (London: Penguin Books Ltd., 1975), pp. 45-46.
8 Ibid., p. 100.

9 Dmitri Merejkowski, *The Romance of Leonardo da Vinci* (New York: The Modern Library, Random House, 1928), p. 9.

10 E. W. Bullinger, *Number in Scripture* (Grand Rapids, Michigan: Kregel Publications, 1967), p. 119.

11 Ibid., p. 243.

12 John Ciardi, *The Inferno* (New York: The New American Library, 1954), pp. 284-285.

13 Arthor Lyons, *Satan Wants You* (New York: Mysterious Press Books, 1989), p. 108.

14 Jane Furth, Mini Murphy and Bureaus, "Satan," *Life* magazine, June 1989, p. 48.

# CHAPTER — 10

[P. 168] Satan, 17, and Prime Numbers:

A prime number cannot be split into factors other than itself and 1. Or you could say a prime can only be divided by itself and 1. The highest prime dividing 153 is 17, and it does this precisely 9 times (i.e., $153 \div 17 = 9$). Also, 7 is the number of completeness; consequently, it is interesting that the 7th prime is 17. The following table lists all primes less than 100.

## THE FIRST 25 PRIME NUMBERS

| 1. 2 | 2. 3 | 3. 5 | 4. 7 | 5. 11 |
|---|---|---|---|---|
| 6. 13 | **7. 17** | 8. 19 | 9. 23 | 10. 29 |
| 11. 31 | 12. 37 | 13. 41 | 14 . 43 | 15. 47 |
| 16. 53 | 17. 59 | 18. 61 | 19. 67 | 20. 71 |
| 21. 73 | 22. 79 | 23. 83 | 24. 89 | 25. 97 |

You can see from the above table that 17 is the 7th prime, and this, plus the fact that $17 = 7 + 10$, implies it represents total completeness or abundance. As was proven in the text, 17 leads directly to the great Fish Number, 153. Surprisingly, it can also lead to the number of Lucifer-Antichrist, 666. Previously we showed that the mathematics of 153 and 666 symbolically mirrored the real struggle between Jesus and Lucifer. Again we see this with respect to 17. For example, consider the sum of the squares of the first 7 primes — the ones up to 17:

$$
\begin{aligned}
\text{SUM} &= 2^2 + 3^2 + 5^2 + 7^2 + 11^2 + 13^2 + 17^2 \\
&= 2x2 + 3x3 + 5x5 + 7x7 + 11x11 + 13x13 + 17x17 \\
&= 4 + 9 + 25 + 49 + 121 + 169 + 289 \\
&= 666
\end{aligned}
$$

Most ancient authorities looked on "2" (the exponent) as the number of opposition, division, or difference. Since 1 symbolizes unity and cannot be divided, 2 says there is another opposing the first. The difference between them may be for good or evil.

1 Saint Augustine, *The City of God* (U.K.: Penguin Books Ltd., 1986), p. 645.
2 O.A.W. Dilke, *Mathematics and Measurement* (London: British Museum Publications, 1987), p. 23.
3 Henry M. Morris, *Many Infallible Proofs* (El Cajon, California: Master Books, 1988), p. 325.

# CHAPTER — 11

[P. 186 and P. 189] Star Numbers:

Star numbers are generated by the following rule:

$$
\text{n} \ \text{----------->} \ 6n^2 - 6n + 1
$$
pre-image                image

For example:

$$
\begin{aligned}
7 \ \text{----------->} \ &6x7^2 - 6x7 + 1 \\
&= 294 - 42 + 1 \\
&= 253
\end{aligned}
$$

$$156 \; ---------> \; 6\times156^2 - 6\times156 + 1$$
$$= 6\times24{,}336 - 936 + 1$$
$$= 146{,}016 - 936 + 1$$
$$= 145{,}081$$

Therefore 253 and 145,081 are star numbers.

Quantities simultaneously star and triangular are very rare. The Flag of Israel Number, 253, is one such; the next is 49,141. Here is a list of the first twenty-four star numbers. Notice the last entries are growing by hundreds:

## STAR NUMBERS

| | | | | | | | |
|---|---|---|---|---|---|---|---|
| 1. | 1 | 2. | 13 | 3. | 37 | 4. | 73 |
| 5. | 121 | 6. | 181 | 7. | 253 | 8. | 337 |
| 9. | 433 | 10. | 541 | 11. | 661 | 12. | 793 |
| 13. | 937 | 14. | 1093 | 15. | 1261 | 16. | 1441 |
| 17. | 1633 | 18. | 1837 | 19. | 2053 | 20. | 2281 |
| 21. | 2521 | 22. | 2773 | 23. | 3037 | 24. | 3313 |

[P. 190] Triangles in the Star:

Recall the definition of triangle numbers and how to add them quickly:

$$n \; ---------> \; 1 + 2 + 3 + \ldots + n$$
$$= (n^2 + n)/2$$

$$13 \; ---------> \; (13^2 + 13)/2$$
$$= (169 + 13)/2$$
$$= (182)/2$$
$$= 91$$

$$46 \text{ --------> } (46^2 + 46)/2$$
$$= (2116 + 46)/2$$
$$= (2162)/2$$
$$= 1081$$

$$155 \text{ --------> } (155^2 + 155)/2$$
$$= (24,025 + 155)/2$$
$$= (24,180)/2$$
$$= 12,090$$

Therefore 91, 1081, and 12,090 are triangle numbers.

[P. 191] The Seals and the Stars:

$$165 \text{ --------> } (165^2 + 165)/2$$
$$= (27,225 + 46)/2$$
$$= (27,390)/2$$
$$= 13,695$$

$$510 \text{ --------> } (510^2 + 510)/2$$
$$= (260,100 + 510)/2$$
$$= (260,610)/2$$
$$= 130,305$$

So 13,695 and 130,305 are also triangle numbers.

1 Hal Lindsey, *The Late Great Planet Earth* (Grand Rapids, Michigan: Zondervan Publishing House, 1973), pp. 99-100.
2 Frederic G. Kenyon, *The Chester Beatty Biblical Papyri* (London: Emery Walker Ltd., 1936), p. 1 – Foreword. The catalogue identification number of the papyrus is $P^{47}$.

# CHAPTER — 12

[P. 200] A Triangular Pi:

Born in what is now Germany, one of the most gifted men of the seventeenth century was Gottfried Wilhelm von Leibnitz (1646-1716).

In youth, his teachers regarded him as a prodigy; in maturity, everyone knew him as a genius at mathematics, philosophy, and science. He was a contemporary of Sir Isaac Newton. Unfortunately, these brilliant men had a long, shameful, public quarrel over who first invented "the calculus," which cast a shadow on both their reputations.

To list all Leibnitz' discoveries and accomplishments would take several pages and wander far from our present purpose. For us, we need only say he discovered an exact formula for pi in terms of an infinite series. Let $T_1 = 1$, $T_2 = 3$, $T_3 = 6$, $T_4 = 10$, $T_5 = 15$, etc., and so the nth triangle number is $T_n$. By replacing his quantities with triangle numbers, the following striking equation results:

$$\pi = (10 - 6)\left(1 - \frac{1}{6 - 3} + \frac{1}{15 - 10} - \frac{1}{28 - 21} + \ldots\right)$$

$$= (T_4 - T_3)\left(1 - \frac{1}{T_3 - T_2} + \frac{1}{T_5 - T_4} - \frac{1}{T_7 - T_6} + \ldots\right)$$

For such a completely erratic decimal as pi, a more regular formula is hard to imagine. You determine the accuracy by how far you take the continued expression on the right side. Exact equality is reached only at infinity. Amazing isn't it. These basic triangular bricks of God's Holy Word provide us with a completely regular, simple formula for one of nature's most unruly numbers.

[P. 221] Hexagonal Numbers:

What follows is a general formula for producing centered hexagonal numbers:

$$n \text{ ---------> } 3n^2 - 3n + 1$$
$$\text{pre-image} \qquad\qquad \text{image}$$

For example:

$$4 \text{ ---------> } 3(4)^2 - 3(4) + 1$$
$$= 48 - 12 + 1$$
$$= 37$$

## HEXAGONAL NUMBERS

| 1.  1 | 2.  7 | 3.  19 | 4.  **37** |
|-------|-------|--------|------------|
| 5.  61 | 6.  91 | 7.  127 | 8.  169 |
| 9.  217 | 10.  271 | 11.  331 | 12.  397 |
| 13.  469 | 14.  547 | 15.  631 | 16.  721 |
| 17.  817 | 18.  919 | 19.  1027 | 20.  1141 |

[P. 222] Cubic and Hexagonal Numbers:

Familiarity with the principle of mathematical induction will allow you to prove the general equation written below. In English it says, "the sum of the first n hexagonal quantities is n cubed." On page 222 you will find specific examples.

$$1 + 7 + 19 + 37 + \ldots + (3n^2 - 3n + 1) = n^3$$

1 Flavius Josephus, *The Complete Works of Josephus*, translated by William Whiston (Grand Rapids, Michigan: Kregel Publications, 1981), p. 233.
2 Ibid., p. 581.
3 Richard N. Ostling, "Time for a New Temple?," *Time* magazine, 16 Oct. 1988, p. 71.
4 Ibid., p. 71.
5 Herbert Silberer, *Hidden Symbolism of Alchemy and the Occult Arts* (New York: Dover Publications, 1971), p. 197.

# CHAPTER — 13

[P. 250] Cheops:

Let's work out the full implications of Herodotus' report that the area of each triangular face is equal to the square of the height. Consider the figure below:

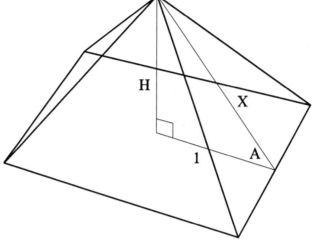

Let X be the slant height of any triangular face,
and assume the base is 2 units long. In no way does this
assumption affect the generality of the conclusion.

Therefore, the face area $= (\frac{1}{2})(\text{base})(\text{height})$
$$= (\frac{1}{2})(2)(X)$$
$$= X.$$

Now the slant height is the hypotenuse of a right-angled triangle
whose legs are 1 (half the base) and H (the pyramid's height).

By the Pythagorean Theorem, $X^2 = 1^2 + H^2$,
and so $H^2 = X^2 - 1$.

When the area of the face equals the square of the height,
we have the following equation:

$$X = X^2 - 1 \text{ or, } X^2 - X - 1 = 0.$$

This is easily solved by the quadratic formula to give the positive root:

$$X = \frac{(1+\sqrt{5})}{2}$$
$$= 1.618\ldots$$
$$= Phi.$$

Because $H^2 = X^2 - 1$,
therefore, $H = \sqrt{X^2 - 1}$ ($H > 0$)
$$= \sqrt{(Phi)^2 - 1}$$
$$= \sqrt{Phi}.$$

So the perpendicular height, H, is the square root of Phi, and the slant height, X, is Phi. Accordingly, this number is built into the basic structure of the pyramid.

[P. 250] The Angle of the Face:

With these ratios, the slope of the pyramid's face with the ground can be found. Call the angle A (see diagram on the previous page):

$$\text{Since } \cos(A) = \frac{1}{Phi}$$
$$= 0.618\ldots,$$
therefore $A = 52$ degrees.

This result agrees with the actual measured angle of Cheops' Pyramid.

1 Herodotus, *The Persian Wars*, translated by George Rawlinson (New York: Modern Library Book, Random House, 1942), p. 179.
2 Ibid., p. 180.
3 Henry David Thoreau, *Thoreau: Walden and Other Writings* (New York: Bantam Books, 1962), p. 148.
4 Howard Eves, *Historical Topics for the Mathematics Classroom* (Washington, DC: National Council of Teachers of Mathematics, 1969), p. 206.
5 E. W. Bullinger, *Number in Scripture* (Grand Rapids, Michigan: Kregel Publications, 1967), p. 284.
6 W. S. Andrews, *Magic Squares and Cubes* (New York: Dover Publications, 1960), p. 123.

7 John Burns, "New Babylon is Stalled by a Modern Upheaval," *New York Times International*, 11 Oct. 1990, p. A-13.

8 Herodotus, *The Persian Wars*, translated by George Rawlinson (New York: Modern Library Book, Random House, 1942), pp. 511-512.

9 E. W. Bullinger, *Number in Scripture* (Grand Rapids, Michigan: Kregel Publications, 1967), pp. 222-223.

10 J. R. Hamilton, *Alexander the Great* (Pittsburgh PA: University of Pittsburgh Press, 1974), p. 151.

11 Ibid., p. 156.

12 Ibid., p. 120.

13 Ibid., pp. 75-76.

14 Ibid., pp. 138-140.

15 Ibid., p. 29.

16 Flavius Josephus, *The Complete Works of Josephus*, translated by William Whiston (Grand Rapids, Michigan: Kregel Publications, 1981), p. 244.

17 Tacitus, *The Annals of Imperial Rome*, translated by Michael Grant (Great Britain: Penguin Books, 1962), p. 354.

18 Ibid., p. 273.

19 Flavius Josephus, *The Complete Works of Josephus*, translated by William Whiston (Grand Rapids, Michigan: Kregel Publications, 1981), p. 540.

20 Ibid., p. 587.

21 Robert Payne, *The Life and Death of Adolf Hitler* (New York: Praeger Publishers, 1973), p. 258.

22 Leo Tolstoy, *War and Peace*, translated by Constance Garnett (London: Pan Books Ltd., 1972), p. 720.

23 Robert Payne, *The Life and Death of Adolf Hitler* (New York: Praeger Publishers, 1973), p. 392.

# CHAPTER — 14

[P. 306] The Great 2000-Digit Period:

PROVE: The digits in the 3rd column of the triangle
numbers are periodic with a length of 2000.

PROOF:                     Let the period be p.

We denote the nth triangle number by $T_n = \dfrac{n^2 + n}{2}$.

Therefore $T_{n+p} = \dfrac{(n+p)^2 + (n+p)}{2}$.

If both sides of the equation are divided by 100,
the 3rd digit moves to the 1st postion.

So, $\dfrac{T_{n+p}}{100} = \dfrac{(n+p)^2 + (n+p)}{200}$.

Now show that $\dfrac{T_{n+p}}{100} - \dfrac{T_n}{100}$ ends in zero for some value of p.

$$\frac{T_{n+p} - T_n}{100} = \frac{(n+p)^2 + (n+p) - (n^2 + n)}{200}$$

$$= \frac{n^2 + 2np + p^2 + n + p - n^2 - n}{200}$$

$$= \frac{2pn + p^2 + p}{200}$$

$$= \frac{p(2n + p + 1)}{200}$$

$$= \frac{p}{200}(2n + p + 1).$$

For our difference to be a whole number and end in a zero, the
minimum possible value for p is 2000. Therefore, the trinity column
of the triangle numbers has an enormous period of 2000 digits.

Now that we have proven the period has a length of 2000, let's
also show it forms a chiasmus (more correctly, a palindrome).

PROVE: The 2000 digit period of the 3rd column
of the triangle numbers is palindromic.

PROOF: Observe: $T_0 = 0$ and $T_{1999} = 0$

$T_1 = 0$ and $T_{1998} = 0$

.

.

.

$T_{85} = 3{,}655$ and $T_{1914} = 1{,}832{,}655$

.

.

.

$T_{225} = 25{,}425$ and $T_{1774} = 1{,}574{,}425$

Notice the sum of the subscripts of each pair equals 1999 (e.g., $225 + 1774 = 1999$). This subscript pattern implies we should test to see if $T_{1999-x} - T_x$ is always zero in the hundreds column. Or we could divide by 100 and inspect the first column. By using x in the range from 0 to 999, we produce 1000 pairs of terms.

$$\frac{T_{1999-x} - T_x}{100} = \frac{(1999 - x)^2 + (1999 - x) - (x^2 + x)}{200}$$

$$= \frac{1999^2 - 3998x + x^2 + 1999 - x - x^2 - x}{200}$$

$$= \frac{2000(1999) - 4000x}{200}$$

$$= 10(1999) - 20x$$

$$= 10(1999 - 2x).$$

Therefore, the difference ends in zero implying the digits are the same, and so the entire period is a palindrome. Both proofs combine to say the third column of the triangle numbers forms a magnificent 2000 digit palindrome.

1 Sir Robert Anderson, *The Coming Prince* (Grand Rapids, Michigan: Kregel Publications, 1986), pp. 51-129.

2 C. I. Scofield, *Scofield Reference Bible* (New York: Oxford University Press, 1919), p. 5.

3 C. I. Scofield, *Rightly Dividing the Word of Truth* (Oakland, CA: Western Book and Tract Company, n.d.), p. 18.

4 Irenaeus, *Against Heresies — The Anti-Nicene Fathers* (Grand Rapids, Michigan: Eerdmans Publishing Co., 1987), Vol. 1, p. 557.

5 Barnabas, *The Epistle of Barnabas — The Anti-Nicene Fathers* (Grand Rapids, Michigan: Eerdmans Publishing Co., 1987), Vol. 1, pp. 146-147.

6 E. W. Bullinger, *Number in Scripture* (Grand Rapids, Michigan: Kregel Publications, 1967), p. 204.

7 Ibid., pp. 219-233.

8 Ibid., p. 44.

# CHAPTER — 15

[P. 327] Negative Triangle Numbers:

Dates labeled B.C. are really negative since they are below (the missing) zero. This poses no problem for the definition of triangle numbers. Consider the −90th such quantity:

$$-90 \quad ---------> \quad [(-90)^2 + (-90)]/2$$
$$= [(-90) \times (-90) + (-90)]/2$$
$$= [8100 + (-90)]/2$$
$$= (8010)/2$$
$$= 4005$$

So, the −90th triangle is the same as the +89th.

[P. 328] The Bible's Last Verse:

In the gematria of Revelation 22:21, 90 was used for the "$o$" in $\tau o \upsilon$. The letter *koppa* (90) was written as "$o$," identical to omicron. See the Greek alphabet on page 49.

[P. 328] 990 and 8001:

$$44 \; \text{---------->} \; (44^2 + 44)/2$$
$$= 990$$

$$126 \; \text{---------->} \; (126^2 + 126)/2$$
$$= 8001$$

Therefore, both 990 and 8001 are triangle numbers.

# SCRIPTURAL INDEX

# NUMBER INDEX

Daniel with his three friends, 58; dispensational cycles and, 298; the empire of the Antichrist and, 314, 326; biblical examples of, 52-53; in 1 Peter, 159; gematria of "Jesus" and, 51-54, 60-61, 98-99, 125, 156, 164, 180, 184, 191, 223, 225, 236, 302, 304, 327, 329-332; gematria of "King Cyrus" and, 260; gematria of "truth" and, 226; the Holy of Holies and, 198; Jewish day of circumcision, 223; the *Last Supper* and, 125; the Millennial Reign and, 301; the millennium and, 156; Noah's family and, 127, 159, 162-163, 164, 169-170; Prologue to Revelation and, 304; Psalm 119 and, 84-85; the Resurrection and, 156; as the Resurrection Number, 60-61, 103, 226; high Black Sabbats and, 156; Salvador Dali's symbolism of, 241-243; and the seal of the Lamb as the Savior, 192-193; Shakespeare and, 45; the sign in John's Gospel, 87; the sign of infinity and, 125; the Three Laws of Biblical Mathematics and, 330-332; all the titles of Jesus and, 53

**9**: the Bible's last verse and, 329; biblical symbolism of, 325; secular and sacred examples of, 326; gematria of "Amen" and, 326; gematria of "My Wrath" and, 325-326

**10** (ten): number 13 and, 138-139, 144; number 70 and, 204; number 490 and, 295; in the Bible, 19, 41, 88, 160; and the Bible's last verse, 329; the biblical symbolism of, 137-138, 295; in the Holy Tetractys, 115-116; Lost Tribes, 254, 260; and the Most Holy Place, 196, 198; and Noah, 160; and our number system, 137; self-evident truths, 35; sons of Haman, 263; the symbolic number of horns or toes, 246-247, 280-281, 314, 315, 316, 317, 323; as a triangle number, 15-17, 21

**12**: number [37] and, 224; number 153 and, 182; the 144,000 and, 172, 176-179, 189-190; the Apostles and, 156; in the Bible, 118-119; children of the

Greek gods and, 280; the chosen and, 173-176; the dodecahedron and, 116-117; governmental power and, 270, 310; New Jerusalem and, 213-217; the 23rd Psalm and, 119; Star of David and, 190, 310; symbolic meaning of, 119; the tribes of Israel and, 185, 187, 189

**13**: number 153 and, 145, 320; number 351 and, 151, 305; number 666 in Ezra's 13th verse, 257; number 666 in Revelation's 13th chapter, 60, 193; Alexander of Macedonia and, 265-266, 269-270; the Apostles and, 173-175; attributes of Satan's number and, 116, 126; coven members, 156; in Esther, 262-263; first mention in the Bible, 139; full moon and, 156; gematria of all the names of the "Antichrist" and, 317-320; Haman the Agagite and, 263; Lucifer's Roman gematria and, 134; Napoleon and, 315; Nero Caesar and, 273-274; Noah's family and, 169-170; origins of the fear of, 137; people at a table, 125, 131; probabilities and, 135-137; rebellion and, 137-139; relationship to 666 and Phi, 140-142; Franklin D. Roosevelt and, 131; Satan's gematria and, 130-135; all Satan's names and, 135; Solomon's palace and, 197; triangle numbers and, 144; Trinity Function and, 143-144

**15**, Abraham, Hagar and, 296

**17**: number 153 and, 32, 89, 357; number 666 and, 358; biblical meaning of, 167; Resurrection and, 293; security and, 167-168, 241

**21**: and the archangel Gabriel, 262; the Bible's last verse and, 328-329; and Black Sabbats, 156; and the gematria of "David," 186-187, 309-310; John's Gospel chapter, 98, 243, 309; and the next century, 313; and Paul's letters, 42; and the letter Tau, 127; and the theater at Epidaurus, 122; as a triangle number, 16, 17, 21

**490**: Abraham and, 296; Age of the Gentiles and, 298-299; Sir Robert Anderson and, 293; as the Covenant Number, 295; Daniel's seventy "sevens," 292-293; David and, 298; Jesus and, 295-296; Moses and, 297; and perfect numbers, 295; symbolic meaning of, 294-295

**666**: the number 13, Phi and, 141-142; number 17 and, 358; number 42 and, 287, 321; number 153 and, 88-94, 96, 99, 142, 358; Alexander and, 276; the Antichrist and, 15, 18, 102-103; Assyria's control over Israel and, 254; Christ, Antichrist and, 145, 256; digital root of, 350; European Union's trade symbols and, 316; Ezra 2:13 and, 257; fascination with, 191; gematria and, 317; gematria of "Hitler" and, 288; gematria of "Lateinos" and, 278; gematria of "Little Beast" and, 318; gematria of "Napoleon" and, 287; gematria of "Nero Caesar" and, 55, 58-59, 274; gematria of "Romiith" and, 278; gematria of "Titan" and, 280; "Jesus," the "Cross" and, 60-61, 304; 1 Kings 11:5 and, 276; Lucifer and, 59, 109, 144, 153-154, 358; the Magic Square of the Sun and, 255; New Agers and, 275; NIV comment on, 60; Phi and, 352; and Revelation, 31, 54, 153, 171, 191, 319, 323; reverse triangle numbers and, 348; Roman numerals and, 55, 277; Rome's control over Israel and, 277; as the sum of triangles, 93, 144; ancient secret religious symbol, 275; as a triangle number 16, 32, 102, 140-141; the year 1998 and, 311, 328, 330

**777**: Antichrist, Cross, Jesus and, 60-61, 93, 304; biblical meaning of, 60-61; gematria of the "Cross" and, 59; NIV comment on, 60; as the sum of triangle numbers, 61

**864**: the Cube of the image, 217; gematria and, 215-216; gematria of "God's Temple" and, 215-216; gematria of "Jerusalem" and, 215; gematria of "saints" and, 215; the image of the Cube, 217

**1081**: the 144,000 and, 189; God's Holy Spirit and, 15-16; an infinite triangle family, 183-184; probabilities and, 335-336; proof of triangularity, 360; triangle numbers and, 18-19

**1260**, 178; Daniel and, 293-294; the *last days* and, 253, 321

**1729**: as the double cube, 221; as the gematria of the "body of Jesus," 218

**1998**: the middle of the Tribulation and, 327; and its relationship to Revelation's last verse, 330; the year of the triple Antichrist, 311

**2000**: 2000-year old puzzle, 88; apocalyptic event *around* the year, 292; Christ's return and, 313; near the end of Daniel's seventy weeks, 299; and the frequency of triangle numbers, 16; gematria and, 301; the great period and, 303, 305-308; not the end of the millennium, 313; proof of the great 2000digit period, 366-367; near the end of the Great Sabbath Week, 300; triangle numbers and, 309-310; the watershed number, 95-97, 311-312, 350

**2001**: or 2000 as the beginning of the third millennium, 313; as a triangle number, 309

**2701**: as a chiasmus, 305; in the First and Third Laws, 331-332; gematria of Genesis 1:1, 230, 329-330; and Jesus, 233; as a triangle number, 230-231

**8991**: number 9 and, 329; number [37] and, 330; number 666 and, 330; number 1998 and, 330; the Bible's last verse and, 329; in the Second and Third Laws of Biblical Mathematics, 331-332

**144,000**, 309, 311; number 153 and, 182; David's Star and, 183-185, 187-191; Revelation and, 171-172; the Tribulation saints and, 176-177

# SUBJECT INDEX

*The Ark on the Flood*, 162; St. Augustine on, 159-160; in 2 Peter, 163; symbolism of, 164

Forming and filling: in Genesis 1:2, 73-74; in Pascal's Triangle, 81, 345

"Fountain of wisdom," gematria of, 233

Friendly numbers: definition of, 28; and Jacob's gift to Esau, 28-29; table of, 339

Friendly pair, 28-29

Gabriel, the archangel: and Daniel, 333; delivers the Annunciation, 50, 236; and the spirit world, 262, 264; supports Israel, 262

Gadarene swine, 303

Galatians, Epistle to the, 228, 275, 296

Galileo, Galilei, 62; quoted from *The Assayer*, 8-9

Garden of Gethsemane, 10

Gematria. *See* Greek language, gematria; Hebrew language, gematria

Genesis, 1, 11, 13, 52, 56, 57, 91, 102, 177, 253, 296; and the 7th day, 38; number 9 and, 326; number 13 and, 139; on the number 70, 204; accuracy of, 20-21; on the biblical year, 293; chiasmus in, 303, 305; first and second verses of, 2, 38, 40, 42, 71, 235, 300, 305, 328, 329; forming and filling in, 65-66, 73-74; gematria and, 18, 61; gematria of the first verse, 229-231, 330; gematria of the second verse, 232; and Ham's rebellion, 170; Irenaeus on, 301; and Jacob and Esau, 26-28; the many numbers in, 160; on Nimrod, 251; and Noah, 160-161, 165, 166; on the Serpent, 109, 132; on the stars, 86; and the Three Laws of Biblical Mathematics, 331-332; Bishop Ussher and, 327; The Word in, 233

Goat of Mendes, 105

Godhead, 4, 5, 25, 65; and the 144,000, 191; Ark of the Covenant and, 222; and the Big Bang, 71; deep mystery of, 65, 224, 237; Jesus as the, 225; mark of, 332; and the Triangle of Creation, 66, 70; Trinity in, 2, 4, 214, 231

Goebbels, Joseph Paul, 286

Goliath: number 40 and, 166; David and, 186

Gorbachev, Mikhail, 317

Gore, Tipper, 152

Goren, Chief Rabbi Shlomo, 210, 212

Gospel(s), 4, 42, 52, 53, 176, 248, 282, 333; number 9 and, 326; number 153 and, 88; St. Augustine on John's, 189; Jesus confronts Peter in, 187; John's, 83, 87, 326; beginning of Matthew's, 40-41; Mark's, 3; and the name "Jesus," 50

Great Commission, 13, 333

Great Sign (in John's Gospel); the 8th, 53; the 9th, 87

Great Tribulation, 253, 267, 298; middle of the, 330

Greek language (major entries only): alphabet, 49, 326, 368; and the "Fish" acrostic, 85, 100; gematria, 30-31, 48-51, 53-55, 59-60, 130-133, 137, 177-179, 181, 186, 214-218, 223-229, 233-234, 253, 265-266, 270, 273, 278, 280, 288, 301-302, 317-320; and the first verses of Matthew, 40; New Testament written in, 10; poetic forms, 221, 303-304; special nature of, 18, 47, 137; letter Tau, 93, 127; and the symbol "SSS," 275-276

Greek(s), the: number 4 and, 115-116; number 7 and, 42; and the dodecahedron, 116-118; and Satan, 120

Hadrian (emperor), 279

Hagar (mother of Ishmael), 208; Abraham and, 296

Ham: gematria of, 169-170; Noah's second son, 162, 251

Haman the Agagite, 262-264, 322; "the enemy of the Jews," 262; gematria of, 263

Hanging Gardens of Babylon, 269; one of the 7 Wonders of the World, 256

256-257; and Daniel's three friends, 57; and the destruction of the Temple, 198, 200, 293; diagram of his dream, 247; the famous dream of, 246-248, 323; and Jerusalem, 200-202; Saddam Hussein and, 257-259

Negative triangle numbers, 368

Nero, Caesar, 280, 322; number 13 and, 273-274; as the Antichrist, 54; career of, 271-275; coin with image of, 274; and the great fire that destroyed Rome, 271; Greek gematria of, 55, 273; Hebrew gematria of, 58-59, 273; and the torture of early Christians, 272

New Age: number 666 and, 275; and Cheop's Pyramid, 249; the false promise of, 103; and the occult, 254-256; and the pentagram, 105-106; relationship to Satanism, 158

New Agers: number 666 and, 275; and astrology, 86; use of magic, 256; and the worship of the mother-goddess, 252

New Jerusalem: number 12 and, 119; a perfect cube, 213-214, 215, 218, 237, 246; as described in Revelation, 213-214; and gematria, 214-216; as the Most Holy Place, 218

New Testament, 10, 133; number 7 and, 40-42; and the 8 names of our Lord, 53; authors of, 223; references to the coming Son of Man in, 302; earliest copies of, 176; the word *dragon* in, 320; and gematria, 47, 55; first and last human name in, 186, 309; Greek language of, 145; trinities in, 3-4

Newton, Isaac, 62, 174-175, 361; anti-Trinity views of, 10-11, 12, 62; career of, 9-12; knowledge of the Bible, 10, 198; on God's Works, 19, 33-34

Nimrod: number 42 and, 253; called "another beast," 253, 280, 318; career of, 251-254; gematria of, 253; and Semiramis, 252; Tower of Babel and, 251, 267. *See also* "another beast" and False Prophet

Nostradamus, and Adolf Hitler, 285

Number of completeness (i.e., 7): number 70 and, 202, 204; biblical symbolism of, 40, 52, 60; secular and sacred examples of, 98, 131, 357. *See also* 7 (seven) in the Number Index

Number of rebellion (i.e., 13), 263, 305; biblical symbolism of, 139; first occurrence in the Bible, 139; in the many names of the Antichrist and Satan, 317-320; as the sum of triangles, 144. *See also* 13 (thirteen) in the Number Index

"Number of the beast," 191, 270; chapter and verse of, 193; as an example of gematria, 54-55, 153, 319; gematria of, 319; many ancient people used, 275; popularity among teenagers of, 153; from Revelation, 31, 54; and Roman numerals, 277-278. *See also* 666 in the Number Index

*Observations upon the Prophecies of Daniel and the Apocalypse of St. John*, a forgotten book by Isaac Newton, 9

Occult, 155, 183, 362; and Alexander, 267; and the Chaldeans, 254; and Hitler, 285; in the music business, 152; and Napoleon, 284; and the New Age, 254-256; nonsense and the Great Pyramid, 249; swastika as the symbol for the, 285

O'Connor, John Cardinal, 150

Old Testament, 10; the 3 resurrections in, 52; number 7 and, 38-40, 98; number [37] and, 229-233; accuracy of, 20; Apocrypha on numbers, 47, 197; and modern archaeology, 12; and gematria, 47, 98; and God's Creation, 66; Latin translation (Vulgate) of, 134; and the Messiah, 187; in the New Testament, 304; patriarchs of, 63; the Septuagint translation of, 205; trinities in, 2-3

Olympias (Phillip's wife and Alexander's mother): gematria of, 266; legends of Alexander's conception and, 266

One: God's three-in-one-ness, 183; three rules in, 35-36, 340-341; triangle symbolizes three-in-, 15

Orion (Nimrod), 44; constellation of, 251-252

Osbourne, Ozzy: and the song "Suicide Solution," 150; stage antics of, 151

Pacioli, Luca (friar, mathematician, and friend of Leonardo da Vinci), and the number Phi, 116, 126-128, 129

Palindrome (a chiasmus with numbers), and the great 2000-digit period, 366-367

Palm Sunday, rejection of Jesus on, 293

*Paradise Lost* (by John Milton): Lucifer as the fallen archangel in, 101, 143; Satan as a terrifying creature in, 102-103; Satan's attitude in, 90

Parthenon, the number Phi in, 121, 129

Pascal, Blaise: number/year 2000 and, 305; the famous triangle of, 21-22; the next row of, 336; properties of the triangle of, 345-346; and the Triangle of Creation, 79-81, 111

Pascal's Pyramid, 346-347

Patmos, Island of, 115

Paul, 42, 120, 157, 176, 205, 277, 301; on the Antichrist, 210; on changing someone's mind, 23-24; on the Creation, 71-72; death of, 272; and the Greeks, 121, 122; on The Holy Spirit, 182; on immortality, 7; knowledge of the Lord's designs, 63; on the *last days*, 146, 158, 313, 319; Sir Isaac Newton on, 10; physical persecution of, 275; said "Prove all things," 47; on Satan, 102, 108, 132; and his shipwreck, 19; on the time of the Gentiles, 298

Pentagonal numbers, 92

Pentagram: the apple's core and the, 114; connections among Phi, the navel and the, 110-111, 114, 285; the Devil's associations with the, 105-111, 153, 185; the dodecahedron and the,

116-117, 175-176; in M.C. Escher's *Reptiles*, 117-118; the inverted, 90, 92, 109; "Man in the," 110, 129; man's and Satan's image relate through the, 106, 153; the New Age and the, 106; Phi and the, 107-109, 126, 140, 251, 268; a proof that Phi is in, 351-352; the Pythagoreans and, 115, 120; Satanists and, 106, 153

Pentateuch, 162; chapter and verses of, 30; generations of the patriarchs in, 327; middle word of the entire, 20

Pentecost Day, and gematria, 239

Perfect numbers, 52, 92, 143; the Days of Creation and, 25; definition and examples of, 25; friendly numbers and, 28, 339; Genesis 1:1 and, 38; the moon's revolution and, 25-26; in Pascal's Triangle, 345-346; proof that every perfect number is also a triangle number, 336-337; table of all known, 338; triangle numbers and, 26

Persia (Iran): Alexander and, 264-265, 268, 269; conqueror of Israel, 248, 260, 314; Cyrus ascends to the throne, 201; and queen Esther, 262-263; and the Jews, 261-262, 264; in Nebuchadnezzar's dream as the silver shoulders and arms, 246, 257; the "prince" of, 264; symbolized as a two-horned ram, 247, 264

Peter, Simon: number 490 and, 295-296; death of, 272; denied Christ three times, 5; and the famous 153 fishes, 83, 88; Jesus confronts, 188; and Matthias, 173; witnessed the Transfiguration, 4

Peter, First Epistle of: "born again," 85; Noah's Ark in, 159; value of "God's flock," 216

Peter, Second Epistle of: how God views time, 299-300; Noah, the 8th person in, 163

Pharaoh (Rameses the Great): Joseph interpreted the dreams of, 38, 246; pursuer of the Jews, 281. *See also* Cheops

Shirer, William R., *The Rise and Fall of the Third Reich*, 282

Shrouds, 195

Six-Day War, 210

Solomon, King, 1, 200, 202, 261; a tragic figure of apostasy, 276; drawing of the Temple of, 197; and the Temple, 10, 119, 197-198, 211, 297, 298

Solomon, David (modern Jewish historian), 213

Solomon's Seal, 193. See also David's Star

Son of God: number 12 and, 173; in the famous "fish" acrostic, 85, 87, 98, 191; gematria of, 228

Son of Man: gematria of, 228; Jesus' favorite title for Himself, 302

Son of morning or the dawn (Lucifer in Isaiah 14), 102, 134

SSS, ancient satanic symbol, 275-276

Star Number(s): the 7th, 187; [37] as a, 231-232; the famous 144,000 and, 189; King David's, 309-310; definition and examples of, 186; formulas, table and proofs, 358-359

Star of David, 193; drawing of, 185; patterns in the, 190; relationship to David's name, 186; and the Tribulation saints, 187, 189; universal image for Jews, 222

Stigma (ς), used for the number 6 by the Greeks, 49, 50, 275

Stigmata, 49

Swastika: Hitler and the, 285-286, 315; and the number Phi, 286

Tabernacle, 209, 297; definition and drawing of, 195-196; the Lord's design instructions for, 195, 237; Most Holy Place of, 196, 198, 200, 214

Tacitus (ancient Roman historian), 365; on Nero Caesar's succession to emperor, 273; on the persecution of Christians, 272

Tau Cross: Jesus crucified on, 93; relationship to the Ark/Cross, 127, 161; and triangle numbers, 127, 164, 188

Temple, 261, 362; number 12 and, 119; number 70 and, 202, 205; and the Antichrist, 209-210, 257, 267, 293, 317, 330; Caligula and the, 278; Ezekiel's, 200; gematria of, 214-217; Herod's, 206-207; a drawing of Herod's, 206; Jesus predicts the destruction of, 207, 279; Josephus on the destruction of Herod's, 207; the Most Holy Place of, 214, 235, 237; king Nebuchadnezzar's armies destroy Solomon's, 201, 256; the New Jerusalem as God's, 213, 215-218, 237; the New (Third), 209-210, 212-213, 281; Isaac Newton's knowledge of Solomon's, 10; the phrase *hep, hep, hurrah* and the destruction of, 208; plan of the First superimposed on the Temple Mount, 211; the Second (Zerubbabel's), 200-202, 257, 260, 293; Solomon and the, 276; drawing of Solomon's, 197; King Solomon's, 197-198, 199, 297, 298; Titus' armies destroy the Second, 203, 204, 207, 278-279, 292

Temple Mount, 210; David buys, 213; plan of the First Temple superimposed on, 211; Western (or Wailing) Wall, 201, 207

Tempter (Satan), 101 and the number Phi, 120-121

Ten Commandments: the Ark of the Covenant and, 222; the beginning of a new covenant and, 296; divisions in, 41; the legal system and, 35; Moses and, 166; the movie, 83; the Second Commandment in, 128

Thessalonians, First Epistle to the, 47; last days in, 313

Thessalonians, Second Epistle to: Paul on the Antichrist, 210, 267; the rebellion, 319; Satan's many counterfeit miracles, 89

## Speaking Engagements

James Harrison is available for seminars or other
speaking engagements for churches, conferences, and colleges.

Subjects include the following:
- A New Vision of the Holy Scriptures
- God's Great Code • Numbers in the Bible
- Biblical Symbolism • Apologetics
- Gematria • Prophecy.

Please Contact:

James Harrison
Isaiah Publications
P.O. Box 1221
Peterborough Ontario,
Canada K9J 7H4

Phone: 1 (800) 537-5489
Fax: 1 (705) 741-1444